FOUNDATIONS

of

TUDOR POLICY

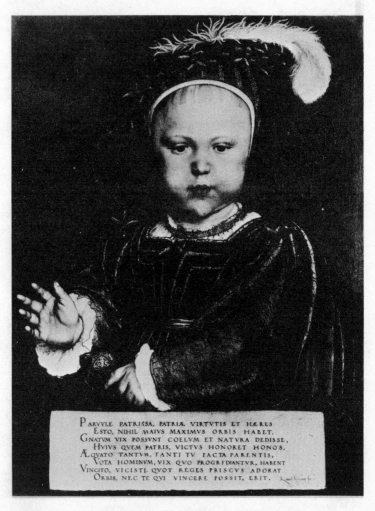

PARVVLE PATRISSA, PATRIÆ VIRTVTIS ET HÆRES
ESTO, NIHIL MAIVS MAXIMVS ORBIS HABET.
GNATVM VIX POSSVNT COELVM ET NATVRA DEDISSE,
HVIVS QVEM PATRIS, VICTVS HONORET HONOS.
ÆQVATO TANTVM, TANTI TV FACTA PARENTIS,
VOTA HOMINVM, VIX QVO PROGREDIANTVR, HABENT
VINCITO, VICISTI. QVOT REGES PRISCVS ADORAT
ORBIS, NEC TE QVI VINCERE POSSIT, ERIT. *Richard Morison f.*

EDWARD VI AS A CHILD, BY HANS HOLBEIN
National Gallery of Art, Washington, D.C.
(Mellon Collection)

FOUNDATIONS
of
TUDOR POLICY

W. Gordon Zeeveld

METHUEN & CO LTD
11 New Fetter Lane London EC4

FIRST PUBLISHED BY HARVARD UNIVERSITY PRESS U.S.A. 1948
COPYRIGHT, 1948
BY THE PRESIDENT AND FELLOWS OF HARVARD COLLEGE

FIRST PUBLISHED AS A UNIVERSITY PAPERBACK 1969 BY
METHUEN CO. LTD., 11 NEW FETTER LANE, LONDON E.C.4

SBN 416 27880 9

PRINTED IN GREAT BRITAIN BY
FLETCHER & SONS LTD, NORWICH

Distributed in the U.S.A.
by Barnes & Noble Inc.

PREFACE

This book is the story of obscure men. Yet their work, published anonymously or surviving only in manuscript, and rarely republished in recent times, had the immediate object of implementing in theory the most momentous government decision in the Tudor period, while at the same time it succeeded in orienting the whole Tudor policy in the light of past and current thought. This would of course be the work of humanists, and their writing abundantly confirms Professor Douglas Bush's conviction that there was no appreciable break in the humanistic tradition after the deaths of More and Fisher. Evidence for this continuity has been demonstrated in the careers and personalities of these men. But throughout I have kept the larger object in view, to assess their contribution to the history of thought; and this properly constitutes the core of the book. It seemed best to deal with both of these interests chronologically and synchronously, tracing the personal careers of the humanists concerned through the years of their greatest influence ideologically, and pausing at convenient points in the narrative to discuss the nature and influence of their ideas. Thus, it will be possible to read Chapters VI, VIII, and IX, where these ideas are analyzed, without reference to biographical detail.

Two words used in the text need explanation. The current pejorative connotation attached to the word *propagandist* is wholly irrelevant to my purpose, which is not to blame or exculpate but to evaluate. The reader need not be reminded that the use of evidence in the sixteenth century cannot be measured by the standards of scholarly integrity of the twentieth, and it is well to remember that, in this respect, the practice of Henry's propagandists was no different from that of other controversialists of their time. Again with due regard to the time and to present feelings toward the events in which they played a major role, I have characterized their point of view as liberal, both by temperament and by current exigency. The age was not without its spokesmen for freedom of speech, as More's opening oration as Speaker of the House and Starkey's defense of the liberty of speaking and writing prove. But Henry's break with the Pope offered an opportunity for speculation which in effect redefined the liberal point of view in England. The Act of Supremacy did not of course set in motion the powerful political and social forces operative in England in the sixteenth century; but it did polarize them, and where it did not unite opposition, at least revealed its conservative character. The effect was to accent the inherently liberal tendencies of those who sustained the government.

Chapter VI was first published in the *Journal of Modern History* for September 1943, and Chapter VIII in the *Journal of the History of Ideas* for January 1946, both of which journals and the University of Chicago Press I should like to thank for the courtesy of reprinting in this present form. I should like also to make a similar acknowledgment to the *Publications of the Modern Language Association* for permission to reprint portions of "Richard Morison, Official Apologist for Henry VIII," published in June 1940.

I wish to make personal acknowledgment here to Professor Garrett Mattingly for his careful and discriminating reading of the manuscript, and for the appreciably increased authority the text has gained thereby. To Professor Bush of Harvard University both for that stimulating paper of 1937 referred to above, and for his keen grace notes throughout the text, to Professor Roland H. Bainton of the Yale Divinity School for his help on ecclesiastical history, and to Professor John Randall of Columbia University for useful suggestions in Chapter VIII I am especially indebted, and to a number of others whose help I hope will not be lost among the notes. I should like also to acknowledge the courtesy of the staffs of the Library of Congress and the Folger Shakespeare Library of Washington, D. C., and of the Public Record Office, London, especially to Mr. Charles Drew for copying out certain manuscripts incapable of mechanical reproduction. Finally, I wish to express my thanks to President Harry C. Byrd of the University of Maryland for a grant of six months' sabbatical leave in order to complete the task.

Yet the book is mine, and I acknowledge it, still hoping that it will escape that dourest of comments:

It is yours;
So like you, 'tis the worse.

Brookeville, Maryland
November, 1947

PREFACE TO THE 1969 EDITION

It is obviously impossible within a brief preface to this reprint of *Foundations of Tudor Policy* to do more than point the directions scholarship has taken in the interim. Nevertheless, it would be remiss on such an occasion wholly to ignore it. Evidence of the new emphasis on the secular rewards of humanistic study in the early Tudor period was presently to appear in Fritz Caspari's *Humanism and the Social Order in Tudor England* (1954), which from a different point of view emphasized the importance of some of the same scholars, especially Thomas Starkey. G. R. Elton had begun to publish the result of his researches on Thomas Cromwell as practical administrator of governmental affairs, the most important new approach toward that controversial figure since Merriman. In Cromwell's program of reform, patronage of scholars was essential. Corroborative support came in H. R. Trevor-Roper's review in *The New Statesman and Nation*, reprinted in his *Men and Events* (1957); and Christopher Morris gave it general currency in his summary of Tudor political thought in 1954. Meanwhile, A. G. Dickens' studies of northern provincial politics in the late 30's led to his *Thomas Cromwell and the English Reformation* (1959) and *The English Reformation* (1964), both of which revealed the religious fabric supporting Cromwellian politics. Since that time, the idea of commonwealth as a social and economic organism, a characteristic aspect of English humanism after Thomas More, has received a good deal of attention from S. T. Bindoff, A. B. Ferguson, and others. On the dawning

ix

idea of state, J. H. Hexter has made a significant start in his semantic study of Machiavelli's *Il Principe* (*Studies in the Renaissance,* IV (1957), 113–138). Although the mediaeval backgrounds of statecraft have recently been elaborately explored by Ernest Kantorowicz and Gaines Post, no comparable study exists for Tudor thought. However, my reference to Richard Morison's knowledge of Machiavelli (and therefore Cromwell's) has now been extended to the end of the century by Felix Raab (*The English Face of Machiavelli, 1500–1700*); and Cromwell's use of Marsilius of Padua has been further underlined by Elton (*Transactions of the Royal Historical Society,* 5th Series, 6, 114–140). The Erasmian strain in Tudor humanism has been traced by J. K. McConica (*English Humanists and Reformation Politics under Henry VIII and Edward VI,* 1965).

As for particular studies of the English humanists at Padua who either became involved in the new politics or turned to Rome, only Reginald Pole has received adequate attention. W. Schenk's biography (1950) may soon be superseded by Sr. Noëlle-Marie Egretier's, and her French translation of Pole's *Pro ecclesiasticae unitatis defensione* has just appeared with a valuable introduction. An English translation is also in print. Thomas Starkey and Richard Morison are yet to receive their due, though several studies are now under way. Among Pole's Italian friends, Sadoleto has been the subject of a new study by Richard Douglas; hopefully, others in the liberal group at Rome will attract scholars.

I wish to express my thanks to Professor A. G. Dickens for suggesting a reprint in paperback, and to the publishers, Methuen & Company, for incorporating this acknowledgment of the passage of time.

W. Gordon Zeeveld

Deep Meadow
Woodbine, Maryland

CONTENTS

ILLUSTRATIONS

FOUNDATIONS

of

TUDOR POLICY

I

HUMANISM UNDER HENRY VIII

The basic assumption of this book is the continuity of the English humanistic tradition in the early Tudor period; its primary intention is to establish the place of those who represented that tradition in the history of English thought. The history of humanism in the fifteenth century has received considerable attention in recent years;[1] its continuation into the reign of Henry VIII by the Erasmian circle at Cambridge and the so-called Oxford reformers is now a familiar story. But the importance of the period after the break with Rome has been generally underestimated in tracing the intellectual history of England during the Renaissance. The declaration of royal supremacy was the most far-reaching event in terms of the history of ideas in the Tudor period, yet the humanists who played the major role in implementing it have remained in obscurity.

There have been reasons for this neglect. Many of the documents, having served the occasion for which they were written, were never republished after their first printing. As a consequence, present-day estimates of Thomas Starkey's work are based, almost without exception, on the *Dialogue between Pole and Lupset,* the only work of Starkey's ever reprinted; whereas the equally important *Exhortation to*

[1] W. K. Schirmer, *Der englische Frühhumanismus* (Leipzig, 1931); Roberto Weiss, *Humanism in England during the Fifteenth Century* (Oxford, 1941).

Unity and Obedience, which has not been reprinted since its first publication in 1536, has been all but ignored.[2] Richard Morison was not known as the author of his two tracts on the Pilgrimage of Grace, *A Lamentation of Seditious Rebellion* and *A Remedy for Sedition,* until 1936, four centuries after their first and anonymous publication, and only *A Remedy* has been reprinted. Other important writing by these men has remained in manuscript.

Literary history has likewise conspired against them. In assaying a period of minor achievement in poetry, scholarship has not always appreciated the major achievement, the rise of a flexible and articulate native prose style. The historical importance of a period that includes the great prose of More, Tyndale's translation of the Bible, the sermons of Latimer, Ascham's *Scholemaster,* and Cranmer's Book of Common Prayer need not be argued. The writers dealt with in this book will be found not unworthy members of that company, with more than one of whom, in fact, they were personally associated. Their simple, unmannered prose has a vitality far removed from the anemic, featureless Ciceronian periods fashionable among humanists of the day, and at its best, it pulsates with a vigor unexcelled in contemporary letters. Judged from a literary point of view alone, their mastery of the vernacular is impressive.

The supposed barrenness of this period in literary history has led, however, to highly speculative inferences concerning the history of Tudor humanism. Sufficiently attributable, as Douglas Bush reminds us, to the inscrutability of the purposes of God, this barrenness has nevertheless been

[2] J. W. Allen, *A History of Political Thought in the Sixteenth Century* (London, 1928), makes a single reference to the *Exhortation.* Franklin L. Baumer, "Thomas Starkey and Marsilius of Padua" (*Politica,* II [1936], 188-205), a study of the Marsilian influence on Starkey, is based entirely on the *Dialogue.* In a more recent work, Baumer makes use of both the *Dialogue* and the *Exhortation* and describes Starkey as "the most outstanding exponent of the new attitude" (*The Early Tudor Theory of Kingship* [New Haven, 1940], p. 148).

ascribed to causes more human than divine. Indeed, a serious effort has been made to explain the alleged gap in the tradition of humanism as the direct result of some kind of diabolical disregard of learning on the part of Henry VIII. It has been assumed that by killing off the important literary figures of his day, he caused a cessation of humanistic activity in England until it was taken up again during the reign of Mary and thence went forward to its triumphant flowering in the age of Elizabeth.[3]

The danger of this point of view has been persuasively demonstrated so far as formal education was concerned,[4] and the thesis becomes no more tenable when one considers humanistic endeavor outside of university walls. Far from being impeded in the later years of Henry's reign, the study of the classics received constant and notable encouragement from Henry himself and from Cromwell, his chief minister. There can be no doubt that the execution of More and Fisher and Surrey was a grave loss to the sum total of humanistic accomplishment in the period, but to conclude that their deaths caused any serious break in the scholarly tradition must be regarded at best as a partial view of the evidence. A merely cursory examination of the Privy Purse expenses [5] and the *Letters and Papers of Henry VIII* in the span of years before and after More's death will reveal a continuous and substantial royal patronage of scholarship.

[3] J. S. Phillimore, "Blessed Thomas More and the Arrest of Humanism in England," *Dublin Review*, CLIII (1913), 1-26; R. W. Chambers, *Thomas More* (New York, 1935), and *The Place of St. Thomas More in English Literature and History* (London, 1937).

[4] Douglas Bush, "Tudor Humanism and Henry VIII," *University of Toronto Quarterly*, VII (1938), 162-177.

[5] *The Privy Purse Expenses of King Henry the Eighth, from November MDXXIX, to December MDXXXII*, edited by H. N. Nicolas (London, 1827); "Household Book of Henry VIII," *Trevelyan Papers Prior to 1558*, edited by J. Payne Collier, Camden Society, no. 67 (1857). "Among the few redeeming traits in Henry the Eighth's character," Nicolas conceded, "was a love of learning, to which each of these entries bears additional testimony."

Indeed, throughout his reign, Henry continued to support scholars at Oxford and Cambridge, at Paris and Padua, far more generously than his father.

It is not to be supposed that these gratuities proceeded —in spite of Erasmus' praise—from a pure love of learning for its own sake. Henry, like most princes, expected a return on his investment. Ludovico Vives' competence of £20 a year ceased abruptly when he opposed the divorce, and Reginald Pole's princely stipend of £100, bestowed ostensibly for study abroad, dried up at once and for the same reason in 1536. This, of course, is to be expected. If *Tottel's Miscellany* is a melancholy tribute to the vigilant axe, it is also a testimonial to the law of political necessity which characterized Henry's attitude toward the scholars whom he chose to subsidize. One need not defend his business ethics to point out that throughout his reign he regarded the relation between humanism and affairs of state as indispensable. The important fact is that his primary consideration in encouraging learning was not belles-lettres but the commonwealth, and in the most critical years of his reign, far from being indifferent to learning, he turned to it as the very keystone of his policy.

For the divorce involved much more than Henry's conscience. To think of it in terms of a royal whim is to ignore the fact that in pursuing it he enjoyed the tacit approval of the great majority of the English people. Had it been otherwise, there would have been revolution. And there was no revolution. Only the abortive Pilgrimage of Grace two years later testifies the existence of concrete opposition, and even then, at the very height of the uprising, the official attitude was hardly more than contempt for a disgruntled minority whose heat would dissipate itself in divided counsels. Weighing heavily on the government's side were some of the deepest and dearest of English convictions, and in every case the national safety was paramount. For all Englishmen, memories of the civil conflicts of the fifteenth century were still too green not to invest the whole matter of the divorce of Catherine with potential danger to the commonwealth as long as the hopes of succession rested solely in the monstrous regiment of women. The popular sympathy for Catherine's plight was great; but Henry's plight was a national concern. For most Englishmen, again, the formalization of the royal supremacy was fully justifiable as a safeguard against foreign domination; if evicting the Pope now worked to Henry's personal interests, so much the better. At stake, of course, was the fabulous prize represented in the wealth of the Roman empire in Britain in the sixteenth century. Monastic plums, ripe for picking, would bring out the worst of venality before the harvest was reaped. Nevertheless, predatory instincts were secondary; most Englishmen regarded the papal recession as a vindication of traditional English liberties. Henry's cause was their cause, and England, not the monastic riches, was the major stake; the major issue, in both cleric and lay opinion, was national independence. It is not surprising that the consciously nationalistic note should sound strong and clear for the first time in the writings of Henry's defenders.[6]

[6] At this late date, the point need not be labored that patriotic sentiments were not a product of the defeat of the Armada; and I am inclined to think that Hans Kohn has overstated his case in insisting that nationalism did not appear in England until the Puritan Revolution. *The History of Nationalism* (1940), pp. 166-173. Within the bounds of his own definition, Kohn himself finds nationalistic expressions in books of wide circulation. See, for example, Lyly's identification of England as "a new Israel, his chosen and peculiar people" in *Euphues' Glass for Europe*. And a preference for the common law as over against the Roman law can be traced back of Starkey's *Dialogue* to the practice of Wolsey. On this point and on the evidence of a sense of equality, I have dwelt elsewhere in the present work. See the index.

Hence, while the King relied instinctively—and rightly as it proved—on overwhelming popular support for his new program in practice, that very fact made him acutely conscious of the necessity for theoretic vindication from the scholarly world. Throughout the protracted negotiations for the divorce, he had exhibited a characteristic sensitivity to European scholarly opinion. Now, in annulling the papal power, he was almost painfully insistent on academic approval, except that, as might be expected, he appealed particularly to English scholars to erect the foundations for an English policy.

It is in this direction, then, that one must look for a continuation of humanistic endeavors in England after 1534. Indeed, it is the practical application of scholarship to the immediate and pressing affairs of state that gave new purpose and vitality to the scholarly profession. Fifteenth-century scholars were not unaware of the classical ideal of putting learning to use in the conduct of government,[7] and humanists like Thomas Bekynton, Robert Flemmying, and John Free had carved out successful political careers. But Henry deliberately sought out men of learning for the creation of policy, and thus opened the way of preferment directly to the throne itself. In another respect, this was a marked innovation. Hitherto, the one means of political advancement for scholars was through the church. Now a student in the civil law might just as easily win the ear of the King. Men with neither social standing nor ecclesiastical pretensions suddenly found themselves under direct and intoxicating royal solicitation, and the effect on humanistic studies was profound.

It was inevitable, under these circumstances, that the

[7] Roberto Weiss remarks, "A utilitarian conception of the humanities is the main feature of humanism in England during the fifteenth century." *Humanism in England during the Fifteenth Century*, p. 182.

supremacy should have been defended on a jurisdictional rather than doctrinal basis, in which national sovereignty was the issue; for on this ground, popular support would effectively neutralize radical Protestants as well as intransigent conservatives, both of whom were God's liegemen before the King's. Henry would have preferred to keep questions of doctrine out of the struggle altogether. Indeed, since he had no disposition to surrender the title of defender of the faith, anything short of doctrinal orthodoxy would have been unthinkable. The apologists approximated this ideal as closely as possible. Essential dogma was to remain unchanged; it was only in *adiaphora*, the things that did not matter, that any changes in doctrine would be permitted. Theologically, both before and after 1534, they felt at one with the church catholic. Theological questions thus conveniently removed, the supremacy could be justified without the reservations that would otherwise hinder a free orientation of theory with practice, and Henry's propagandists could confine their attention to a purely political settlement.

Needless to say, there were some who could not so confine it, though many for the time being accepted this limitation of the question on grounds of personal expediency alone. Stephen Gardiner, for all his legal dexterity, and Thomas Cranmer and Cuthbert Tunstal, disposed by their training to view the issue in ecclesiastical terms, in the end would have a limited usefulness as theorists. Straddling simply would not do in an exigency that so clearly required conviction. Furthermore, where there was a genuine conviction, but concealed, pressure for a declaration never subsided. Henry angled long for Reginald Pole; he would have moved earth, and possibly a little heaven, for Thomas More.

But what were the motives of the men to whom Henry's

cause seemed just? It is easy to understand why for those who saw the old order disintegrating before their eyes, compliance was impossible, and just as easy to misunderstand men like Thomas Starkey and Richard Morison with much to gain and little to lose, for whom support of the King meant an unprecedented opportunity to advance themselves in the service of the state. Had this been their only motive, their contribution to English thought might have been little more than a narrow *étatisme,* a dogmatic defense of the state rather than the faith. The fact that they laid deep enough foundations for a state church to last until the Commonwealth, and outlast it, is an adequate measure of the broadness of their humanistic training. As a matter of fact, a liberal point of view is recognizable early in their careers. It is not without significance that their educational backgrounds may be traced to Wolsey's college at Oxford during the time when it was shaken by heterodoxy, and that some four years later they were enjoying the hospitality of Reginald Pole at Padua in a period when the University of Padua was renowned throughout Europe as a center for liberal and speculative thought.[8] This temper did not abate when they found themselves standing in the sun of royal favor. Elevated to the place of intellectual advisors to the crown, they were in a strategic position to exert an immediate and powerful influence on contemporary policy. The effectiveness of their answer to the problems they faced cannot be accounted for solely on grounds of urgency, though it is true that their solutions were for the time, not the future, expediential rather than consciously theoretical. As a matter of fact, by royal commission as well as by tem-

[8] Hastings Rashdall, *The Universities of Europe in the Middle Ages* (Oxford, 1936), II, 21; John H. Randall, "The Development of Scientific Method in the School of Padua," *Journal of the History of Ideas,* I, 183-186.

perament and training as humanists, they invariably sought an anchor for expediency in tradition. But tradition would have to be resurveyed in a new and more liberal context for which present events seemed to constitute a prelude. To this objective, in spite of their official status, they could address themselves freely. For this reason, their contribution to the history of ideas was extraordinarily germinal.

When the hallmark of that policy, Henry's religious supremacy, unexpectedly divided private and public loyalties, the community of scholars also divided. Pole returned to Rome; but by that time, those ambitious grafts from the Paduan stock had taken root and were flourishing in English soil. It is an ironic commentary on the vicissitudes of learning during the Tudor period that doctrinal differences made reconciliations impossible. When Pole came to England as cardinal at the accession of Mary, his former associates, uprooted, went into an exile from which some of them never returned. Nevertheless, their enthusiasm for learning continued abroad. Transmitted to such younger scholars as John Cheke, Thomas Wilson, and Thomas Hoby, all of whom studied in Padua during the exile,[9] to Thomas Smith, to Roger Ascham, secretary to Morison, and to John Ponet, who shared exile with them under Mary, its perpetuation in the reign of Elizabeth was assured.

II

But when Pole first went to Padua in 1519, these differences had not yet emerged. On the contrary, a fortuitous set of circumstances had created a community of scholars in which the intellectual atmosphere was wholly congenial to the growth of a liberal spirit. For this, Pole himself was partly responsible. It is difficult to read the opinions Starkey

[9] C. H. Garrett, *The Marian Exiles* (Cambridge, 1938), p. 116.

attributes to him in the *Dialogue between Pole and Lupset* without arriving at that conclusion. On his first coming to Italy, it was the liberals in ecclesiastical circles to whom Bembo introduced him, and it was their company that he continued to find most congenial. Gian Matteo Giberti, Bishop of Verona, and Giacomo Sadoleto, Bishop of Carpentras, occupied an intellectual position not unsympathetic with the moderate church reformers of the stamp of Melanchthon. The counter-Reformation to which they dedicated themselves remained an ideal unrealized, yet in the years before intransigence set in, the possibility of church unity put Catholic and Protestant liberals within reach of agreement. Sadoleto has been described as well disposed to the reformation, a great favorer of Melanchthon and Bucer, and regretful at the death of Zwingli and Oecolampadius.[10] To Starkey, he was "one of the wisest men of our time." [11] In Pole's desire for a reform from within toward the purity of the early church, in his willingness to examine the original texts of the Scripture for light on the necessity of certain traditional doctrines, he stood on common ground with both Sadoleto and Melanchthon. His dismay must therefore have been less on account of the suppression of the monasteries than on account of Henry's break with the Pope, representing as it must have seemed to him an irrevocable rupture of church unity. That act obliterated the identity of his interests and those of the moderate Lutherans, the influence of whose ideas was to prove so powerful in the creation of the Anglican *via media*. Otherwise, Pole's difference with Henry might conceivably be resolved into a question of aesthetics. At any rate, his liberalism in the

[10] "Pole" in *Biographia Britannica,* edited by White Kennett (London, 1760), V, 3388; W. F. Hook, *Lives of the Archbishops of Canterbury* (London, 1868), VIII, 58.

[11] *Dialogue,* p. 203.

matter of church reform emphasizes his tolerance within his own household. Sadoleto, in speaking of Pole's personal preference for those works "whose emolument extended not only to this life but to futurity," added the comment that he had nevertheless been "long conversant with a set of men who are rather averse to these studies." [12] This is patent understatement for the utter- rather than other-worldliness of most of those who profited by Pole's hospitality. Suddenly they discovered that scholarship was a commodity, and further, that it had a royal bidder. The success of Starkey, who immediately after leaving Padua to become chaplain to Pole's mother found himself chaplain to the King, was electrifying.

III

It would be unjust to the scholarly sincerity of the group at Padua to attribute their enthusiasm for learning to wholly utilitarian motives. The intellectual atmosphere in Pole's household was immensely stimulating. Indeed, any such set of miscellaneous prejudices and temperaments combined with an avidity for learning was bound to be an excellent breeding ground for ideas. But *esprit de corps* will hardly account for the fact that from this group dynamic ideas sprang, more far-reaching perhaps than any of the individuals in it could know at the time. For the impact of the world outside their scholarly circle had broken with crushing force into academic discussions on the ideal state and the ideal society. The entire political and social structure was in fact undergoing radical shifts, and it is precisely because of these shifts that the younger scholars assumed primary importance to the crown.

[12] [Thomas Phillips], *The History of the Life of Reginald Pole* (London, 1767), I, 95.

Their empirical attitude toward Machiavelli is a case in point. All three of Machiavelli's works on political theory, *The Prince, The Discourses on the Decades of Livy,* and the *Florentine History* were known in England, and, as will be seen, through Morison's use of them exerted a direct influence on Cromwellian policy.[13] Of this influence, Pole was extremely apprehensive. About 1539, in a letter to Charles V, perhaps too impassioned to be taken as a strictly historical account, Pole described with horror a conversation with Cromwell some ten years previously in which Cromwell arrogantly suggested that Plato's idealisms in politics were now outmoded. At the same time, he recommended a book of more practical politics, apparently Machiavelli's *Prince,* which Pole later discovered to his dismay was written "by the finger of Satan as the Holy Scriptures are said to be written by the finger of God." What this letter reveals is not merely a fundamental incompatibility between Machiavelli's philosophy of government and his own, but a striking and significant rift that contemporary events had brought about among liberals. Men like Morison understood Machiavelli and accepted the pragmatic implications of his doctrine. To them he was an admirable master of practical politics, and they let moral considerations alone. Pole likewise understood him, but sensed in the application of such principles moral chaos.

It was this feeling that impelled Pole to warn John Leigh, a henchman of Cromwell's "against reading the story of Nicolo Matcheuello, which had already poisoned England and would poison all Christendom." [14] Pole could see only an unscrupulous line of conduct described in Machiavelli,

[13] For the evidence on this point, see below, pp. 184-189.

[14] *Letters and Papers, Foreign and Domestic, of the Reign of Henry VIII, 1509–47* (London, 1862–1932) XV, no. 721. (Hereafter referred to as *L&P.*)

a line of conduct abhorrent to him as a threat to the existing order. And indeed, for him personally, this was so. The dissolution of the monasteries meant for him the loss of Bisham,[15] his family seat; the destruction of the older nobility meant the destruction of his family and his own mortal danger; the royal supremacy meant the destruction of the only world he knew. Yet he could not see, as some of his fellow students in Padua could, that Machiavelli was willing to accept the fact of unscrupulous conduct to maintain a new order already in being. In their willingness to accept the irrevocable, the direction, not the objectives of scholarly endeavor had changed, in some respects markedly, from the tradition of More.

At this distance in time, one is inclined to regard this exigency rather than abstract theory as creating the real line of cleavage between scholars. The continuous lament running through the *Utopia* is the failure of the intellectual to obtain a hearing from a king absorbed in the practical affairs of state. Where, indeed, outside of Plato's *Republic* and More's *Utopia* was that state where kings would be philosophers? Knowing no answer, Hythloday retired. Pole, facing the same dilemma and in full realization of its implications, also retired. One may give due respect to this point of view without forgetting that the practical problems of government remained. After 1534, the old order had legally ceased to exist. If traditional modes of thought no longer wholly fitted the current situation, a practical *modus vivendi* had yet to be found. Never in the history of English thought was it more imperative to stride resolutely ahead. When Pole, like More, saw no answer, it was inevitable that Henry should turn for justification of this new social and political world to the bright young minds in

[15] Geoffrey Baskerville, *English Monks and the Suppression of the Monasteries* (London, 1937), p. 158.

Padua with a respect for the past but the courage and will to face the world they lived in. They performed the great task of binding that new world of fact created by Henry to the old world of tradition to which More and Pole clung. In their efforts we must find the continuity of humanism in the sixteenth century; in their solutions, an intellectual bridge from the Middle Ages to the Renaissance.

Thus while it is true that these writers were propagandists, and that their most significant work was propaganda, officially approved and published anonymously from the King's press, they laid foundations far deeper than the current situation demanded, partly because of their humanistic training, partly because they sensed the fundamental character of the issues at stake. They were propagandists but not charlatans. They wrote a program, but they wrote it with honesty and conviction. At times they quoted out of context, but so did their opponents. For beyond the bounds of formal logic, there was this kind of rightness in their cause: that they spoke in the last analysis, not for Cromwell, not for their king, but for the English people. Whatever the argument, they spoke in the accents of an English mores.

The primary concern of the chapters that follow will be to measure the importance of those accents in intellectual history. But since the achievement of these men would have been impossible without a broad humanistic training, the prerequisite to judging their place in the history of ideas must be an examination of their scholarly careers from their beginning at Oxford in the most ambitious gesture toward learning of that most ambitious of Henry's policy-makers, Cardinal Wolsey.

II

THE CARDINAL'S COLLEGE
AT OXFORD

Abbot Macy of the Cistercian Abbey of Bruerne was well satisfied. The last of the two hundred eighty great oaks felled in the forests of the monastery were on their way to Oxford where they would presently rise again in the noble interiors of Cardinal Wolsey's new college. It had taken these plus a consideration of two hundred fifty marks to make him an abbot, a heavy price but a great reward. The transaction was symbolic of the ecclesiastical property that was to be converted to the support of the project nearest to Wolsey's heart. Eventually, the wealth of twenty-one monasteries would be lavished on it. Cromwell well knew how to tickle his master's vanity when some three years after ground for the buildings had been broken he wrote: "The buyldings of yor noble Colledge most prosperouslye and magnyfycently dothe arryse in suche wise, that to euery mannes iudgement the lyke thereof [hath] neuer [been] sene ne ymagened hauing consederacyon to the largenes, beautie, sumptuous, curyous, and most substauncyall buylding of the same." [1]

<hr>

[1] *Original Letters Illustrative of English History*, edited by Henry Ellis (London, 1846), third series, II, 139.

Disgrace and death would shortly interrupt the Cardinal's plans. But sharper fear than these to him was the possibility that in the general debacle his college, still unfinished, might sink into neglect and desuetude. In his distress, he pleaded to the now firmly established Cromwell last and only for the preservation of his foundations at Oxford and Ipswich, "for they are in a manner, opera manuum tuarum." [2]

Cardinal's College, Wolsey's most ambitious formal project for the advancement of learning, represented the culmination of an habitual patronage of scholarship within his own household, marked by an unprecedented liberality both in a material and an intellectual sense. Pollard, estimating the total number of Wolsey's servants as "little if at all short of a thousand," concluded that "no college would have compared in size or splendour with the household he maintained." [3] What this meant to learning hardly needs underlining. The practical nature of his contribution to learning, however, has not been generally appreciated, and sometimes it has been misrepresented. By comparing his humanistic activity with that of his predecessor, Archbishop Warham, who in addition to being a patron of the great humanists of his generation was himself a scholar, Hook has conveyed a disparaging impression of the patronage of Wolsey. "Although Wolsey was too great a man not to be a patron of literature," he wrote, "his time was so completely occupied by political business that he was the Maecenas rather than the companion of learned men." [4]

[2] *L&P*, IV (3), no. 6076. See also his appeals to the King and others in *Original Letters*, second series, II, 32-38; *L&P*, IV (3), no. 6578; V, no. 456.

[3] A. F. Pollard, *Wolsey* (London, 1929), pp. 326-327. Brewer was more modest, but estimated Wolsey's household expenses at "something over £30,000 a year, modern reckoning"; *The Reign of Henry VIII* (London, 1884), I, 270, n. 1.

[4] *Lives of the Archbishops of Canterbury*, I, 265.

This description is literally accurate enough. Wolsey cared little for formal scholarship as such.[5] But this disposition in no way lessens his importance as a patron of learning; and it is low praise for the man of whom Erasmus, beneficiary of Warham, could say to Gonell, beneficiary of Wolsey: "O vere splendidum Cardinalem qui tales viros habet in consiliis, cuius mensa talibus hominibus cingitur."[6]

The fact of the matter is that Wolsey's occupation with political business was precisely the element that lent impetus to those who, in benefiting by his generosity, were shrewd enough to see that his patronage of scholarship was a way to fortune. Actually, the point of difference between the patronage of Warham and Wolsey lay not so much in purpose as in emphasis. Since the middle of the fifteenth century, humanistic training had opened the way to political and eventually to ecclesiastical preferment.[7] But Wolsey's brilliant secular career at a time when the papal dominion was losing its preëminence in England offered a living example of politics and diplomacy as ends in themselves. Wolsey's household consequently reflected his natural inclination to look at learning as a preparation for service in the state rather than the church, and this disposition established a solid secular basis and direction for scholarship which was to become only more pronounced as the church fell under the influence of the crown.

This practical influence is apparent in Strype's remark that Wolsey's household resembled a university, "for those

[5] Brewer remarked (*Reign of Henry VIII*, I, 58): "It is hard to find any statesman of his eminence who manifested less interest in the revival of letters, and cared less for Ciceronianisms and Latin elegancies."

[6] *Opus epistolarum*, edited by P. S. Allen (Oxford, 1906–), III (1), no. 968, p. 356.

[7] Weiss, *Humanism in England during the Fifteenth Century*, pp. 179–181.

many accomplished men in all kinds of knowledge and good learning, that were his domestics." [8] Men like Richard Sampson, Richard Pace, Cuthbert Tunstal, William Gonell, and John Clement, specifically mentioned in Strype's list, worthily carried on the tradition of Warham's scholars; Pace, Tunstal, and later Clement by study in Padua, Gonell and Clement as friends of Erasmus and members of More's circle. Wolsey's influence is revealed in the fact that Sampson, Pace, and Tunstal all achieved ambassadorial rank. And, as will be seen, they in their turn influenced those who were to transmit the humanistic tradition in the next generation. His household served, in Strype's phrase, "as a nursery for the court." [9] One historian of the reign has held that most of the officials of Henry VIII's reign passed an apprenticeship in Wolsey's household,[10] and there is some confirmation of this opinion in the extant subsidy rolls for the years 1525 and 1527,[11] which show a great increase in the number of his household servants,[12] though the lists, in another respect, are disappointing. Thomas Cromwell appears there (E 179/69/8), but no scholars of importance.

How practical a role humanists were expected to play in Wolsey's scheme of preferment is illustrated in his exchange of letters with his servant, Richard Sampson. One summer day in 1514, Sampson, then Wolsey's commissary, accompanied the Cardinal to the staple in Bruges. For some time .he had found his job irksome, his natural taste being for study; and for some time the Cardinal had ignored his

[8] *Ecclesiastical Memorials* (London, 1822), I, 194.

[9] *Ecclesiastical Memorials*, I, 188.

[10] J. S. Brewer, as quoted in P. V. Jones, *The Household of a Tudor Nobleman* (Cedar Rapids, Iowa, 1918), p. 33.

[11] PRO, E 179/69/8 Subsidy, 20 March 18 Henry VIII; E 179/69/9 Subsidy, 20 March 18 Henry VIII; E 179/69/10 Subsidy. *L&P*, IV (2), no. 2972.

[12] Not as great, however, as those estimates which have neglected the fact that many names are entered more than once.

wishes, unwilling to release a good servant. When, then, during the course of their walk, Wolsey chose to criticize his lack of assiduity, Sampson took the occasion to unburden his heart. At his first entry into Wolsey's service, Sampson reminded his patron, he had begged to be allowed time to study the civil and canon law. Yet since then, with more need for those studies than ever, he had found that his time was wholly absorbed in a world of business which he heartily disliked.[13]

Sampson's dissatisfaction is understandable. Since graduating Bachelor of Civil Law at Trinity, Cambridge, in 1505, he had continued in the same study at Paris and Sens, and in the year preceding had become Doctor of Civil Law at his alma mater. Wolsey's reply was an appointment in the Arches, and later the management of his household. Again, this time more boldly, Sampson reminded Wolsey of his lifelong determination to devote himself to letters, and begged that he be granted this indulgence, at the same time insisting that he was satisfied with his present condition, that he had no desire for the exaltation which others coveted. A court life, he frankly confessed, was disagreeable to him.

But there was no escape. How ironic that having refused Wolsey in 1519, Sampson should find himself in 1522 under request from the King for "some personages about him, as well to receive strangers that shall chance to come, as also that the same strangers shall not find him so bare without some noble and wise sage personages about him."[14] This was a summons that could not be avoided, and that same year he was trapanned into the diplomatic service at last. Writing from Valladolid, he accepted the new honor with grace, thanking Wolsey for his kindness in educating him.

[13] *L&P*, I, no. 5251.
[14] *L&P*, III (2), no. 2317.

The following spring, he was promoted to the deanery of Windsor.[15]

How genuine a casualty to Wolsey's importunities Sampson's experience represented is of no importance. Perhaps Sampson resigned himself without too great difficulty to the practical and remunerative task of defending Henry's supremacy, a task for which his exhaustive reading in the civil law preëminently fitted him. For what is important in Sampson's career is the evidence of an increased value placed on the civil law as an instrumental learning during Wolsey's term of office. It foreshadows the hard-bitted attitude of that other servant of Wolsey's, chief agent in establishing his college and greatest of his civilians, Stephen Gardiner. "Is not that that pleaseth the King, a law?" he was asked by Cromwell on an occasion when they were together in the royal presence. "Have ye not there in the Civil Law 'quod principi placuit'?" To a younger ambitious scholar, such a question might be an open invitation to the study of the civil law. From Gardiner, it drew a warning to Henry against "a new manner of policy," but it was a policy for which Wolsey's encouragement of the civil law may well have been responsible.

II

It is to be expected that the lavishness and practicality that characterized Wolsey's household would likewise inform his project for a new college at Oxford. His prodigality in its construction was the subject for raillery even in his own day, but he was not, as the criticism would seem to imply, merely a hewer of stone and drawer of water. He was equally generous in providing for its scholarly excellence. Its size alone is impressive. The original plan called for the incorporation of a dean and sixty canons, for forty

[15] *L&P*, III (2), nos. 2661, 3006.

petty- or junior-canons, for forty-two servants of the chapel, including choristers and a teacher of music, and for six public professors. There was provision also for twenty rich young commoners, to be maintained at their own expense. Poor commoners were supported as petty canons, with tutors to look after their funds.[16] The salaries were generous. Edward Hall, though unfriendly, expressed one contemporary opinion when he described the project as begun "so sumpteous and the scholers . . . so proude, that euery persone judged, that thende would not be good." [17]

Fortunately for the history of humanism, when Wolsey turned his attention to the curriculum and to academic appointments he exhibited the same healthy interest "in all kinds of knowledge and good learning" that he had shown within his own household, though in this respect his policy was apparently quite at odds with his expressed zeal against the Lutherans. There is no mistaking his announced intention in founding the college not only to promote good learning but "to extirpate the many heresies and schisms which had spread themselves over the christian world," [18] and his prejudice against the "hellish Lutherans" has led the historian of Christ Church to draw the not unreasonable inference that the Cardinal was "unequivocally hostile" to the new learning.[19] At the French court, Wolsey was confidently cited as authority for the opinion that no one could attain excellence in philosophy or theology without studying the schoolmen.[20] But such statements more properly

[16] C. E. Mallet, *A History of the University of Oxford* (London, 1924), II, 37-38.

[17] *The union of the two noble and illustre famelies* (1548), sig. Cxxxvii.

[18] Richard Fiddes, *The Life of Cardinal Wolsey* (London, 1724), p. 374.

[19] Henry L. Thompson, *Christ Church* (London, 1900), p. 7.

[20] *L&P*, IV (2), no. 5019. Winter to Wolsey, December 9, 1528.

reflect Wolsey's deep-seated distrust of religious extremism, a feeling held without exception by all the royal servants in England at the time. His conduct when Lutheranism presently sprang up in his own college is otherwise unaccountable.

As early as 1518 he declared to Queen Catherine that he proposed to found new professorships to meet the requirements of the age. In addition to medicine, philosophy, mathematics, Greek, rhetoric, and humanity, he planned to erect new chairs in theology and in civil law,[21] the study of which had already made Richard Sampson indispensable, and would distinguish the training of the new servants of Henry VIII. The Queen's continuing interest augured a brilliant future for the project. In the year of its founding, John Longland, Bishop of Lincoln, gave her a glowing prospect of "what learning there is and shall be, and what learned men in the cardinal's college," and assured her that "literature would be so encouraged that men would resort to England from all parts of Christendom for learning and virtue." [22] The university authorities in acknowledging Wolsey's gift indulged in even more fulsome praise:

If ever a Way was opened to true and solid Learning, this is the Time wherein the Dispositions of Providence to that End, appear more remarkable: Since no Age ever discovered a more forward Inclination in Men to Letters, or afforded greater Advantages for learned Improvements; For what can more excite the Ardor of Men in pursuit of them, than to understand, that their Endeavours do not only recommend them to the Approbation of their Superiors, but to the sensible, to the most generous, Effects, of their Favour and Encouragement. What indeed can contribute

[21] Hook, *Archbishops of Canterbury*, I, 273-274.
[22] *L&P*, IV (1), no. 995. January 5, 1525.

more to animate Men in their Search after Knowledge,
than when they consider they are pursuing those very
Methods, by which your Eminency hath gradually raised
yourself to so transcendent a Pitch of Glory,[23] etc., etc.

It is just possible that these great expectations inspired
the Queen, herself a patron of learning, to suggest for the
new chair in civil law the appointment of Juan Luis Vives;
he was in favor with Wolsey shortly afterward [24] and was
established in Oxford in March 1525, "amidst the studies
and leisure of a scholar." [25]

Fully as enthusiastic as Catherine for the new project was
the youthful scholar-nobleman, Reginald Pole. Soon after
the founding, Thomas Lupset, his devoted friend and fellow
student in Padua, succeeded John Clement in the chair of
rhetoric; and in 1529 Wolsey appealed to him for help in
procuring a professor of oratory from Italy. Pole accordingly
wrote to Romolo Amasei, professor of Greek and Latin at
Padua and a member of his household there. The Cardinal
of York, he informed Amasei with frank admiration, had
commenced a most magnificent work. The place was grand
in itself, but much more so by virtue of the multitude of
faculty and students. Two hundred were to be supplied
with food and clothing. No class of learning was to be excluded, and each was to have its own compensation. To
Amasei, Wolsey had authorized an offer of five hundred
ducats a year plus his traveling expenses and benefices for
his sons if any of them were destined for the church. These
inducements notwithstanding, Pole was sincere, one feels

[23] Fiddes, *Wolsey,* p. 375.
[24] On May 26, 1520, More expressed his pleasure to Erasmus that
Vives stood so well with his friend the Cardinal, and hoped that this
would be a means of mending his fortune. *L&P,* III (1), no. 838.
[25] *L&P,* IV (1), no. 1177. See also *L&P,* IV (1), p. 520, n.;
Fowler, *The History of Corpus Christi College* (Oxford, 1893), pp.
87-88.

sure, in recommending the place, as much for the good of his country as for Amasei's welfare.[26]

III

Pole had already assumed the role of patron of learning, and his unreserved praise of the broad policies of Wolsey is an anticipation of the character of the humanistic tradition after Wolsey's death. But the more immediate results of Wolsey's policy were revealed in an episode, hardly concluded as Pole wrote to Amasei, which tested not only Wolsey's tolerance but eventually, by force of circumstance, Pole's. Not long before, in order to insure a high level of scholarship in the student body, Wolsey had resorted to an unprecedented importation of scholars from Cambridge. Under the date February 17, 1527, in an itemized account of disbursements of the college, is the following entry: "The expences of Dr. Thorton [Shorton] in conveying of sundry scholars from Cambridge to Oxford, £11, 12s." [27] Robert Shorton, D.D., was master of Pembroke Hall and dean of the Cardinal's chapel.[28] His task was to invite "scholars of ripe wits and abilities to study and read there, with promise of great encouragement and reward." [29]

The Cambridge draft in the name of learning was a characteristic extravagance. Undertaken at the same time as Pole's effort to strengthen the faculty, it was only a part of Wolsey's general plan to obtain the best minds wherever they might be found. According to Foxe, Wolsey brought in "many others out of other places, most picked young men,

[26] *L&P*, IV (3), no. 5224. January 27, 1529.
[27] *L&P*, IV (2), no. 3536.
[28] *L&P*, IV (1), no. 4685.
[29] John Strype, *The Life and Acts of Matthew Parker* (Oxford, 1821), p. 10.

of grave judgment and sharp wits." [30] Some of them had already been established at Oxford when the Cambridge men arrived, among them, Rudolph Gualter, Thomas Starkey, and Richard Morison. Gualter was probably the son of the "D. Gualter anglius" mentioned by Andrich as consiliarius of the English nation at Padua from 1500 to 1502.[31] A learned man, according to Foxe,[32] he apparently continued his scholarly career abroad, where he was associated with Protestants, for he returned to England in 1537 as the foster-son of Henry Bullinger, the Swiss reformer.[33] Starkey had spent "that greater part of his youth" at Oxford in the study of philosophy and the classics,[34] and in 1521 he had become Master of Arts there.[35] In the following year, Wolsey, ignoring university custom, stepped into an intramural struggle over proctorships at Oxford and deferred their election, meanwhile appointing two "masters of the schools" who were not of a "turbulent, aspiring temper." One of these was Starkey.[36] Morison, we know from his praise of Wolsey's devotion to clerical duty,[37] was a former member of the Cardinal's household. Others were

[30] John Foxe, *Actes and Monuments,* edited by S. R. Cattley and George Townsend (London, 1837–1841), V, 5.

[31] Io. Aloys. Andrich, *De natione Anglica et Scota iuristarum Universitatis Pativinae* (Padua, 1892).

[32] *Actes and Monuments,* V, 5.

[33] Theodore Vetter, *Relations between England and Zurich during the Reformation* (London, 1904), p. 5.

[34] *L&P,* VIII, no. 214.

[35] John A. Gee, *Life and Works of Thomas Lupset* (New Haven, 1928), p. 147.

[36] Fiddes, *Wolsey,* p. 309, collections (in appendix), p. 122; *L&P,* III (2), no. 2267.

[37] *A Remedy for sedition, wherein are conteyned many thynges, concernynge the true and loyall obeysance, that commes owe unto their prince and soveraygne lorde the kynge* [London, 1536], sig. E ii^v–E iii.

brought in, according to Wood,[38] only after "certain pauses
and delays, that he might make choice of the sharpest (as
'tis reported) and quickest wits," among whom Wood mentioned John Taverner and "William" Tyndale, an error for
Gervase Tyndale.[39] Morison and Tyndale were both appointed petty canons.[40]

The importation of scholars from Cambridge, however,
represented Wolsey's only attempt at wholesale acquisition.
About seventeen scholars have been attributed to Shorton's
efforts, though the list is certainly defective and probably
incomplete. Strype listed in his *Life and Acts of Matthew
Parker* (p. 10) Richard Cox, John Friar, and Henry Sumner, all of whom were mentioned by Anthony à Wood as
excellent scholars,[41] John Clerk, who, with Sumner, Strype
labeled as an excellent divine,[42] William Betts, Richard
Harman,[43] Richard Taverner, Florentius, a Dominican,[44]
John Drumm, John Akars, and John Frith. To this list
should be added Richard Baily, Godman (no first name

[38] *The History and Antiquities of the Colleges and Halls in the
University of Oxford* (Oxford, 1786), p. 423.

[39] J. R. Bloxam, *Register of Magdalen College* (Oxford, 1863),
III, 41, repeated the error, but see reference cited in Note 40.

[40] *L&P*, XIII (2), no. 817, p. 325.

[41] *Fasti oxonienses*, edited by Philip Bliss (London, 1815), p. 72.

[42] *Parker*, p. 10.

[43] "Harman, afterwards fellow of Eaton," in Strype's *Memorials of
the Most Reverend Father in God Thomas Cranmer* (Oxford, 1812),
p. 4; "Nicholas Herman" in Strype's *Parker*, p. 10; "Godf. Harman"
in Wood's *Fasti*, p. 72, and in Joseph Foster's *Alumni Oxonienses: the
Members of the University of Oxford, 1500–1714* (Oxford, 1891–
1892). J. and J. A. Venn, *Alumni Cantabrigienses* (Cambridge, 1927),
suggested the possibility of two Harmans at Cardinal's College. See
also Thomas Harwood, *Alumni Etonienses* (London, 1797).

[44] So Wood's *Fasti*, p. 72. Strype's *Parker*: "Flor. Dominick." This
is possibly Florentius Volusene, who had been one of the tutors to
Thomas Winter, Wolsey's natural son, in Paris in the previous year
(see pp. 59 ff. below), though his biographers make no mention of
it, tracing his scholarly career from the University of Aberdeen to
Paris.

mentioned), and Thomas Lawney from Strype's *Cranmer* (p. 4), and Winmer Allen, Edward Staple, and possibly Edward Wotton from Wood's *Fasti* (p. 72). According to Strype, Thomas Cranmer, John Skip, Walter Haddon, and Matthew Parker were invited but refused the offer "by the persuasion of their friends." [45] They were not green scholars. Out of the number, Cox, Friar, Sumner, Clerk, Betts, Harman, Frith, Allen, Baily, and Wotton had already earned degrees before their incorporation in Cardinal's College. All were young and gifted. Shorton had every reason to believe that his work had been done well.

In such a group and in view of subsequent events, it would be natural to expect convictions. As to their nature and source, however, authorities differ. Since the new appointees were hand-picked for Wolsey, Gordon Goodwin's statement [46] that at their arrival three of the new M.A.'s were "violent Lutherans" is putting a hard name on what seems to have been little more than youthful inquisitiveness. More credible is the Coopers' claim that they adopted Lutheran opinions soon after their arrival.[47] At any rate, there is no evidence that in his effort to obtain "ripe wits and abilities," Shorton exceeded his commission in either intent or fact. Indeed, on the basis of existing evidence, it is highly likely that he was not acting on Wolsey's direct orders at all, but by direction from Edward Fox, and that Fox's approval would therefore have been determinant in their choice. As Wolsey's servant, possibly already as his secretary, Fox had aided Wolsey in founding his colleges

[45] *Parker*, p. 11. In his *Cranmer* (p. 3), Strype explained Cranmer's refusal as "choosing rather to abide among his old fellow-collegians, and more closely to follow his studies and contemplations here."

[46] *DNB*: "John Friar."

[47] C. H. and T. Cooper, *Athenae Cantabrigienses* (Cambridge, 1858–1861), I, 225. Perhaps on the authority of Foxe (V, 423): "tender and lately born little flock in Oxford."

at Oxford and Ipswich; and after the Cardinal's death, he had induced Henry to finish King's College Chapel.[48] It is hardly coincidental that Cox, Friar, Sumner, and Harman all came from Eton and King's where Fox matriculated and where a year later he would be installed as provost by recommendation of Wolsey and the King. And this connection is confirmed by Fox's patronage of Friar at a later point in his career.

What sort of aid Fox gave to Wolsey is not a matter of record; but if on the basis of the known facts we may assume that the King's continental agent for the divorce in 1530 and the author of *De vera differentia regiae potestatis et ecclesiasticae* of 1534 was influential in getting the Cambridge scholars to Oxford in 1527, then it seems reasonable also that they would reflect his opinions as of 1527, and that those opinions would be liberal. For lack of more concrete evidence Fox's influence must remain a speculation, but it is a speculation worth consideration, for it suggests his acquaintance as early as 1525 with Starkey and Friar's friend, Morison, both of whom were presently to lend their talents to the propaganda campaign for the royal supremacy.

Cardinal's College seemed assured of a brilliant future. But bright young collegians are unpredictable, and from the point of view of the college authorities their minds often move in mysterious ways. Late in February 1528, barely a year after Shorton's draft from Cambridge, John Longland, Bishop of Lincoln, received a long letter from Dr. London, Warden of New College,[49] a man whom the Bishop especially trusted for his wisdom. It appeared that since his last letter on university affairs many things had occurred to make him pensive. Thomas Garrett, curate of All Souls, in Honey Lane, London, and a B.A. from Oxford in 1517, had

[48] *Athenae Cantabrigienses*, I, 66.
[49] *L&P*, IV (2), no. 3968. February 25, 1528.

visited his alma mater at Easter. Seeking out those who knew Hebrew, Greek, and Latin, on the pretense of learning these subjects, he had distributed a great number of books tainted with Lutheranism. It was London's suspicion that Garrett had been asked to come by John Clerk. Clerk was a questionable fellow, anyway, having been known to read the Pauline epistles in his chamber to young men as well as to those of two, three, and four years standing in the university. And Higdon, the dean, knew some of them to have a shrewd name. The perennial accents of college wardens are recognizable in his exasperated dictum: Would that Wolsey had never called Clerk or any other Cambridge man to his most towardly college; it had shown a clean record till they came. Like all good wardens, however, he swallowed his irritation and searched for excuse. These youths, he assured the Bishop, had not long been conversant with Garrett, nor had they greatly perused his books. Actually, he was sorry for them; they were the most promising young men in Oxford.

The Bishop of Lincoln was in far from good health when this disturbing letter reached him. Wolsey had in fact recently allowed him special dietary indulgence for his ailment, a kindness which he acknowledged before laying the affair of the Cardinal's College before the Cardinal himself. It was not his first letter concerning the matter, but another seemed necessary in view of the information that had been coming in from various quarters in the meantime. His sorrow arose from Garrett's Socratic offense, "the great corruption of youth," but he named also "Master Clarke, Master Freer, Sir Fryth, Sir Dyott, and Anthony Delabere" as "famylyarly acquaynted in this mater," and suggested for the good of the university that Wolsey call some of them before him for examination and judgment. The others, "bycause of the multytude and that they be yong and penytent, and by other malicious persones seduced" should be dealt with on the spot by Wolsey's commission.[50] On March 5, Longland was able to report to Wolsey that Garrett and Friar had both been seized and were now in prison, though he feared that their influence had infected many other parts of England.[51]

What must have been particularly ironic for Wolsey was the identity of those "infected" within the college. At least twelve of the Cambridge men installed in Cardinal's College were in some way implicated. But John Higdon spared no feelings in the face of duty. With Garrett and Friar already in custody, he seized Clerk, Sumner, Betts, Frith, Baily, and Lawney.[52] Then he listed Friar's books, locked them up, and sent the list to Wolsey so that Friar's word could be checked against the fact. Some of those wanted had escaped to the continent. But even there the search continued. In July, Harman was arrested in Antwerp. John Hacket, reporting the incident to Wolsey, was anxious to prove him guilty of treason, since on a heresy charge revocation would free him. He was of the opinion that Lutherans should be included with traitors in the statutes of intercourse of 1505, "for as soon as they have passed the sea they know neither God nor King." [53]

IV

Hither and yon the offenders were rounded up to await Wolsey's disposition of their offenses. But there the cases seemed to rest. His officers were puzzled. Only recently the Cardinal had excommunicated the Lutheran sect; now it brazenly lifted its head in his own college and he was

[50] Ellis (ed.), *Original Letters*, third series, II, 77-80.
[51] *L&P*, IV (2), no. 4017.
[52] *L&P*, IV (2), no. 4074.
[53] *L&P*, IV (2), no. 4511.

doing nothing. As time lapsed, the situation became embarrassing. To what purpose had the guilty been harried down if they were not brought to justice? At the university, Higdon observed the approach of Easter and asked if they were to be absolved. There is no record that Wolsey was shocked into a reply.

Eventually, no doubt to the vexation of the college authorities, they were acquitted. In August, Clerk was writing from Poghley, where he had preached without satisfactory ecclesiastical license before the trouble arose, asking Cromwell's favor with Wolsey for a letter to the dean to admit his brother Richard to a petty canonry. The request was granted, though ironically sickness struck in Cardinal's College immediately after, carrying away not only Richard [54] but Henry Sumner and Richard Baily as well, a circumstance hardly chargeable to Wolsey. The other three culprits, Betts, Frith, and Lawney, still remained in Higdon's custody on September 1, but they too were soon released.[55]

Outside the college walls, Wolsey exercised a similar leniency. By the end of the year one of the chief offenders, John Clerk, had been reëstablished as a canon in the college.[56] Richard Taverner, who was accused of "hiding the books of one of the parties under the boards in his school," was forgiven, if *Athenae Cantabrigienses* can be believed, on the grounds that he was a musician.[57] John Friar, confined in the Fleet, was pardoned personally by Wolsey. His

---

[54] According to Foxe (*Actes and Monuments,* IV, 617), Richard Clerk was "a tender young man, and the most singular in learning amongst them all." Foxe is also responsible for the story that the unfortunates were infected from the smell of salt fish in the college prison.

[55] *L&P,* IV (2), nos. 4074, 4607, 4690; Foxe, *Actes and Monuments,* V, 4.

[56] *L&P,* IV (3), no. 6100.

[57] The story would seem more likely for John Taverner, who was brought to Cardinal's College for his ability as an organist.

letter of gratitude, written from the prison on September 16, overflows with praise for Wolsey's generosity "which he had often experienced before" and which had now caused him to break the silence occasioned in part by his grief at these sad times. Wolsey's memory "will be dear to all posterity," and as for himself, Wolsey had saved him from destruction which he had brought on himself by his own folly.[58]

In Flanders, Harman's case continued to wait on Wolsey's judgment. Finally, early in February, John West, an Observant friar acting for Hacket, wrote impatiently to Wolsey that unless new charges of treason could be preferred against him, he would be released in three weeks to do more mischief; and again, on February 8, he warned Wolsey of the great encouragement to Lutheranism if Harman were delivered.[59] There is no evidence that Wolsey acted, and Harman later was in the employ of Cromwell.[60]

Wolsey's impeachment in November 1529 would conceivably have distracted him from consideration of other people's troubles; yet all the facts seem to argue the reliability of Foxe's explanation for Wolsey's apparent unwillingness to back up the punitive measures of his officers: "Frith, with others, by cardinal's letter, who did not want them so straitly handled, was dismissed out of prison, upon condition not to pass above ten miles out of Oxford." [61] Under this sentence, one must presume, they might continue to contaminate the university to the vexation of the good dean, but Wolsey had thereby saved his scholars to fight another day.[62]

It was a day which Wolsey would never see. Before the

[58] *L&P*, IV (2), no. 4741.
[59] *L&P*, IV (3), nos. 5462, 5275.
[60] *L&P*, XIII (1), nos. 1055, 1056.
[61] *Actes and Monuments*, V, 5.
[62] Brewer (*Reign of Henry VIII*, I, 58; II, 267) felt that whereas before 1528 Wolsey was indifferent toward Lutheranism on the

year was out, he had lost all and died a broken man. Yet the echoes of grandeur run through his appeal to the King's secretary, Stephen Gardiner: "In the wey of charite, & for the love that ye bere to vertue, & *ad bona studia,* be meane to the kyngs highnes for my poore colleges; and especially for the college of Oxford. Suffer not the things, which by your greate lernyng, studie, counsaile & travaile, hath bene erected, founden, & with good statutes & ordinances, to the honour of God, increase of vertue & lernyng establisshed, to be dissolved or dismembred." [63] His motives in establishing his college may well be questioned; the Cardinal's coat of arms patterned in the great windows is proof enough that self-aggrandizement was undoubtedly a strong incentive, and the futile efforts of men like Sampson to escape the rigorous demands of office for the freedom of the study may have had the effect of harnessing rather than liberating the scholar. But these are flaws in the grain which characterize rather than detract from the permanent service he did for scholarship. As one looks back at the episode of the Cambridge scholars, a patron of learning emerges, genuinely interested in its advancement. His emphasis on the usefulness of the scholar was ultimately a healthier influence on scholarship than an over-scrupulousness for religious opinions, and it is to his credit that to this end he was willing

---

grounds that societies of scholars, amply endowed like his foundation at Oxford would be a better preventive than repression, after 1528 he took up active persecution. But there is no evidence in his handling of the incident at Oxford of any such change. Burnet (*History of the Reformation,* edited by Nicholas Pocock, Oxford, 1865, I, 261-262) suggested that he may have refrained from persecution because of the King's order. In any case, his earlier record of liberalism in education is confirmed by his policy in affairs of state. With regard to his retention in office of Sir Robert Wingfield after his failure to carry out orders, Brewer remarked (I, 120): "To the credit of the reign, a freedom of opinion and dissent was allowed to official men, which disappeared in after times."

[63] Strype, *Ecclesiastical Memorials,* V, 456.

to protect "grave judgment and sharp wits" against even the dread name of heresy. One gains the impression that London and Higdon, conscientious in their duties, were more frightened by the dangers of Lutheranism than was Wolsey.

Nor did their fears prove groundless. According to one of Wolsey's best biographers, "none were more active and instrumental in opening a Way to the Reformation in England, than the very Members of that Society, which the Cardinal had founded with an intention of doing eminent Service therby to the papal Cause"; [64] and a recent historian of the Reformation in describing the entrance of the New Learning into England has asserted that "the continental teachers and the scholars from Cambridge who were brought in by Cardinal Wolsey to staff his great new college, were probably the chief source of such views." [65] From a narrowly ecclesiastical point of view, the dean was right. But for Wolsey, the irony of the situation was undoubtedly tempered by his desire to propagate learning, and in this respect the dean's agitation serves to emphasize Wolsey's fundamental broad-mindedness as a factor in the history of learning in Renaissance England.

They were more than reformers, these scholars who were brought together under Wolsey's patronage in his new college at Oxford. Disappointing as their penchant to Lutheranism may have been, they were nevertheless Wolsey's men in their urge to put their learning to use in the service of the state. Where his elder servant, Richard Sampson, was reluctant, they were eager to participate in public affairs. If only for the fact that Cardinal's College brought Edward Fox, Richard Cox, Thomas Starkey, Richard Morison, and Richard Taverner into scholarly contact with each other,

[64] Fiddes, *Wolsey*, p. 374.
[65] L. E. Elliott-Binns, *The Reformation in England* (London, 1937), p. 43.

CARDINAL WOLSEY
National Portrait Gallery, London

CARDINAL POLE
National Portrait Gallery, London

Wolsey's practical aims in patronage would seem to have been satisfied. For it was out of this small group of enthusiasts that justification of the new Tudor program was to spring.

There was little to prevent the disintegration of Wolsey's establishment at his death. His household did indeed fall apart, and the results are observable in the years following. The college, for which he made his last abject pleas, suffered also, though support gradually rallied. In August 1530 John Higdon appealed to the King for its preservation, "but not so great and of such magnificence as Wolsey intended to have, for it is not thought meet for the common weal of our realm." [66] Not until July 1532 did Henry reëstablish Cardinal's College as King's. Then, as Anthony à Wood put it, "upon the desires of several well wishers to the Muses, and especially at the most humble request of the dispersed remnant of the Cardinal's Scholars," [67] the King granted patents with twelve canons and John Higdon as dean.

Such a petition argues that at least a small company of Wolsey's scholars survived at Oxford three years after his death, a melancholy comment on the vicissitudes of patronage and patrons. But they are of little if any interest in the history of scholarship. For it was not the petitioners of the King who were destined to make intellectual history. What, it might reasonably be asked, had happened in the meantime to the men of "grave judgments and sharp wits"? It is not to be supposed that they would find the atmosphere of King's College under Higdon precisely inviting. And even so, there were more pressing wants than a congenial atmosphere to determine their careers. Moreover, those who were able had fled to the continent where, if they really were Lutheran by conviction, as Frith certainly was, they could

[66] *L&P*, IV (3), no. 6579.
[67] *History and Antiquities . . . of Oxford*, p. 428.

establish themselves and maintain well-organized contacts with England, but where, if their "Lutheranism" were merely a term of opprobrium flung at a liberal temperament, a shift of patrons would be relatively more difficult than in England. They would appeal to Cromwell as a matter of course. But in the meantime, it is not strange that, by one means or another, they began to appear in Italy during the years after Wolsey's fall, either in the household of Thomas Winter, Wolsey's natural son who gravitated discontentedly between London, Paris, and Padua, or in that of Reginald Pole, whose house in Padua had already become a center for English students in Italy.

The harvest of Wolsey's liberal policy thus began to be apparent in the careers of those young expatriates. They were the visible sign of the continuity of humanism after his death. Pole's satisfaction at the fact that no class of learning was excluded from Cardinal's College was an earnest of his continuation of that policy when Wolsey's men, deprived of his patronage, should find in Pole's household new encouragement to learning. Tunstal, now ambassador to the Emperor, Sampson at Bruges, and Pace, ambassador to Venice and Pole's closest friend, demonstrated the material success to which a younger generation of Wolsey's scholars might attain. His spirit must have rested benignly on them. They remembered him with affection. And well they might. For few of the scholars who directed Henry VIII's policy in his break with Rome did not find themselves recipients at some time in their careers of his great minister's generosity. On a less magnificent scale, the gracious and undiscriminatory life at Padua and Venice was no less welcome as an asylum for Wolsey's deprived exhibitioners. The story of how Pole became sponsor of their intellectual activity can best be told by turning back to the time of that young nobleman's first arrival in Italy.

III

PADUA, PARIS, AND
THE DIVORCE

Reginald Pole's arrival in Padua in 1519 heralded a renaissance of English scholarship in Italy. It had been more than twenty years since Grocyn, Colet, and Linacre had returned to England, and in the intervening time few Englishmen had made the journey to the nursery of arts and recognized school for English diplomats. True, the line of continuity of English scholars had never been completely broken; Richard Pace, John Clerk, his close friend, and Cuthbert Tunstal were all recent arrivals while Latimer of the older generation was still there,[1] and Latimer and Tunstal were presently to combine efforts to see that Pole of the next generation was properly certified. Occasional notices indicate that the English colony was certainly larger than this. "An English doctor" lectured in Padua in 1502;[2] Thomas Buclam matriculated there in 1507 or 1508;[3] and in 1512 and 1513 the son of James IV of Scotland was writing letters from Padua to his royal father without giving his father's

[1] Jervis Wegg, *Richard Pace* (London, 1932), pp. 8-9; Charles Sturge, *Cuthbert Tunstal* (London, 1938), pp. 10–11.

[2] *Calendar of State Papers, Venetian* (London, 1864–1898), I, 828. (Hereafter referred to as *Ven. Cal.*)

[3] Andrich, *De natione Anglica et Scota*, p. 21.

title, in order to avoid suspicion "in consequence of the war." [4] Evidence of the state of English scholarship in Italy during this period may be found in the correspondence of Erasmus with the utterly academic John Watson in Venice, who had been following the strict pattern of the academician in his study of Quintilian under Raphael Regius and of Greek under Musurus. When Erasmus twitted him lightly for his love of Duns Scotus, Watson readily acknowledged it, "having resolved to devote the rest of his life to Latin theology." [5] This was the fitful *nachtschein* of the English tradition in Italy of the fifteenth century. There were extenuating factors. For several years after 1510, war in Italy and the conditions consequent upon it brought about almost complete discontinuance of university life. [6] But the record is sparse enough, the years lean enough, to account Pole's arrival as an event of the first magnitude in the history of English scholarship in Italy.

Pole's first journey to Padua in 1519 was without fanfare and of short duration. [7] Henry financed it, apparently on an increased allowance from the £12 annual stipend which he had furnished for his support since his entrance to Magdalen in 1513. Pole was then nineteen years old. He had lived gracefully and quietly in the commodius quarters of the president of the college, enjoying such deferences and conferring such favors as befitted his social station. Now he found himself in a cultured society, in which his royal blood enhanced his dignities and made him at once the recipient

[4] *L&P*, I, nos. 3479, 3828.

[5] *L&P*, II, nos. 2728, 2772, 3420.

[6] Sturge, *Tunstal*, p. 15.

[7] *L&P*, III (1), no. 198. So Martin Haile, *Life of Reginald Pole* (London, 1910), and Athanasius Zimmerman, *Kardinal Pole, sein Leben und seine Schriften* (Regensburg, 1893). Gee, *Thomas Lupset*, p. 112, n. 47, concludes on the basis of new evidence that Pole's first visit to Italy was in 1521, but the 1519 letter referred to above seems decisive.

of new and flattering attentions. Of "Monsigr. Anglese," Peter Bembo wrote: "He is always with Messer Leonico, or with Monsignor Stampa, or with Monsignor Prothon de Rossi, a gentle, studious youth of his own age, or with Count Ludovico in San Bonifacio and other scholars and very worthy gentlemen of the same kind, who willingly follow and escort him [*lo seguitono e corteggiano volontieri*]." [8] In his letter to Henry announcing his arrival, he spoke of the embarrassments these courtesies involved in view of the fact that he had been provided only with an exhibitioner's maintenance; and expressed the hope that the King would not allow him for lack of funds to abandon Padua for some obscure place in Italy.[9] But if Pole was finding it difficult to make extended ends meet, ill health may have forced his decision to return home.[10]

The request for more money met with success. In the King's book of payments for February 1521 is a grant of £100, finding for one year,[11] a sum which continued to be granted as long as Pole was a student in Italy. Most munificent among the King's benefactions, it proved to be also the most significant in the history of Tudor humanism. Pole's preparations were quickly made, and on March 5 *The Gabriel* sailed from Dover to Calais with him aboard.[12] This second visit was full of promise. His quasi-diplomatic importance may be judged by the fact that he bore Henry's personal recommendation to the Signory of neighboring Venice.[13] The Venetian Council, anxious to compliment the

[8] Bembo to Cardinal Chigi, 1519–1520, cited in Haile, *Reginald Pole*, p. 22.

[9] *L&P*, III (1), no. 198.

[10] *L&P*, III (1), no. 411. Edward Laborne to Pole's mother, the Countess of Salisbury, August 7, 1519, from Wimborne, to report on affairs there to her son, "whom I beseche God restore too helthe."

[11] *L&P*, III (2), p. 1544.

[12] *L&P*, IV (3), p. 3105.

[13] *Ven. Cal.*, III, no. 184.

King's relative, granted him permission to export purchases, and somewhat later, to carry weapons for the security of his person.[14] This precaution was not overly solicitous. When rumors were already in circulation in Italy that Henry mistrusted Pole's popularity "lest he prove disloyal," [15] his personal safety was a state consideration. No doubt Pole's social rank diverted attention from his humanistic interests. It was not every English student coming to Padua for whom the Signory of Venice expressly provided a tutor, to whom the English ambassador extended hospitality, and who received a personal word of encouragement in his studies from the Pope.[16] But though Pole was aware of his position and was perfectly willing to capitalize on it, he came as a scholar, not as a relative of Henry. It was the recommendation of the great English Paduans, Thomas Linacre and William Latimer, his instructors at Magdalen, that he presented as credentials to Nicolo Leonico, their Greek teacher and Cuthbert Tunstal's while they were in Italy. And certainly from the first, scholarship was the common meeting ground for those who gathered about him. Richard Pace hastened to extend social amenities, not only as the English ambassador in Venice, but as a former student of Latimer and Tunstal.[17] Thus, in his person, Pole continued the tradition of English scholars who had studied in Padua before him, but with the unique and immense prestige that his lineage brought. Continental scholars likewise recognized the importance of his arrival. While Pace entertained Pole in Venice, Christopher Longueil, the Ciceronian, delayed his visit solely out of respect for their

[14] *Ven. Cal.*, III, no. 218; IV, no. 1053.
[15] *Ven. Cal.*, III, no. 204.
[16] *L&P*, IV (1), no. 79.
[17] Wegg, *Richard Pace*, pp. 4, 8; Sturge, *Cuthbert Tunstal*, pp. 9, 12.

intimate friendship.[18] Erasmus, to whom Padua was now "the Athens of Europe," expressed pleasure to find in such times a person so devoted to studies and piety, and while recommending the young Polish scholar, John à Lasco, to his company as a kindred spirit, deplored the necessity of staying in Basle away from the scholarly fraternity now gathered in Italy.[19] Peter Bembo described Pole as "the most learned, mature, and virtuous young man in Italy," and complimented him for his indefatigable studies and the vast extent of his reading.[20] Allowing for a degree of sycophancy in such remarks, the fact still remains that the intellectual aristocracy of Europe were interested, and that interest gave Pole's household in Padua an international standing.

This deference was the more conspicuous in that Pole made no distinctions in social rank. "His house," said Hook, "became the resort of the great and the learned, who were pleased to share his hospitality; and, as the custom then was, he afforded board and lodging to several poor scholars, who for the sake of sharing in the instruction given in common, were willing to discharge, without any derogation of their dignity, menial offices, a place below the salt being supplied to them at meal times." [21] Enthusiasm for learning was their only qualification. He had always shown this same disarming lack of condescension. Beccatelli, one of Pole's servants and his first biographer, remarked that "the meanest servants of his household were the objects of his care, in case of sickness even of his personal attention," and that because of his kindness of heart, he was sometimes imposed upon by "bad men, who palmed themselves upon him as

[18] *L&P*, III (2), no. 2460.
[19] *L&P*, IV (1), no. 1685; IV (2), no. 2953; V, no. 382.
[20] Phillips, *Reginald Pole*, I, 25.
[21] Hook, *Archbishops of Canterbury*, VIII, 21.

poor scholars." [22] While his establishment in Padua was rather more gracious than luxurious,[23] it was always open to commoners. Among Englishmen there, only Richard Shelley and Michael Throckmorton were gentlemen by birth, and neither of them made any pretensions to scholarship. Shelley was sent abroad to complete his education but took little interest in it; [24] and Throckmorton was a scapegrace family friend whom Pole tolerated as his messenger.[25] The rest of Pole's dependents were all of humble origin. Thomas Starkey's father had been granted an annuity by Henry VII "at his first entry into this his realm," but the family had since fallen into straightened circumstances.[26] Henry Phillips, son of a former mayor of Hereford, was a rapscallion whose scholarly career in Louvain was colored by a reputation for having betrayed Tyndale; who had spoken of the King as a tyrant and spoiler of the commonwealth; who had committed other grievous crimes against the King and his neighbors; and who had with egregious effrontery offered an acquaintance service with Pole on the strength of his friendship with Throckmorton. He seems to have been the only person ever to be refused help when he turned up at Pole's house in Padua several years later, and the circumstances seem wholly to exonerate Pole from blame.[27] Richard Morison, Henry Cole, John Friar, and George Lily were all of low birth, though Lily enjoyed the rather dubious advantage of having been preceded at

[22] Ludovico Beccatelli, *The Life of Cardinal Reginald Pole* (London, 1766), p. 149.

[23] Beccatelli, *Pole*, p. 133.

[24] A. F. Pollard, "Sir Richard Shelley," in the *DNB; L&P*, XIII (2), nos. 724, 847.

[25] *L&P*, VIII, no. 536; XI, no. 4; XII, no. 430.

[26] *L&P*, II (2), no. 3354.

[27] *L&P*, VIII, no. 1151; X, no. 535; XII (1), no. 1293; XIII (2), nos. 507, 509.

Padua by his renowned father.[28] When the Signory's governors of Padua addressed "the most Illustrious and Reverend Reginald Pole" as "a student in our university," they were paying him the respect he most valued. He had the satisfaction of knowing that at Padua in his time was preserved the same democracy among scholars that had characterized the generation of Erasmus, Colet, and More.

Perhaps the most stimulating aspect of Pole's household was the temper and range of its learning. Under the tutelage of Leonico, they were viewing the great classics for the first time free from the commentaries and insertions of the Arabic philosophers which had obscured them during the Middle Ages. With the same excitement that Colet read the Pauline epistles in the original, they were rediscovering Aristotle and Plato. They joined Joannes Baptista Opizo in printing Galen, the standard medical authority, in the original tongue.[29] One can feel the enthusiasm of a young Grecian in George Lily's report to Starkey in England that he had read without assistance seven tragedies of Sophocles, five of Euripides, three comedies of Aristophanes, and the moralia of Xenophon and Plutarch.[30] This was the boast of a beginner, anxious to impress his recent companion in study. But the same zest is apparent in the commonplace books of Morison, a more mature fellow student, where snatches of Greek interlard the customary Latin.

Furthermore, their enthusiasm in rediscovering the Greek classics in Greek set the mood of approach toward the classics of medieval and modern Europe. Soon after Morison left Padua, he was quoting Chaucer and commending the learning of Vives and Erasmus. Lily, in his letter to

[28] A cause of occasional personal discouragement. *L&P*, IX, no. 292.

[29] Gee, *Thomas Lupset*, p. 117; Wegg, *Richard Pace*, pp. 254-255.

[30] *L&P*, IX, no. 1034.

Morison on the progress of his studies, spoke of the novel experience of hearing lectures on Faustus in Greek. As students in Italy, their familiarity with the great works in Italian literature was to be expected. For one who felt such misgiving at the prospect of return to England that he could write, "I, for so many years, thanks to my misfortunes, have been an Italian," [31] a casual citation of Dante in a hastily contrived political tract is no more surprising than that he had come across the passage in his reading of Machiavelli, whose works were just off the presses in Italy. Precisely in the same mood of discovery was their interest in the current revival of the Roman civil law, shorn of its medieval commentaries.

Yet always this intellectual curiosity was animated by a typically humanistic impulse, the desire to make their knowledge useful in the state. Their learning was not for the ivory tower but for the market place. Life in Padua was only a sojourn, not an aesthetic end in itself. "Nothing [was] too difficult, no labour too great, while I had that hope," said Pole; "but nothing would have been easy, nothing pleasant, if that hope had been withdrawn." [32] Starkey's offer of his services in a letter to Cromwell is literally a dedication:

In dyuerse kyndys of studys I haue occupyd my selfe, euer hauyng in mynd thys end & purpos at the last here in thys commynalty where I am brought forth & borne to employ them to some vse; and though in them I haue not most profyted, yet dylygence & wyl hathe not lakkyd therto: but what so euer hyt ys that I haue by the gudenes of god attaynyd vn-to I schal most gladly . . . apply hyt to

[31] Morison to Starkey, *L&P*, IX, no. 102.
[32] Haile, *Reginald Pole*, p. 22.

*the seruyce of our prynce, and therby rekun my selfe to
attayne a grete parte of my felycyte.*[33]

Pole's own accomplishment in scholarship was not to be
of lasting importance, but his generosity with his wealth
and his tolerance of free inquiry among those to whom he
gave harborage would multiply the King's investment many
times over. Meanwhile, he settled into the life of an affluent
nobleman in this pleasant land of adoption where he would
pass the next five years. Not all of his time was spent in
study. There were frequent visits to the city of the Doges,
and occasionally his leisure hours were diversified by a
comedy or a pageant.[34] But these *divertissements* do not
obscure the portrait of a young man seriously and funda-
mentally absorbed in intellectual pursuits.

From the first, there were moods in him which his
scholar-companions did not understand. Longueil praised
his learning and discernment, but noted also that he remained aloof from the general topics of conversation, and
that while he was "endowed with marvellous modesty," he
was also "prodigiously taciturn."[35] So the English members
of his household were to find him—to their cost. Open
natures were completely deceived by him.

On the other hand, everyone testified unreservedly to the
excellence, almost fastidiousness, of his mind. In the exag-
gerated praise lavished on him by his Italian friends,[36] there
is more than a suggestion of the Ciceronian pose so highly
valued among Pole's contemporaries.

[33] *England in the Reign of Henry VIII: Starkey's Life and Letters,*
edited by S. J. Herrtage, Early English Text Society, extra series,
XXXII (1878), x. (Hereafter referred to as "Herrtage.")

[34] *Ven. Cal.,* III, no. 941.

[35] F. A. Gasquet, *Cardinal Pole and his Early Friends* (London,
1927), pp. 29-30.

[36] See above, p. 43.

*Cicero you must read now and ever, Sadoleto advised,
and not only read; you must absorb him and make him your
own by every intimate sense and method; for there is no
crown of learning, no brilliance of oratory, no magnificence
of sentiment, no charm of word and phrase, no quickness
of wit, no vigor of mind, which does not clearly, nay, with
unrivalled lustre, exhibit itself in him, and exercise so swift
and irresistible an influence, that the ear, and indeed the
heart, of the reader is overwhelmed as though by a torrent
of delights.*[37]

Pervasive as Cicero's conception was of the learnings as
ancillary to service in the state,[38] his eloquent periods might
prove irresistible to a person, like John Watson, of academic
rather than practical tastes. This tendency to effete imita-
tion is observable in Pole's correspondence with his Italian
friends. Bembo, "in whom our age finds its chief orna-
ment," [39] had sent Pole's letters to Giberti, who expressed
delight in them and suggested that Pole write to him and
to Sadoleto. Further correspondence disclosed Sadoleto's
willingness to include Pole among his friends, although
Bembo could not persuade him to let Pole see the first
part of his book, an attack on philosophy, until he had writ-

[37] *Sadoleto on Education*, edited by E. T. Campagnac and K.
Forbes (Oxford, 1916), p. 98.
[38] *Ibid.*, pp. 85-86: "If it was your lot to live alone, by yourself,
philosophy, or that which is the object of our quest—virtue or wisdom, would suffice for itself and ask for nothing more; but you have
to live in a large society, and have to enter into and maintain a
traffic with men in regard to every interest, concern, and common
duty which bind them and you together, and if so, if this human
society is to be maintained in easy effectiveness, there is no instrument in more signal use than the art of speech. And that is why I
often make it my business (and indeed I shall often make it) to com-
mend you before all else to these studies from which a distinguished
and lofty mode or style of speech can be acquired."
[39] *Ibid.*, p. 133.

ten the rest. Bembo declared that he had never read anything better or more Ciceronian than the first book. In the
literary correspondence following this introduction, Sadoleto and Pole traversed the scope and distinctions of philosophy and religion in a spirit too consciously imitative to
escape wholly the criticism of preciosity.[40] Concerning one
member of Pole's household, Lazaro Bonamico, Thomas
Winter had declared that to hear him one would think that
Cicero had returned to Italy.[41] But when Bonamico decided
to lay his studies aside to take up active service for his
country, it was a deeper instinct than his taste for neo-
Ciceronianism that prompted Pole's appeal to Sadoleto to
rescue Bonamico "from the benches of the rhetoricians and
restore him to philosophy." [42]

II

Padua, during the years of study now in prospect for Pole,
could gratify his deeper instincts in a way impossible during the civil disturbances of the previous decade. The wars
of the League of Cambrai were now over, and the university was undergoing a rapid expansion, both in numbers of
lectures given and in students to hear them. This healthy
renaissance was undoubtedly due in great measure to its
location outside the Papal States, and to the tolerant attitude of the Venetian republic.[43] It was the period of Pom-
ponazzi and Leonico in philosophy, of Vesalius in surgery.
Under the influence of such men, both humanistic and

---

[40] *L&P,* IV (1), nos. 54, 938; V, 1453, 1479.
[41] *L&P,* VI, no. 314.
[42] Haile, *Pole,* p. 129, citing *Epistolae Reginaldi Poli . . . et aliorum
ad se,* edited by A. M. (Giralamo) Quirini (Brescia, 1744–1757), I,
408.
[43] Frederic C. Church, *The Italian Reformers* (New York, 1932),
p. 7.

scientific learning at the university were immensely stimulated.[44] Impressionable young foreign scholars were delighted by the glittering anti-Thomist neo-Aristotelians
"wherin the most parte of men lettred" there occupied
themselves.[45] John Clerk, with the responsibility of Wolsey's
son, Thomas Winter, on his hands, may have been unduly
cautious when he reported to Wolsey from Rome in 1523
that the universities were still so disquieted with the wars
that Winter and his retinue, who had just arrived in Italy,
would profit as much, perhaps more, in other places.[46] Yet
only ten years later, Winter himself wrote to his then
patron, Cromwell, from Padua: "There are professors of all
sciences here, such as [I have] never hitherto heard; philosophers into whom the mind of Aristotle seems to have
migrated; and civil lawyers and physicians than whom there
are none more learned." [47] If Winter's glowing picture was
colored by his urgent need for more money, Leonico's account to Pole in 1531 was not, and yet it tallies in all but
one respect. Leonico could not remember when the university was so well equipped. "The study of humanities and of
letters are held in the highest honor; many devote themselves to these studies, and especially Greek. The law
schools are carried on well." As against Winter's comment
on reincarnated Aristotles, Leonico professed to find the
study of philosophy frozen up for lack of good professors
and because of a barbarous fashion of reading.[48] But the
criticism should not be taken too literally. After all, the

[44] In the opinion of Sir George Newman (*Interpreters of Nature,*
London, 1927, p. 24), Vesalius' *De humani corporis fabrica* "began
in a true sense the renaissance of medicine." See also Maclaren
Thompson, "A Glimpse of Padua," *The Diplomate,* XVI (1944),
302.

[45] Herrtage, p. x.

[46] *L&P,* III (2), no. 3594.

[47] *L&P,* VI, no. 314.

[48] Gasquet, *Pole,* pp. 114-115.

restorer of the text of Aristotle could well afford to make his complaint to a favorite absent student.

For the first two years Pole indulged his scholarly tastes in a pleasant renewal and enlargement of the society of his foreign acquaintances, many of whom enjoyed the hospitality of his spacious living in Padua and Venice, and chiefly those who "could be of use to him in his favorite studies of eloquence and polite letters." [49] These would have included beside his tutor Leonico, Longueil, Bonamico, Amasei, and Flaminio. Aside from his occasional contacts with Richard Pace, there is no record of Englishmen in his household until 1523. That he was accompanied in his journey to Italy by a staff of personal servants is certain, though it is doubtful if there were any among them who could be called companions or fellow students. Then, in May 1523, over the arduous passes of the mountains from Trent, came Wolsey's Thomas Winter.[50] It was not his first visit to Italy, though if the advice of his physicians meant anything, it might be his last. On the journey from Trent, he had contracted a fever which forced delay in the mountains for an indefinite period and finally resulted in a flat statement from the physicians that he could not spend another summer in Italy. Clerk, who was managing the expedition, then ordered Winter back to Louvain with instructions to be ready to return to Italy in March. Probably Winter was then about thirteen years of age, certainly not over fifteen,[51] and at least ten years Pole's junior, so that his change in plans should have made little difference to the older scholar. But with him as his tutor was Thomas Lupset, with whom Pole may have struck up an acquaintance first at Magdalen,[52] and who, in

<hr />

[49] Phillips, *Pole,* pp. 13-14.

[50] *L&P,* III (2), no. 3594.

[51] A. F. Leach, *Memorials of Beverley Minster: the Chapter Act Book,* Surtees Society, CVIII (1903), xcv.

[52] Gee, *Lupset,* p. 109.

the interim of Winter's illness, was obviously free to proceed independently. Lupset arrived about May 8, and, like Pole, had letters from Latimer and Tunstal to Leonico.[53] He went first to Venice to pay his respects to Pace, his fellow student at Padua eight years previous, and in November [54] to Padua and Pole, whom he may have accompanied there on the occasion of Pole's first visit.[55]

It was a happy meeting of scholars. Lupset was fresh from Bruges, where the famous Vives was at the moment in residence. What is more, he brought first-hand accounts of Oxford, where he had been lecturing, at first in rhetoric and humanity, then, since the granting of his Master of Arts, in Greek. For Lupset, returning to Italy, there was the attraction of the revivified university life, which must have been as exhilarating for the youthful scholar as Pole's company. Together, they spent the time in study until Winter's return to the mountains above Padua in the spring of 1524; and when the time came for Lupset's departure, Pole not only accompanied Winter and his tutor but remained with them in the fall when they returned to Louvain.[56] In December, he was back in Padua.[57]

There can be little doubt that the meeting of these two scholars was significant in terms of the continuity of humanism in the third decade. For Leonico it was a joyous reunion also, and he saw to it that the Paduans of the earlier generation were informed. To Latimer he wrote with satisfaction of the younger men's diligence in study; to More, his proposal of a scholar's exchange of his edition of Aristotle's *Parva naturalia* for More's *Utopia* was spiced with the ob-

[53] Gee, *Lupset,* p. 109.

[54] Gee, *Lupset,* 110, n. 36, pp. 116; Gasquet, *Pole,* p. 54.

[55] Gasquet, *Pole,* pp. 47-49.

[56] Gee, *Lupset,* p. 110; *L&P,* IV (1), no. 618; Gasquet, *Pole,* pp. 56-57.

[57] *L&P,* IV (1), no. 938.

servation that Pole constantly referred to More as "one of the most learned men alive." [58] When More acceded to his request, Leonico informed Pole, observing that the Utopian republic was better than that of any ancient writer, and exclaiming in words to which both More and Pole would have concurred, "Would that in some place or other in the world there might really exist a true republic of philosophers!" [59] Erasmus heard about the meeting from the lips of Lupset himself in an account so vivid that the elder scholar wrote to tell Pole that he now knew him well, and found pleasure in these deplorable times that someone was devoting himself to the cause of learning and piety. [60]

Some idea of the nature of their studies may be inferred from Leonico's reading after Pole had left Padua to join Winter and Lupset in their mountain retreat. The emphasis was on Greek: Plato's *Timaeus* and *Phaedrus*, Chrysippus, Pontius, Posidonius. Cicero and the Greek and Latin historians were reserved for "lighter reading." [61] What the teacher of Linacre and Latimer read doubtless guided the younger scholars. In Leonico's letter to Pole in May 1524, is perhaps the first suggestion for their participation in a project which was to occupy their attention and to enlist that of others when Lupset and Pace rejoined Pole in Venice early in 1525 after a stay in Trent. [62] Leonico informed Pole that he had read all of Galen, noting in particular "those points which seemed to belong to Philosophy," and, in accordance with Galen's own belief "that the best Physician is also a Philosopher," he concluded, "It appears to me, in the wisdom of my old age, that he is the most skilful exponent of

---

[58] Gasquet, *Pole*, pp. 58-59.
[59] Gasquet, *Pole*, pp. 69-70.
[60] *L&P*, IV (1), no. 1685. October 4, 1525.
[61] Gasquet, *Pole*, p. 66.
[62] *Ven. Cal.*, III, nos. 921, 1042; Wegg, *Pace*, p. 255; Gee, *Lupset*, p. 117.

the teaching of Plato." [63] Linacre's polished translation of
De sanitate tuenda (Paris, 1517) had been reprinted several
times, Lupset acting as corrector of the press;[64] and more
recently, Linacre had translated *De naturalibus facultatibus*
(London, 1523). In the meantime, Lupset had brought out
Methodus medendi (Paris, 1519).[65] Now the time seemed
ripe for an edition of the whole works in the original tongue.
Three weeks after Leonico had expressed his admiration of
Galen to Pole, John Clement, son-in-law of More, who, after
a brief stay at Cardinal's College teaching Greek and Latin,
had devoted himself entirely to the study of medicine,[66] visited Leonico in Padua on his way to Venice.[67] It is incon-
ceivable that Clement would not have shared Leonico's fresh
enthusiasm. The fact is that Pole and Lupset in the company of Pace arrived in Venice early in February 1525, and
soon after, a project for a Greek Galen was under way.

For a work of such size—it took up five folio volumes [68]—
scholarly collaboration was needed. Andreas Torresanus,
father-in-law and successor to Aldus Manutius, undertook
the immense labor of collecting and collating the manuscripts,[69] assisted by Giovanni Baptista Opizo of Pavia,
whom Andreas credited with the original suggestion for

[63] Gasquet, *Pole,* p. 66.
[64] Gee, *Lupset,* p. 59.
[65] Gee, *Lupset,* p. 65.
[66] *L&P,* III (1), no. 1109.
[67] Gasquet, *Pole,* p. 69.
[68] Through the kindness of Mr. Scott Adams, Acting Librarian of
the Army Medical Library, Washington, D. C., the first volume of
this work was made available for my use in Washington whence it
had been removed for safekeeping during the war.
[69] In his dedication to Clement VII, he wrote: "Quotquot usq̃ fere
tota Graecia, simul atq; Italia reperiri codices potuerunt: incredibili
cura, sumptuq̃; supraq̃ dici absq; ulla mendacii aut uanitatis suspi-
cione possit: conquisiui. atq; ita multiplici eorum collatione primum
omnium quae in uno Galeni medicorū praestantissimi desiderarētur,
ex aliis suppleui: quae inuersa deprauate legerentur, prout in pluribus
se recte haberent, restitui."

undertaking the project as well as a major part in carrying it out.[70] And though their work went without formal acknowledgment, others in Pole's circle beside Lupset and Clement shared editorial labors: a certain "Roseus" of whom nothing further is known, and "Odoardus," probably Edward Wotton,[71] a recent arrival in Italy, who had made a brilliant record at Magdalen, Pole's college, as a student and lecturer in Greek, and who would return to Oxford the following year as an M.D. from Padua. Work on the project may have been completed by the time Pole left for the Jubilee in Rome in August; before the end of the year, it was coming from the Aldine press in Venice.

In spite of Erasmus' derogatory remarks about it,[72] a first edition of the standard medical authority in the original Greek was an event of the first importance in the scholarly world. It remains one of the inevitable ironies of the history of learning that a scant twelve years after the Paduan Leonico rediscovered in Galen a connection between philosophy and science, Galen was already being superseded at the same university by the studies of Vesalius in experimental surgery. But in the meantime, the association of English medical scholars in a major project of the Aldine press raised the prestige of Pole, their friend and supporter. Quite suddenly he was elevated to a status of importance as a patron of learning, and even though the stay of Clement and Wotton was temporary, his household at Padua gained perceptibly in stature. One may judge somewhat of Opizo's reputation by the fact that Clement appealed to him for a prescription for Pole, and of his modesty by his reply that he knew no secrets and that he could leave the patient to

[70] "Qui, ut uerum fatear, me & ad suspiciendũ hoc munus apprime hortatus est: & ad proficiêdum 'q maxime iuuit."
[71] Gee's conjecture as to his identity (*Lupset*, p. 118, n. 84) is unlikely.
[72] Gee, *Lupset*, p. 117, n. 83.

Clement who understood his constitution.[73] Opizo's recollections of his English associates remained warm long after "M. Edoardo" and "M. Clemente" had returned to England.[74] John Clement's career aside from the short period of contact with Pole's household has no further interest here; but that contact helped to knit relations between English scholars at home and abroad, and the definite connection of his name with the English Paduans has therefore a special importance.

Of Wotton, more needs to be said. The scholarly talents of the man who was later to become physician to Henry VIII and president of the Royal College of Physicians, had first come to the attention of Richard Fox, Bishop of Winchester, through Claymond and Morwent at Corpus Christi in 1524, a year after Fox had admitted Pole as fellow.[75] The statutes of Magdalen did not permit giving Wotton the same standing, but Bishop Fox circled the provision and made him "socius compar," with a license to travel in Italy to improve his learning, and chiefly to learn Greek, for a period of three years from May 1, 1524, and for five years more if at the end of that time he wished for an extension. Leland, who apparently profited by Wotton's instruction in Homer, Cicero, and the rhetoricians, called him "cultor maximus Galeni," [76] and Sir George Newman has hailed him as the first eminent naturalist among English physicians, and the first to include the study of zoology in the medical curriculum.[77]

Pole himself seems not to have engaged in the Galen proj-

---

[73] L&P, VII, no. 1016.

[74] L&P, X, no. 945. May 23, 1536.

[75] L&P, IV (1), no. 4; Thomas Fowler, *The History of Corpus Christi College* (Oxford, 1893), pp. 84-85.

[76] *Encomia*, p. 130: "Ad Thaliam, ut Eadueardum Ododunum medicum invisat."

[77] *Interpreters of Nature*, p. 16.

ect. Nor did two of his traveling companions: one, a friend of Bembo and Erasmus, known to them as "Dr. Marmaduke," [78] and the other, Pole's secretary, Thomas Starkey, who would presently exceed them all as a servant to the state. It is significant that the first notices of the author of the *Dialogue between Pole and Lupset* should associate his name with theirs. Starkey had been educated at Magdalen, where in all likelihood he first made Pole's acquaintance;[79] he had obtained his Master of Arts there in the same year in which Lupset obtained his. It is a matter of conjecture why he relinquished his proctorship by Wolsey's appointment at Oxford, but it is no surprise that he should have appeared in Pole's household in Padua, where he distinguished himself in the classics and attained to his doctorate.[80] Leonico paid tribute to his learning along with Tunstal's and Latimer's after Starkey had left for England,[81] and among his lifelong friends was Edward Wotton, whom he may well have met at Padua at this time.[82]

In any case, the year 1525 brought a brilliant company of scholars together at the house of Pole, and it saw accomplished in the editing and publishing of Galen a notable use of Greek scholarship for a practical end. But although Pole had thereby become a patron of learning, he could hardly forget that his patronage was possible only because of two others: Henry, of course, for his assured grant as long as Pole might be in Italy; and, significantly in the year of the founding of Cardinal's College, Wolsey. Pole's acknowledgment of Wolsey's help was made in July when it became apparent that Pace would have to return to England. In-

[78] *L&P*, IV (1), no. 938; IV (2), nos. 2953, 3820, 4756.
[79] Herrtage, p. viii, n. 4.
[80] Anthony à Wood, *Athenae Oxonienses,* edited by Philip Bliss (Oxford, 1813–1820), I, 451, n. 3.
[81] Gasquet, *Pole,* p. 107.
[82] Herrtage, p. viii, n. 4.

dicative of the extent of Wolsey's patronage is Pole's expressed hope that he would not be forgotten, or alone thought ungrateful out of the many who had received Wolsey's favors.[83]

III

Before the end of the year, many of the English Paduans had departed for England, an exodus instigated perhaps by the poor health of Pace. The Doge urged Pace's recall, and Pole was under the impression that he would leave in August; but he did not start until October and finally arrived in November.[84] Wotton was in Oxford at the end of the year;[85] Lupset was in Paris in 1525 or early in 1526.[86] Pole apparently remained in Padua for the rest of 1525 and most of 1526.[87] In the late fall, he met Lupset in Paris, and together they too crossed the Channel to England.[88]

There was good reason why Pole and Lupset should linger in Paris through the autumn. Sometime during that summer—Lupset may have timed his arrival to suit—Thomas Winter settled there, dignified by the new and lucrative title of Dean of Wells. Only recently he had become archdeacon of Richmond and provost of Beverley.[89] Altogether, Winter's was the highest clerical subsidy, amounting to £40

[83] *L&P*, IV (1), no. 1529.

[84] *DNB:* "Pace"; *L&P*, IV (1), nos. 1529, 1587; Gasquet, *Pole*, p. 70.

[85] Wood (*Athenae Oxonienses*, I, 226) stated that he was granted Doctor of Physic at Oxford at the end of 1525. W. D. Macray (*Register . . . of Magdalen College*, London, 1894–, new series, I, 153) added that he was incorporated in Magdalen as an M.D. from Padua on May 16, 1526. The date of March 3 in Wood's *Fasti*, p. 72, is probably an error.

[86] Gee, *Lupset*, p. 120.

[87] Phillips, *Pole*, I, 27.

[88] Gee, *Lupset*, p. 120; Gasquet, *Pole*, p. 95.

[89] Leach, *Memorials of Beverley Minster*, pp. xcv–xcvi.

yearly.[90] Most of his then fifteen years of age had been spent in comparative obscurity under tutors on the continent, but he had now reached an age when dignities must be conferred proper to the son of the first minister. The King of France took an interest in his welfare, and hinted at "very large offers." [91] Giberti, Bishop of Verona, expressed great affection for him.[92] "He is in the face of the world," Russell wrote to Wolsey early in 1527, "and many learned and worshipful men resort unto him, besides the English." [93] He was of the opinion that Winter should have a house of his own, "since men here take him for your kinsman and honor him therefore." [94] During Wolsey's lifetime, Winter's household was to be as important as Pole's for the maintenance of English scholars abroad.

Housing "for Mr. Dean and all his company" had been a difficulty from the first. The death of one of his servants soon after his arrival had forced him to move temporarily into the house of the Scottish humanist, Florentius Volusenus or Volusene, a kind, very gentle, and well-learned person,[95] possibly the Dominican, Florentius, presently to be drafted into Wolsey's college at Oxford.[96] John Taylor, master of the Rolls, who was arranging for Winter's quarters, described Volusene's residence in a manner calculated to please Wolsey. It stood "in a very wholesome soil, with a fair and a large garden, sequestrate from recourse of people, having a church within them and daily service, and"—

[90] *L&P*, IV (2), no. 2922.
[91] *L&P*, IV (2), no. 2568.
[92] *L&P*, IV (2), no. 2868.
[93] *L&P*, IV (2), no. 2805.
[94] *L&P*, IV (2), no. 2806.
[95] *L&P*, IV (2), no. 2545. Sadoleto spoke of him as "modestus, placidus . . . certe enim eiusmodi modestiam, prudentiam, compositionem oris atque vultus, vix in Italo homine talem expectare potueramus." *Sadoleto on Education*, p. xxi.
[96] See above, p. 28.

with a touch for a solicitous father—"every night the gate shut." [97] If Wolsey had any qualms, they could hardly have been set at rest by Russell's reference to it as "bare and uncommodious";[98] better assurance could be found in Taylor's continuing reports of a house inside Volusene's gate belonging to William Shelley, the current Grand Prior of the Knights of St. John, and legal counsel for Wolsey's college at Oxford. "My lord of St. John's" place seemed to Taylor as satisfactory as any in Paris, and here apparently Winter's household was finally established.

Housing troubles were minor, however, by comparison with Winter's inaptitude for the scholarly life. Wolsey, faced with what he suspected were far from candid reports on his son's *gradus ad Parnassum*, dispatched Lupset to Paris in February 1528,[99] to investigate at first hand. While admitting Winter's good will, Lupset was frankly disappointed in the whole situation: Winter's house was still insufficiently furnished, he was squandering money, and he was not "strong enough" to undertake the plan of studies Lupset had in mind for him. But this much admitted, it is significant that he pleaded nevertheless for the maintenance of Winter's household, even though it was larger than Wolsey had planned for. Gardiner and Fox on a later visit both deferred to Lupset's judgment that "none of them could be spared." [100] Clerk also, in spite of Winter's scholastic record, sent a similar report: "Your grace's scholars doth excellently well." [101]

This concurrence of opinion in two men of learning on the intellectual achievement of Winter's household raises tantalizing questions with regard to its personnel, especially

[97] *L&P*, IV (2), no. 2545.
[98] *L&P*, IV (2), no. 2806.
[99] *L&P*, IV (2), nos. 2805, 3955, 4015.
[100] *L&P*, IV (2), no. 3955.
[101] *L&P*, IV (2), no. 2587.

since Pole was presently to break his journey to England at Winter's residence in Paris, and in all probability became acquainted at that time with some of the scholars whom he took into his own house on his return to Padua. We are by no means in the dark in that respect. The tutorial staff maintained by Wolsey eliminated the possibility that his heir, however indisposed to learning, should escape being exposed. All activities, tutorial and otherwise, centered in Volusene, Winter's taciturn host, though whenever Wolsey called Volusene to England, the mood of both tutor and student was likely to lighten. In thanking Cromwell for a loan of horses on his return from London in October 1528, Volusene expressed a sly hope that Vincent de Cassilis would not get along too well with his English, "lest with his eloquence and other gifts he ingratiate himself too much with that girl of mine, the daughter of Mrs. Lauson, who supped with us day before yesterday." [102] Included in that conviviality was Anthony Bonvisi, well-known Italian merchant and moneylender, whom George Lawson referred to as "my gossip," and entrusted with instructions to Volusene regarding his son's application to study in Winter's household.[103] As for Winter himself, Volusene found that his titled guest had seized the occasion of his absence in England for an extended vacation from study.[104]

Beside Volusene, Wolsey supported two others in Winter's household on a tutorial basis, Thomas Lupset and an Italian called Cyprian. The Cardinal's concern over Winter's scholarly ineptitude made even the most competent tutor's life difficult, and neither Lupset nor Cyprian escaped criticism. It is to Winter's credit that he always interposed in their behalf. On one occasion, Winter acknowledged his

[102] *L&P*, IV (2), no. 4807.
[103] *L&P*, IV (3), app. no. 84.
[104] *L&P*, IV (2), no. 5019.

great obligation to Lupset and insisted that he could not get along without him.[105] And when Lupset defended Cyprian on the grounds that he had done more for Winter than any other since he came to France,[106] Winter generously confirmed the opinion, and at the end of a year of daily tutoring, when the Italian desired to live the rest of his days in England where he had spent his youth, Winter asked Wolsey to benefice him.[107]

Indirectly, then, Wolsey was exercising an important influence on humanistic activity by maintaining the elaborate establishment which constituted Winter's household during his Parisian residence. Aside from the tutorial staff, it included a large and diverse group of students. Some, like John Bekinsau, made their way on the strength of their scholarly ability; some, like Winter himself and Richard Pate, were supported by high ecclesiastics; some (a newer phenomenon) were the sons of wealthy men of business. All were imbued with the common purpose which set the pattern for the age, to employ their learning in affairs of state.

The first record of John Bekinsau in Winter's entourage is in April 1529, when both Winter and Wilson recommended him to Cromwell as a young man of good learning and honest.[108] The recommendation was well deserved. Bekinsau was a permanent fellow of New College, who, three years before, had taken his Master of Arts and journeyed abroad to study, at which time, according to Wood, "he was esteemed in his college a most admirable Grecian." [109] At Paris, he had become reader of the Greek lecture. One year after his recommendation to Cromwell, he was enjoying a

[105] *L&P*, IV (2), no. 4848.
[106] *L&P*, IV (2), no. 4064.
[107] *L&P*, IV (2), no. 4848; IV (3), no. 5382.
[108] *L&P*, IV (3), nos. 5446, 5946.
[109] *Athenae Oxonienses*, I, 307.

stipend from the Privy Purse as King's scholar at Paris, and shortly thereafter he became tutor to Gregory Cromwell, son of Thomas.[110]

Richard Pate, from a different background, was equally successful. Nephew of the Bishop of Lincoln, John Longland, he came to Winter's household from Bruges, where he had been "wonderfully studious" under the tutelage of Vives.[111] It is not clear when he joined Winter, but in July 1528, when Longland wrote to Wolsey in the hope that his charge might be granted a house in the close of Lincoln belonging to the late archdeacon, he added: "If master Wynter were in England I doubt not that he would be a humble suitor to your Grace in this behalf for my said nephew, who hath him in his especiall favor; and he is, in his learning, and otherwise, daily attendant upon Master Dean." [112] Pate had a B.A. from Corpus Christi, 1523, and during his residence in Paris would proceed to M.A.[113] So far as the records show, he continued to spend much of his time in Paris until November 1533, when he received an appointment as "King's ambassador resident in the court of the Emperor." [114]

Most significant of the widening recognition of scholarship as a practical aid to preferment, however, is the presence in Winter's entourage at Paris of the sons of the King's commoner business executives. There was the son of George Lawson, builder of the King's works at Tournai and Berwick, who saw fit to instruct "Mr. Florens to see that my son George be kept continually at school." [115] There was William Belson, probably the son of William Belson of Bryll, who received regular compensation from the Cardinal's Col-

[110] L&P, V, no. 1799, pp. 748-749; V, no. 496.
[111] L&P, IV (1), no. 481. Vives to Longland, Bruges. July 8, 1524.
[112] L&P, IV (2), no. 4514.
[113] Athenae Oxonienses, II, 794-795.
[114] L&P, VI, no. 1481 (12).
[115] L&P, II (1), no. 1940; IV (3), app. no. 84.

lege for Chalford of Wallingford.[116] There was the mild-mannered son of George Hampton, "my father Hampton" to Winter, who on one occasion, being questioned by Cromwell on his alleged withholding of the revenue of Winter and a certain John Eston, replied tartly, "I have neither. As for Eston coming here [Paris], he had better go to Turkey." [117]

Costly and thankless as Winter's continental education must have seemed, it is nevertheless surprising that Wolsey should have been willing to draw on the establishment at Paris as his interests became increasingly absorbed in the larger project at Oxford. In March 1528, Lupset pleaded with Wolsey for "Walter, dear to us all, especially to Winter, who could hardly get along without him." No one, he claimed, understood Winter's health better.[118] Circumstances favor the assumption that the person so highly regarded was Walter Buckler, and that Wolsey was recalling him to serve as one of the canons of Cardinal's College. Wood listed him as both M.A. and fellow in that college, and as being employed by the King in 1534 on matters of state in Paris.[119]

The supposition is strengthened by the fact that Lupset himself was feeling pressure from Wolsey in October and left the group in Paris for England shortly after,[120] to succeed John Clement in the chair of rhetoric at Wolsey's college. The Cardinal's conduct toward Lupset at just this time is so similar that only one conclusion is possible:

[116] *L&P*, IV (3), no. 6788, p. 3067. Both Lawson and Belson apparently remained in Winter's household until 1531, when they accompanied him to Italy. *L&P*, V, no. 338.

[117] *L&P*, VI, no. 649.

[118] *L&P*, IV (2), no. 4022.

[119] *The History and Antiquities . . . of Oxford*, p. 423.

[120] *L&P*, IV (2), no. 4848; Gee, *Lupset*, p. 130. He was with Wolsey in June 1529. *L&P*, IV (3), no. 5642.

Wolsey was making inroads on Winter's household as he had at the University of Cambridge for his project at Oxford.

IV

But two events outside academic circles were now in motion which were seriously to threaten them: the fall of Wolsey, and the beginning of the proceedings for the divorce. It will be apparent from the foregoing analysis of the scholarly activities carried on in the households of both Pole and Winter that Wolsey's influence was all-pervasive, the effect of its sudden removal unpredictable. From the date of the Cardinal's indictment, October 28, 1529, both Pole and Winter had lost a benefactor, and for Winter, whose position depended solely on the Cardinal's gratuities, the loss was perilous.

Precarious certainly, but not irretrievable. As Dean of Wells, Winter was enjoying a prestige which was in all likelihood only a foretaste of the future Wolsey was grooming him for. Leach believed that the losses of preferments at this time were in some degree resignations preparatory to his promotion to the bishopric of Durham.[121] But the King did not give him up, and on July 25, 1530, Wolsey was able to thank Gardiner for arranging Winter's acceptance as the King's scholar.[122] Indeed, as early as April 1529 Winter was expressing gratitude to Cromwell for promoting his affairs; and it would be interesting to know the substance of the message which Winter mentioned sending to Cromwell by way of John Bekinsau in the same letter.[123] Yet even disregarding any assurances he may have received from Cromwell, the

---

[121] *Memorials of Beverley Minster*, p. xcvii.
[122] *Ibid.*
[123] *L&P*, IV (3), no. 5446.

show of royal favor made his position—though not necessarily that of his dependents—secure. At the same time, his
loss of prestige and, as a consequence, his value as a patron,
were hopelessly reduced.

Pole's position, on the other hand, while it could hardly
be seriously jeopardized by Wolsey's fall, was so prominent
that he could hardly hope to remain indefinitely neutral in
the matter of the divorce. It was to be expected that Henry
would exert pressure, and that Pole, his scholarly and retir-
ing instincts for the moment at war with the humanist's
ideal of service to the state, would demur. Pole's intellectual
crisis is not easily defined, chiefly because his actual conduct
during this period must be measured against his rationalization of it after he had broken with Henry in 1536. Of this
we can be certain: he was in Paris in 1528, closely associated with Henry's agents for the divorce. The most important
evidence of this visit is Starkey's ledger for Pole, itemizing
receipts and expenditures over a period of residence there
and en route to London from there.[124] One credit item is from
Lupset, then in London; other items reveal among Pole's
associates in Paris Richard Pate, Winter's companion in
study, and "Martyn," possibly Martin du Bellay, brother of
the French ambassador and resident with him. An item of
twelve francs "for wyne of the cōsalar" may refer also to
Martin.[125] One curious entry under expenses: "Mr. Const for
lokys & durrys [doors] broken," connects Stephen Gardiner

[124] PRO, SP 1/55, fol. 194. This manuscript has never been carefully examined. It was calendared in *L&P*, IV (3), no. 6004 (ii) as
of the year 1529, where it is inaccurately described as "an account
of money expended and received on a journey, evidently to Rouen,
and thence to Paris." With the exception of two letters among the
Edgerton papers in the British Museum, calendared in *L&P*, IV (2),
nos. 4405, 4756, there is no other evidence that Pole was abroad in
1528. But these letters are conclusive.

[125] See *L&P*, IV (3), no. 5541, where he is addressed as "Con-
seiller en la Court de Parlement de Paris."

with the group.[126] An item "for byndyng of the cõseylys," possibly the book that Pole later demanded for Fox from Guillaume du Bellay, and another, "for papyr to wryte the greke boke," indicate the nature of their activity. Payments to servants included Bernardino Sandro, who had been with Pole in Padua and would be again, and Owen, erstwhile serving man of Reginald's brother Geoffrey, Lord Montague, and now serving Pate—"my long countryman," as Pate affectionately called him in a letter to Starkey.[127] The returning party, it is clear from Starkey's ledger, made the journey from Paris to Rouen by boat, and thence to Calais, where they shipped for England.

In the autumn of 1529, soon after Henry moved against Wolsey, Pole went again to Paris. Yet there seems to have been no connection between the two events. His unreserved praise for Wolsey's college at Oxford and his willingness to engage actively in strengthening its faculty from his own recent household did not now bring him to its defense. In fact, his plans to leave England again were already formulated before Wolsey's fall. As early as October 12, Jean du Bellay, French ambassador and Bishop of Bayonne, informed Francis of Pole's expected journey,[128] and the accounts of the Treasurer of the Chamber list a payment of £100 to Pole on October 16 "for one year's exhibition beforehand." [129] Nor did the indictment on October 28 call forth any protest. This does not imply that Pole was indifferent to his patron's fate; but it does confirm the impression that it was not Wolsey's fall that brought his decision to go to France. Ostensibly, his object was to continue his

---

[126] "Mr. Const" is an abbreviation of Gardiner's pseudonym, "Marcus Antonius Constantius." See James A. Muller, *Stephen Gardiner and the Tudor Reaction* (New York, 1926), p. 214.

[127] *L&P*, VIII, no. 785.

[128] *L&P*, IV (3), no. 6002.

[129] *L&P*, V, p. 315.

studies. So Jean du Bellay reported at the time. Pole, he remarked to Francis, was the most learned man known. And it is worth noting that when the divorce commission arrived in France, it was to Pole, the scholar, rather than to John Stokesley, Henry's official representative in the matter of the divorce, that Bellay paid his respects. George Lily, long after Pole had made his mind known on the divorce, recalled merely that he had gone to France, enjoying the King's high favor, to take up his former study of sacred letters.[130]

Indeed, studies would be the most convenient excuse for leaving England, if, as it is generally assumed, he left to avoid the divorce question. In that case, his hand would have been forced by a royal commission, received immediately after his arrival in Paris, to obtain an opinion on the divorce from the Sorbonne. His own explanation of this turn of events is explicit and detailed, part accusation, part confessional, to Henry himself:

I can, God is my witness, truly declare that no commission was ever more displeasing to me in my whole life than that of collecting opinions in favour of the divorce. As I had left England with the object of escaping from the plots and intrigues which, under your own protection and direction, were agitating against your honour and your house, your commands were doubly grievous to me. I thought there would be no such agitation abroad, when suddenly your letter and commission came upon me; I was to undertake your business with the University.

I can still remember that as soon as grief at the unexpected news allowed (for some time the blow robbed me not only of speech, but of the faculty of thinking), I wrote to you, setting forth my ignorance, and entreating you to

[130] *Elogia,* fol. 50, cited in Gee, *Lupset,* p. 136.

*send a more experienced person in such matters. You did so
at once, or I would have considered any torments preferable
to such a service, which I never really took upon myself, as
I only played the part of his representative, until the new-
comer arrived. I took no share in the matter, and was convinced of the unlawfulness of the divorce.*[131]

But if this is a literal report of his feelings at the time, it
does not wholly explain his actions in the matter. Sometime
after Pole's arrival in France, the Duke of Norfolk took occasion to congratulate him on his acting so stoutly in the
King's behalf, especially without royal order; the King, too,
Norfolk went on, had expressed his satisfaction at Pole's
conduct and had paid high tribute to his learning.[132] Haile
(p. 72) has doubted the authenticity of this letter, but other
evidence confirms it. The best clue to the nature of his help
appears in his last-minute instructions "to Mr. Starkey for
Thomas Lupset" just before leaving France at the close of
his mission in July 1530.[133] This document shows his close
coöperation with Edward Fox, who had been sent in answer
to Pole's request, in eliciting a favorable opinion on the
divorce from the Sorbonne. Pole's departure was hurried by
Henry's insistence, first through Lupset and afterward
through Fox, that he return immediately after the decision
was reached. In accordance with the royal summons, therefore, he sent Fox off on July 7 with the news that Henry was
most anxious to hear, and apparently followed shortly afterward himself.[134] "Your grace could not grant me at this time

[131] *Pro ecclesiasticae unitatis defensione,* lib. III, cap. iii. Cited in
Haile, *Pole,* p. 71.

[132] *L&P,* IV (3), no. 6252.

[133] PRO, SP 1/55, fol. 193. This manuscript, together with Starkey's
ledger (PRO, SP 1/55, fol. 194), heretofore cited, has been associated in *L&P,* IV (3), no. 6004, with the journey from London to
Paris in October 1529. But see note 124 above.

[134] *L&P,* IV (3), no. 6505.

a petition more comfortable unto me," he wrote, no doubt with genuine relief, "and so, making what convenient speed I may, my trust is shortly to wait upon your highness." [135] Supposing, as he insisted so categorically in 1536, that he was opposed to the divorce at this time, one can still interpret as a professional courtesy his careful instructions for the carriage of Fox's personal effects.[136] But what punctilio of protocol would require him to further Henry's cause to the extent of asking Lupset "to demande off mõsʳ de langy ii bokes for mʳ fox. Librũ cõciliorum. Librũ maloris [?]. yow must put them in mʳ foxis great chest"? Guillaume du Bellay had been in England during the previous summer [137] to negotiate the treaty of Cambrai, and he and his brother Jean had been active in support of Henry's divorce. Though Guillaume was not himself a reformer, he was sympathetic to the movement, and several years later tried to effect a meeting between Francis and Melanchthon. Pole, we know from other sources, had been in recent contact with him during his current stay in France.[138]

It is possible that his own statement to Henry six years after is an accurate recollection; in that case, his present assistance in an exchange of books between Langey and Fox must be regarded as a part of an elaborate disguise for his real feelings until he should reveal them in 1536, and his letter to Henry on July 7, reporting with satisfaction the conclusions of the University of Paris as well as the great diligence and prudence of Edward Fox, the bearer of his letter, in withstanding the adverse party, represents the same

[135] *Records of the Reformation*, edited by Nicholas Pocock (Oxford, 1870), I, 563, quoted in Gee, *Lupset*, p. 139.

[136] "To haue in mynd that ther be ii coffers for mʳ fox both blakke the tõ short the tother longe."

[137] *Mémoires de Martin et Guillaume du Bellay* (Paris, 1910), II, 34-37.

[138] *L&P*, IV (3), no. 6383.

course of practical wisdom. Reynard against Fox. And what folly to underestimate the Lion's strength! But it is also possible and consistent with his conduct hitherto, that, in spite of a natural desire to antedate his opposition to the divorce once the break with Henry had been made, Pole had not as yet made up his mind. In this light, the record of his conduct in Paris need not be interpreted as purely prudential policy adopted in self-defense so much as an attempt at putting learning to use in a cause concerning which he had not achieved conviction. Hence, although he continued to be reticent on the great question, and, indeed, on all questions of state, he meanwhile found the company of the moderate reformers in all other respects wholly congenial. Such conduct would be characteristic of Pole; he acted in 1535–36 with the same deliberation.

But whatever his real state of mind, in terms of the continuity of humanism the security without commitment thus preserved by both Pole and Winter was vital. Cromwell's position as a patron had yet to be ascertained, and in the interim, when the livings of many scholars were thrown into jeopardy by the sudden loss of Wolsey's support, Pole's good standing with the King as much as his acknowledged preeminence as a scholar, and to a lesser extent Winter's instatement as the King's scholar after July 1530, established them both as centers of gravity when patronage seemed most uncertain. The fact, therefore, that during his stay in Paris Pole maintained friendly contacts with Winter, and may indeed have lived in Winter's house,[139] accomplished as much as the business of the divorce to identify Paris, for the time being, as the centripetal point for scholars. In view of the King's need for scholarly opinion, this concentration of learning can hardly be considered fortuitous. Volusene, who

[139] *L&P*, Addenda, I (1), no. 688.

had rejoined Winter there by April 1529,[140] was the recipient of a reward in May 1530,[141] and John Mason, King's scholar, received the first of a series of royal exhibitions for study in Paris in December of the same year.[142]

The full intellectual capacity of this group should not be judged, however, without consideration of three others, all of whom within reasonable conjecture can be included, all of whom till recently had been students in Wolsey's college at Oxford: John Friar, Richard Taverner, and Richard Morison. The supposition that Friar was in Paris at this time is based on the likelihood that he had already made contact with his new patron, Edward Fox, after his release from prison through the interposition of Wolsey in 1528. There is no record of him until the occasion of the signing of the treaty with France in Calais in 1532, when he was listed as commissioner on charges of the French king's train.[143] Edward Fox was one of the signatories of that treaty. There is therefore a reasonable possibility that when Fox came to Paris in 1529 the penitent John Friar was with him.

Richard Taverner, who had been entered in Cardinal's College from Gonville Hall, Cambridge, as a petty-canon, was a minor offender. Wolsey excused him shortly after he had become a fugitive, and thus he was able to earn his A.B. in 1529 from Cardinal's College, returning in the following year to Gonville for his Master of Arts.[144] He had concentrated in the study of philosophy, Greek, and divinity, and, according to Wood, had attained such proficiency in Greek that when he later studied law at Strand Inn and the Inner Temple, "his humour was to quote the law in

[140] *L&P*, IV (3), nos. 5446, 5946.
[141] *L&P*, V, p. 319.
[142] *L&P*, III (2), p. 747.
[143] *L&P*, V, no. 1492, p. 628.
[144] Wood, *Athenae Oxonienses*, I, 423; Venn, *Alumni Cantabrigienses.*

Greek, when he read any thing thereof." But the death of
Wolsey, for him as for so many scholars, meant dislocation
and migration to the continent. Two years later he appealed
to Cromwell "unknown to you, and in great distress." His
description of his life in the interim makes his presence in
Paris while Pole was there plausible: "I am master of arts
at Cambridge, where I have taught, but was induced to
leave it by my friends to become a student abroad. My
friend who supported me is dead, and I dare not ask for the
King's liberality without first communicating with you." [145]
It would be valuable to know the names of the friends who
counseled him.

Morison's career parallels Taverner's closely enough to
suggest that they may for a time have been together. Like
Taverner, he was a petty-canon in Cardinal's College where
he obtained his B.A. on January 19, 1528.[146] Five years after
the event he wrote, without elaborating the fact, that he had
"left the Cardinal's service for the sake of visiting Latimer at
Cambridge." [147] The statement may have been intentionally
ambiguous, since his letter was a belated congratulation to
Cranmer for Cranmer's elevation to the archbishopric. This,
together with his description of himself in 1533 as young
and inexperienced, suggests that he too may have been one
of the youthful reprobates whose "leaving" in 1528 was
more a matter of compulsion than design. Having settled,
like Taverner, at Cambridge, he made the acquaintance of
William Gonell, amanuensis for Erasmus,[148] tutor of Thomas
More's children, and later a member of Wolsey's household;
and through Gonell he met Thomas Cranmer. Both Taver-

[145] *L&P*, V, no. 1762.
[146] W. Gordon Zeeveld, "Richard Morison, Public Apologist for
Henry VIII," *Publications of the Modern Language Association*, LV
(1940), 407.
[147] *L&P*, VI, no. 1582.
[148] Gee, *Lupset*, p. 50.

ner and Morison studied law at the inns of court, and both went abroad to study.[149] Whether Cranmer responded to his frank bid for patronage in December 1533 is not known; but it is clear that for some years he continued to eke out a hand-to-mouth existence in Italy. His lament to Starkey in August 1535, over his lean years in Italy,[150] suggests that he had no greater success with the Archbishop than he had had through the years with Winter, his acknowledged patron at that time and perhaps as early as the Paris residence.

V

Meanwhile, Henry's order for Pole to return to London had precipitated a crisis.

What thoughts ran through Pole's mind as he hastily scratched down memoranda to Starkey before leaving Paris to wait upon the King's highness, it is impossible to say. Erasmus heard—and he probably had it from Lupset en route to Paris from Italy—that Pole had left Padua and his literary pursuits there unwillingly, and that he had taken them up again on his arrival in England. But Simon Grynaeus brought other information.[151] As I have inferred earlier, these conflicting reports apparently reflect the inevitable perplexity of the scholar in the face of a strong divergent and disengaging interest. And in this case, Pole's acceptance of Henry's invitation meant that he had come to a decision. Perhaps his diplomatic success in the company of Edward Fox had convinced him of his ability in public affairs. Perhaps now the time had come to face Henry with his evil practice. There was yet time for Henry to fulfill

[149] Coopers' *Athenae Cantabrigienses*, p. 143.
[150] See above, p. 46.
[151] *L&P*, V, no. 382.

the wish of Plato and the pious hopes of Erasmus at the beginning of the reign, at least to the extent of listening to philosophers. One fact was clear: the royal summons seemed to open a new and exciting prospect to him as he neared the cliffs of Dover once again.

But on December 27 Lupset's death occurred,[152] and with it Pole's plans underwent radical change. Accompanied by Starkey he retired to the Carthusian monastery at Sheen, where as a child he had received his first education. His friends in Italy could not understand. For several months they received no letters, and they were ignorant even of his whereabouts. Not until June did they know. Then Edmund Harvel, an English businessman in Venice, well acquainted with Pole and his household in Italy, heard from Starkey in a letter delayed since March 29. He wrote at once in protest. Why had Starkey enclosed himself in the Charterhouse, and dedicated all his work to "perpetual philosophy"? Why not come forth to teach others, and make all the land know *quam sit humaniter vivendum*, help to take out all barbarous customs, and bring the realm to an antique form of good living? To Pole, sorrowing at the death of Lupset, he promised to write by every courier.[153]

There were other motives beside Lupset's death that influenced Pole's decision. They are hinted at in Harvel's obvious presentiment that Starkey's news of Pole was not unrelated to the gossip that "men distrust the continual tranquillity of England"; the fact that a son of the Doge of Venice took service with the Turk seemed evidence to him that the practices of princes "tend to the concitation of all the world." Without attaching sinister connotations to Harvel's words, one may safely infer that Pole's return to England marked the beginning of his active opposition to

[152] Gee, *Lupset*, p. 147.   [153] *L&P*, V, no. 301.

Henry's policy, and that whatever had brought it about was serious enough to effect a permanent intransigence. Furthermore, it was serious enough to set him to work in the seclusion of the monastery on a book which Cranmer described, at the same time that Harvel was expressing his misgivings, as "of such eloquence that if it were known to the common people, I suppose they could not be persuaded to the contrary . . . He uses such eloquence that he would persuade many." [154] Five years would elapse before Pole's eloquence would be made public. But Cranmer was right. Though the work would eventually be completed as a plea to the King, there is no escaping the incendiary alternative in *Pro ecclesiasticae unitatis defensione*.

Severe as the shock of Lupset's loss must have been to Pole, a meeting, not a death, was a far likelier cause of his temporary retirement. When Pole returned from Paris the principal change in the complexion of affairs was the jockeying for power that followed the death of Wolsey. So far as a scholar was concerned, the disposition of Wolsey's extensive patronage would have been a matter of critical anxiety. But for Pole, especially in his present state of mind, it was quite as •important to acquaint himself with those who would now have a guiding hand in England's policy. Inevitably, that would lead to the historic meeting with Thomas Cromwell. To Charles V about 1539, Pole described it as taking place about ten years earlier; but Pole was not in England in 1529, and the circumstances all point to a time shortly after his arrival in 1530 as the actual date of the conversation. Some hints of it obviously leaked out by way of Starkey to Harvel; but even Starkey, daily companion of Pole at Sheen, may not have been a witness to Pole's dismay at the discovery that henceforth the guide for

[154] *L&P*, V, app. no. 10. June 1531.

English policy would not be Plato but Machiavelli.[155] That discovery meant the end of his hopes under Henry; it meant an apparent renunciation of his whole course of action up to this point. Little wonder that Harvel, unaware of that meeting, was perplexed.

For Pole, the only alternative, as he later told Charles, was escape to the comparative safety of the continent. In the meantime, he did not—indeed could not—completely immure himself in the Charterhouse. As Dean of Exeter and of Wimbourne Minster, Dorset,[156] he found himself engaged in the ordinary duties of those offices. One of his petitioners was an old friend, John Haly, a prebendary in both deaneries, who had become master of the grammar school adjoining Magdalen in the same year that Pole had entered that college as a student, and had once entertained Lupset there.[157] Through Starkey, his "amico charissimo," he petitioned Pole to effect an exchange of his benefice near Warwick for one of "Mr. Dr. Wilson's" (Volusene's),[158]

---

[155] In spite of Paul Van Dyke's opinion to the contrary (*Renascence Portraits,* New York, 1905, pp. 401 ff.), it is hardly conceivable that Cromwell should not have known the work of Machiavelli while he was still in Florence. Machiavelli's political writings were widely disseminated in Italy, as P. Villari had shown long before Van Dyke undertook to deny Cromwell's knowledge of them. On the basis of evidence presented by Villari (*Niccolo Machiavelli e i suoi tempi,* Milan, 1927, II, 165-175) and Adolph Gerber (*Niccolo Machiavelli: die Handschriften, Ausgeben und Übersetzungen seiner Werke in 16 und 17 Jahrhunderts,* Gotha, 1912, I, 82-97), Professor Garrett Mattingly, in an unpublished article which he has generously placed at my disposal, has concluded that "in the 1520's at least three and perhaps five Italian book-sellers were using professional copyists to multiply copies of *The Prince.*"

[156] Dean of Exeter, 1527–c.1537 (John Le Neve, *Fasti ecclesiae Anglicanae*); Dean of Wimbourne Minster, Salisbury diocese, February 12, 1518 (Hook, *Lives of the Archbishops of Canterbury,* VIII, 18 and n.; *L&P,* II (2), no. 3943).

[157] Gee, *Lupset,* p. 58.   [158] *L&P,* V, no. 212.

assuring Starkey that although he could live on his present income he was anxious to have assistance "to set forward a scholar or twain, and also *ut haberem quo profugerem quoties societas sceleratorum me cepisset Warwici.*" [159]

Haly's correspondence with Starkey is of special interest because it makes clear that Pole and Starkey were planning as early as November 1531 to go abroad again, and for an indefinite period. Apparently in answer to an earlier proposal by Starkey, Haly wrote on November 12 that, because of the infirmities of age, he would rather remain in some safe place in his own country than cross the sea; but he hoped to come to London at Easter "to see Mr. Dean, and bid both him and other my friends farewell for ever." His premonition was correct. Less than a year later he was dead.[160] As for Pole, his face was now resolutely set away from England. In the spring of 1532, accompanied by Starkey, he set out once more for the continent, not to return until the accession of Mary, and then wearing the red hat. As Winter wrote to Runcorne in October 1532, "Pole is at Venice, and is resolved to stay there." [161]

Meanwhile, without Wolsey's support, Winter was not finding his role as King's scholar too satisfying. He had gone to Padua and Venice, where in July 1531 he was pleading his disgrace if he had to sell furniture, clothes, books to live. George Lawson and William Belson, he complained to Cromwell, had both required medical treatment.[162] By the end of the year he was back in England as the King's chaplain. In January 1532 he was granted a license to leave the

[159] *L&P*, V, nos. 529-530.

[160] On October 17, 1532, James Cruse reported to Cromwell "a priest dead in Warwick, named James Haly," and offered 40 marks for the vacant prebend of Wimbourne Minster, "of the gift of Mr. Pole, dean there, of £10." *L&P*, V, no. 1443.

[161] *L&P*, V, no. 1453.

[162] *L&P*, V, no. 338.

country with "three servants, four horses or geldings, am-
bling or trotting, and baggage and necessaries usual," [163]
but by the summer he had resumed his complaints to Cromwell, living so wretchedly, he claimed, that it was an obstacle
to study. "You know the taste of the Italians; they don't
endure shabbiness, nor willingly admit poor people into
their society." Besides, he was enjoying no friendship with
learned men.[164] One tires of the song.

In early February Pole and Starkey had reached Paris,
and Winter spent four days with them there. Warned of the
high cost of living in Italy, Winter sent George Hampton
home before continuing the journey southward.[165] Winter
and Pole may have started out together, but Pole's way led
to the valley of the Rhone, where he stayed during the
summer months, not arriving in Venice until October.[166]
He had two reasons for taking such an unconventional route:
one was the personal desire to visit his dear friend Sadoleto,
the Bishop of Carpentras; the other, the desire to study the
civil law in Avignon where Alciato had been lecturing, and
where now Giovanni Francesco Ripa was directing a renaissance of the *Corpus juris civilis*.[167] Pole's admiration for
Sadoleto's philosophic powers was great; and just now, the
serious mental strain of his recent visit to England had put
him in need of the consolations of philosophy. Sadoleto, he
felt, had "freed his mind of perplexity in very great matters"
and had led him to the entrance of "that sacred harbour in
which he himself lives with tranquillity of mind." [168] Such

[163] *L&P*, V, no. 766 (12).
[164] *L&P*, V, no. 1210. See also a list of "desperat obligations,"
L&P, V, no. 1285 (iii).
[165] *L&P*, V, app. no. 27.
[166] *L&P*, V, no. 1453.
[167] F. W. Maitland, *English Law and the Renaissance* (Cambridge,
1901), p. 6.
[168] *L&P*, V, no. 1479.

was the high aim of philosophic studies in Sadoleto's treatise on education which Pole took with him to read when
he resumed his journey to Italy. In that treatise he read that
those who turn to the civil law or the service of the state
after studying philosophy will have gained facility to enter
and determination to continue in them, but that those who
find in philosophy their abiding habitation are to be
deemed godlike.[169] Both Pole and Starkey became enthusiastic civilians, Pole convinced that the civil law could be
adopted in England.[170] But whereas Pole's inclination at the
moment was certainly to that higher aim of philosophic
study as pointed out by Sadoleto, Starkey's was just as
strongly to its lower and practical uses. "Francis Curtius is
dead, to the grief of those who follow the doctrine of Bar-
tholus," he announced with unction to his Paduan friends,[171]
among whom he was certain of a sympathetic ear,[172] and
he plunged into a study of the civil law with Ripa, the great
civilian, as he explained afterwards, "that I myght therby
make a more stabyl and sure jugement of the polytyke ordur
& customys vsyd amonge vs here in our countrey . . . by-cause
my purpos then was to lyue in a polytyke lyfe." [173] When Pole
decided to renew his journey to Padua he could hardly have
disapproved of Starkey's decision to linger in Avignon for
further study in that subject of all subjects which Pole regarded as "the most auncyent and nobyl monument of the
Romaynys prudence and pollycy, the wych be so wryte

[169] *Sadoleto on Education,* p. 141.

[170] Thomas Starkey, *A Dialogue between Cardinal Pole and Thomas
Lupset, Lecturer in Rhetoric at Oxford,* edited by J. M. Cowper,
Early English Text Society, extra series, XII (1871), pp. 194-195.

[171] *L&P,* VII, no. 900 (ii).

[172] That Richard Morison was searching the Roman law with
equally practical aims is apparent from an examination of his Commonplace Book, PRO, SP 6/4, fols. 126-127.

[173] Herrtage, p. x.

wyth such grauyte, that if Nature schold hyrselfe prescrybe partycular meanys wherby mankynd schold observe hyr lawys, I thynke sche wold admyt the same." [174] And Starkey did stay on in that congenial company [175]—"your Thomas," as Sadoleto affectionately referred to him— [176] presently to make good use of the knowledge there gained in an England from which Pole, for reasons which he did not divulge to his traveling companion, may already have chosen what proved to be exile.

[174] Starkey's *Dialogue,* p. 194.
[175] *L&P*, V, no. 1605.
[176] *L&P*, VI, no. 827.

IV

LONDON OR ROME?

Gossip on the continent did not underrate either the political or the scholarly significance of Pole's third visit to Padua. Chapuys, ambassador in London to the Emperor, thought it worth reporting the rumor that Charles might get into his power this son of the princess's governess, grandson of the Duke of Clarence, who according to common court gossip would marry the not unwilling princess and inherit the kingdom; and he expanded on the great virtue and the influential relatives and "allies" of the English nobleman at Padua.[1] Other reports, though more reserved, were in the same vein. Martin de Çornoça, who had some acquaintance with Pole in Venice, described him to the Emperor as "so learned in letters both divine and human, that no one could be found in England like him," and so endowed with prudence, manners, and every virtue that through him the Emperor would be able to gain control of affairs in England without serious contention of arms, blood, or destruction.[2] But Pole was undergoing a change of purpose which gossip-mongers did not know.

[1] *L&P*, VI, no. 1164, pp. 486-487; *Calendar of State Papers, Spanish* (London, 1862–), IV (2), 813-814; V (1), 323-325 (hereafter cited as *Cal. Span.*)

[2] *Cal. Span.*, V (1), 234, 236, 594.

Having turned his back to England, he set himself assiduously and with a considerable degree of success to cultivating his reputation as a scholar. "There was never gentleman out of England more regarded for his learning and wisdom than is master Powll in these parts, the which may be a great jow [*sic*] to all his friends," wrote one Englishman from Venice shortly after Pole's arrival.[3] And this reputation is borne out in his own correspondence with Sadoleto.[4] While he was resolved to devote himself to learning, he had intended also to renew old friendships; but with Lazaro Bonamico as his tutor, his studies had engrossed his leisure, so much so, indeed, that he presently felt no need for his tutor except as an agreeable companion. Significantly, the company he found most joy in was that of his old friends, Gasparo Contarini and Gianpetro Caraffa, Bishop of Chieti; an association which would certainly direct his studies toward practical ends. Still liberal in spirit but unable to accept the new governmental policy under Henry, the bent of his interests, temporarily at least, began to swing to ecclesiastical reform within the Roman church, and it was with this disposition that he settled himself in Padua once more.

Soon English scholars in Italy gravitated to his household, with ambitions, as Sadoleto would have expressed it, less godlike than in the common way and nature of men. Winter was already there, his cortege probably considerably reduced, his concern, now more than ever, with his financial difficulties and his inability to keep up appearances among his Italian associates.[5] Pole's gift of a horse merely accentuated his poverty.[6] We learn of the presence of Thomas Goldwell—whose continued loyalty to Pole as his chaplain

[3] John a Borough to Lord Lisle. *L&P*, VII, no. 233.
[4] *L&P*, VII, no. 1159.
[5] *L&P*, V, no. 1210.
[6] *L&P*, VI, no. 314.

was eventually to be rewarded by a bishopric when his master returned to England under Mary [7]—through his father's prudent injunction to address "my good lord of Canterbury" (William Warham) in Greek, with such sentence as be commendable for the purpose, and to do diligently whatever service he could in Italy for his natural sovereign lord, adding, "and it may turn to your preferment." [8]

Equally loyal to Pole, but more important in the continuity of humanism was Henry Cole, an old acquaintance of Starkey's and possibly of Pole's, later Dean of St. Paul's by Pole's appointment. Cole had taken up residence in Padua in 1530 soon after being graduated Bachelor of Civil Law at Oxford, and according to the usual accounts, from New College. He certainly knew Starkey then, but his letter in that year to "Dr. Starkey" [9] indicates a previous relationship which may have dated back to 1528 and the "Lutheran" trouble at Wolsey's college when Starkey was a proctor on Wolsey's special appointment at Magdalen. According to Foxe, "One of the aforesaid proctors, called Master Cole, of Magdalen College, who afterwards was cross-bearer unto Cardinal Wolsey, was well acquainted with Master Garret; and therefore, he gave secret warning unto a friend or two of Master Garret's, of this privy search; and willed, therefore, that he should forthwith, as secretly as he could, depart out of Oxford." [10] If the "Master Cole" of Foxe's story be indeed the friend and fellow-proctor at Magdalen with Starkey, then one and possibly both were acquainted with the young students who caused such anguish to Higdon, a

[7] Wood, *Athenae Oxonienses*, II, 822-823; John Strype, *Annals of the Reformation* (Oxford, 1824), I, i, 153; Strype, *Ecclesiastical Memorials*, II, ii, 67.

[8] *L&P*, V, no. 1155.

[9] Wood, *Athenae Oxonienses*, I, 451, n. 3.

[10] *Actes and Monuments*, V, 421.

supposition borne out by Cole's open support of the royal supremacy on his return from Padua.[11] The fact that they both continued under Wolsey's sponsorship would illustrate again the Cardinal's liberal policies. Of the group who were to make Pole's house simmer with intellectual activity during 1535 and 1536, Cole had the longest uninterrupted history as an English Paduan. When Pole and his entourage moved to Venice in March 1536, Cole remained in Padua, though he was the only Englishman there;[12] and when he finally left Padua for Paris in 1537, he had been there for seven years.[13]

These were the only English students known to have joined Pole at his arrival. But the number was shortly to increase, partly because of the great expansion of the university during these years, partly because of the commodiousness of Pole's establishment, but presently also because of the phenomenal success of those who were to discover that, paradoxically enough as it proved, Pole's household in Padua was the threshold to the King's household in London. And of those who sojourned there, no one more deliberately or effectively dedicated his learning to the uses of the state than Thomas Starkey, who now rejoined his patron after his study of the civil law in Avignon.

II

Starkey had given a good account of himself during their separation. On July 14, 1533, Sadoleto wrote to Pole from Avignon, sending his compliments to Starkey, and referring to him as a man well worthy of Pole's intimacy, and of the

[11] John Jewel, *Works,* edited by John Ayre (Parker Society, 1845–1850), I, 60-61.
[12] *L&P,* X, nos. 411, 418.
[13] *L&P,* XII (2), no. 40.

studies to which he daily devoted himself.[14] This daily devotion, it is clear from Starkey's own correspondence with a friend and fellow student in Avignon in August 1534,[15] was to the civil law. It will be recalled that Starkey had remained in Avignon after Pole had left in 1532, for the particular purpose of continuing his civilian studies with Ripa. This persistent interest over a period of two years, soon after his semi-retirement with Pole in the Charterhouse, is a plain indication of a newly inspired ambition to enter into the active life of politics. Later on, Starkey told Cromwell of this turning point in his career in a brief account of "the ordur, processe, & end" of his studies:

Fyrst, here in oxforth a grete parte of my youthe I occu-pyd my selfe in the study of phylosophy, joynyg therto the knolege of both tongys bothe latyn & greke, and so aftur passyd ouer in to Italy, whereas I so delytyd in the contem-placyon of natural knolege—wherin the most parte of men lettryd ther occupye themselfys—that many tymys I was purposyd to haue spend the rest of my lyfe holly therin, tyl at the last, mouyd by chrystyan charyte, phylosophy set apart, I applyd my selfe to the redyng of holy scrypture, jugyng al other secrete knolege not applyd to some vse & profyt of other to be but as a vanyte. wherfor in the study of holy letturys certayn yerys I spent, aftur the wyche, by-cause my purpos then was to lyue in a polytyke lyfe, I set my selfe now thes last yerys past to the knolege of the cyuyle Law, that I myght therby make a more stabyl and sure jugement of the polytyke ordur & customys vsyd amonge vs here in our countrey.[16]

What Starkey here hinted at vaguely as a cause of his

[14] *L&P*, VI, no. 827.
[15] Hieronymus Lopis. *L&P*, VII, no. 900 (i, ii).
[16] Herrtage, p. x.

shift of interest to the civil law becomes much clearer in an examination of his activities in the brief interim between the autumn of 1532, when Pole left Avignon for Padua, and July 1533 when Starkey took up his study of the civil law in Padua again. For some years now, he had been the continual companion of Pole; now the King's interest was to draw him back to England while Pole continued on to Italy as planned. In fact, his desire, expressed after his return to Padua, for "a more stabyl and sure jugement of the polytyke ordur & customys vsyd amonge vs here in our countrey," was apparently a result of his direct participation in the greatest legal question of the day, the divorce of Catherine. In April 1533 Starkey addressed a legal opinion to Henry on the King's cause.[17] There is no indication of where Starkey was when he wrote it; but it is clear that he was making a definite bid for Henry's attention. A scribbled memorandum, which the editors of the *Letters and Papers of Henry VIII* have associated with the opinion, reveals his intention to offer as his qualifications for the King's service his "long study in divers kind of letters," and his "experience had in strange countries."[18] His learning, his travel, Henry must be informed about; but chiefly, his familiarity with the case. The letter to Henry undertook to make this clear. Although many learned men had given their opinions on the divorce, he felt constrained to give his. He asserted that all impartial men were agreed that the marriage was against the law of nature and of God; the real danger, he thought, would arise from two wrong opinions of the vulgar, and measures should be taken to eradicate them: (1) that the King's father would never have arranged this marriage if it had transgressed laws either divine or human, and (2) that the Pope can do no wrong. Inasmuch as such vulgar errors

[17] *L&P*, VI, no. 414 (i).
[18] *L&P*, VI, no. 414 (iii).

exist, Starkey advocated referring the case to a general
council; to decide it elsewhere would be a blot on the
King's reputation.

This is a frank and in some ways original analysis of the
political problems inherent in the divorce question. It faced
the King with the existence of a widespread domestic
opposition to the government policy since Henry had separated from Catherine, a fact which had been reported by
foreign observers for some time though approached with
great caution by his own advisors, and it advocated the
only international court of appeal which would side-step
Catherine's insistence on papal jurisdiction. It was not a
perfect solution of Henry's great question. Even if the Germans could be counted on, a conciliar determination would
be slow, perhaps intolerably slow. Nevertheless, it was
under serious consideration when Starkey wrote his opinion. A general council had been mooted since 1530, but
Starkey was doubtless counting on the fact that in February 1532 Henry instructed Carne and Bonner to use the
threat of an appeal of the divorce issue as a means of
bludgeoning the Pope.[19] At this stage in Starkey's thought,
he was not proposing, as he did later, a council composed
of secular appointees; but it is significant of his awareness
of the trend of current policy that at just this time he should
propose the council as a means of escaping papal domination. Concerning the future course of Tudor policy, he had
raised fundamental questions. As a matter of policy, was
the conduct of a Tudor subject to criticism? As a matter of
policy, was the conduct of the Pope exempt from criticism?
Infallibility, it appeared, was a double-edged weapon. And
for the moment, the conciliar solution to Henry's problem
was a bone for all Henry's advisors to chew on. It was the
direct inspiration for the negotiations with the German

[19] *L&P,* V, no. 836, p. 395.

princes in the following year, the chief negotiator for Henry being Edward Fox, who as early as the summer of 1530, it will be remembered, had received a book on councils by the hand of Starkey.

Starkey therefore well knew the timeliness of the conciliar theory when he wrote to Henry in 1533. And in view of that fact, there is every reason to believe that it was on the strength of his letter that Starkey was called to England by Henry at this critical juncture in the divorce proceedings. The evidence is as follows: On June 17, 1533, Thomas Cranmer wrote to Hawkins, ambassador at the Emperor's court, to give the official explanation of Catherine's conduct in the divorce. She had refused citation before the commission headed by Cranmer and appointed to inform her of the final determination, on the grounds that her cause was before the Pope and that she would have no other judge. She was therefore cited for contempt of court by the commission meeting at Dunstable on May 8. Every printed version of Cranmer's white paper, except one, includes a "Dr. Hewis" among the commissioners,[20] "with diverse other learned in the law being councellors in the law for the king's part"; but in *The History of the Reformation*,[21] Burnet substituted "Dr. Sterkey [al. Hewis]," as one of the "Observations and Corrections of the two Volumes . . . made by Mr. Strype" in the 1816 edition.[22] The evidence is hardly conclusive, but it should not be neglected in the light of Starkey's letter to the King. That he should have been a

---

[20] *Archaeologia* (London, 1817), XVIII, 78; *Original Letters Illustrative of English History*, first series, II, 36; *L&P*, VI, no. 661.

[21] Vol. I, 219, n. 47.

[22] Vol. III, pt. ii, p. 528. That there was a Dr. John Hughes among the men learned in the laws of God and the realm summoned by the King on July 25, 1534, when Starkey is known on other evidence to have been in Padua, makes Burnet's substitution no less interesting. See *L&P*, VII, nos. 945, 1008, 1016.

member of the divorce commission is wholly consistent with the later activities of this new civilian-trained LL.D. with ideas.[23] Cranmer, the head of the commission, had recently risen from obscurity for the same reason.

The fact that Starkey was giving an opinion, and thereby gaining recognition in the highest quarters, on a prejudicial case should not bring his honesty into doubt or obscure the originality and independence of his mind. In that same year, he dared to make the novel suggestion that Henry distribute ecclesiastical first fruits among the poor "so that that inequality which formerly obtained might be duly proportioned." [24] And he did not forget the suggestion three years later when it had become clear that the revenue of the suppressions was being used for other purposes.

But the best evidence of the temper of the man who was to lay the foundations of English polity is a discourse on the liberty of speaking and writing as a means for securing and stabilizing a commonwealth.[25] It was written, one would infer from its place in the *Letters and Papers of Henry VIII*, at about the same time as his letter to the King. Starkey took the position that the unrestrained opinions of good men have always strengthened the commonwealth of

[23] Starkey had his doctorate in both civil and canon law when he went to England late in 1534. Shortly after his arrival, one of his friends in Italy addressed him as "Honorar. domino Thomae Starkeio, utriusque Juris Doctori peritiss." *Original Letters*, second series, II, 73.

[24] *L&P*, VI, no. 414 (ii): "Primi fructus distribuendi pauperibus ecclesiae cuiuslibet, ut inequalitas illa olim quae fuit aequitate temperetur."

[25] PRO, SP 1/75, fol. 240. A fragment of only ten lines remains. It is recorded in *L&P*, VI, no. 414 (ii) as "Conclusion of some discourse on the liberty of speaking and writing." Mr. Charles Drew of the Public Record Office remarks: "The writing is very faint, and several words on the right hand margin are mutilated on account of the document having perished."

good men and would overthrow the effrontery of bad men.[26] It is a limited freedom: inexperienced, unconsidered opinion, and abuse of the privilege of speaking and writing ought to be restrained; but freedom has always proved itself in place and time, and though it is a great question whether severity or clemency should be used in a commonwealth, [liberty] permits the wise man to bring all time and means to the matter, and thus by comparing he discovers more easily what is best to be done and most beneficial for the common wealth.[27]

There is no better indication of the liberality of the group around Pole with whom three months later Starkey was once more to be associated. With Starkey, Pole was soon to find himself in serious disagreement. Yet not only does there seem at no time to have been any cessation of the amiable personal relation which had held them together since the death of Lupset, but when Starkey returned to England early in December 1534 [28] it was to become chaplain to Pole's mother, the Lady Salisbury. In the "leisure and quietness" of Howgate, recuperating from the illness that had forced him to leave Italy,[29] he composed the work which

[26] "Libere eae bonorum sententie bonorum rempublicam semper confirmarunt sed contra temeraria malorum everterunt."

[27] The present condition of the manuscript makes a literal translation difficult. The legible portion of the manuscript reads as follows: "viz. quod libertas semper fuit proba . . . loco et tempore, hoc est apud eos qui rei publice presunt sed apud vir . . . imperitum coercenda est temeritas et licentia illa loquendi scribend . . . Sed de severitate et clementia in respublica que cui sit preferenda longo major est difficultas et in summa prudentis viri est observa [L&P: observari] . . . et tempus et rationes omnes negocio adjectas et ita ex collatione facilius inveniet quid sit factu optimum et rei publice salutarissi . . ."

[28] L&P, VIII, no. 132.

[29] L&P, VIII, no. 785.

drew the attention of Cromwell and inside of two months had made him chaplain to the King.

III

Leisurely and quiet Howgate must have been, by comparison with the increased intellectual activity in Pole's residence in Padua in the months before Starkey left Italy. Some idea of the pitch and scope of their studies can be gained from Starkey's letter in August 1534, answering the eager inquiry of a friend and fellow student at Avignon.[30] Pole he described as engaged in the study of theology, Matthew Curtius in reading Galen in Greek, Bembo in writing a history of Venice, and he himself in reading the civil law. Furthermore, even before he left, the circle of scholars had been notably augmented by Richard Morison, erstwhile servant to Winter.

Morison's shift of patronage was governed by more than mere necessity. For Winter's periodic interruptions of study for trips to Verona or to Ferrara when gratuities arrived from Cromwell, or to England when they didn't,[31] had long made it evident that his devotion to learning was as questionable as his patronage was erratic and precarious. He had paid a price for freedom from priestly orders, he announced, but he had no intention of giving up his preferments. He was devoted to letters, he insisted to Cromwell, but at the same time he added cantankerously that if he had trusted his friends' advice, rather than Cromwell's fidelity, he would have returned home to look after his business interests.[32] Plainly, whatever fleeting glimpses of learning the King's scholar would get henceforth were to be inci-

[30] L&P, VII, no. 900 (i, ii.).   [32] L&P, VII, no. 280.
[31] L&P, VI, no. 315; VII, no. 100.

dental to his butterfly flights between England and Italy. In the summer of 1534 he was at court, enjoying the King's inquiries about his life in Italy and sipping the nectar of the Queen's "Vintere carissime." [33] At the same time, he was soliciting Cromwell for funds to support him in Padua. Less than a year after, he was back in England again, pinched, at least according to his own standards, by poverty.[34] In 1537 his frustrations had assumed a fixed pattern: he would like to return to the learning from which he had been absent for forty-four months, a loss of time tolerable only because of Cromwell's conversation and favor.[35]

It is understandable, then, that Winter's dependents in Padua should have found in Pole a steadier patron. Such was the case of William Belson,[36] who until August 1532, while Winter was soliciting Cromwell for a year's support for him, had performed the duties of a trusty servant to Winter without pay.[37] But of far greater consequence in the history of English scholarship was the kindness of Pole toward Richard Morison. Unlike Belson, he was probably wholly dependent on patronage, and patronage in the period since his appeal to Cranmer in December 1533 had been slim. He had done his best. He had sought to align himself with the new archbishop by a bland assertion that the nobility of England were now opposed to superstition, that ceremonies that had once been good were now degenerate. The opinion would have been less suspect if it had not been accompanied by a request for help.[38] Whether Cranmer responded is not known; but in October of the following year he was soliciting aid from Cromwell, in tones, however, far from sycophantic. While the news of the imprisonment of More and Fisher was filling more timid

[33] *L&P*, VII, no. 964.

[34] *L&P*, IX, no. 345; X, no. 2.

[35] *L&P*, XII (1), no. 447.

[36] *L&P*, IX, nos. 659, 1034.

[37] *L&P*, V, no. 1210.

[38] *L&P*, VI, no. 1582.

Englishmen abroad with dismay and foreboding,[39] Morison
boldly offered Cromwell the gratuitous suggestion to act so
that all men would honor him: Banish "England's enemies,"
he counseled, rather than put them to death;[40] and after
the executions had taken place he wrote a highly critical
letter, reporting unfavorable opinion abroad.[41]

Brash as it was, Morison's confidence in his own ideas, an
eagerness that outran discretion throughout his career, was
characteristic. His was not a temper either conducive to
agreeable relations between dependent and patron, or easily
adjustable to the circumstances imposed by Winter's strin-
gency. Within a month, Cromwell had received complaints
from Winter of Morison's poverty (*tenuitas*),[42] and pleas
from Winter's friends to be good to him, "which, God know-
eth, hath a very small living." [43] He had even pawned his
books.[44] But destitute as he was, his linguistic ability and
his zest for learning won him the respect of his associates.
From his long residence abroad he had acquired a native
fluency in Italian, and if Lloyd's remark refers to this period
in his career, the very "virtues and port of a German, as if
he had been a native of that place." [45] He wrote readily in
Greek and Latin. Of his feverish appetite for study, one
catches glimpses: in his impatient request for the Greek
Commentaries, in his resolve to read "all of Aristotle," [46] in
his reading of Euripides and Aristophanes with the admir-

[39] John Mason to Starkey, July 3, 1534: "What will be the end of
this tragedy God knows." *L&P*, VII, no. 945.

[40] *L&P, VII*, nos. 1311, 1318. The attainders of More and Fisher
were presented at the prorogation of parliament on November 3,
seven days after Morison had written. *L&P*, VII, no. 1377.

[41] *L&P*, IX, no. 198.

[42] *L&P*, IX, no. 103.

[43] *L&P*, IX, no. 345.

[44] *L&P*, IX, no. 102.

[45] David Lloyd, *State Worthies* (London, 1766), pp. 113-114.

[46] *L&P*, IX, no. 103.

ing George Lily.[47] Confidently he boasted to Starkey that with books and freedom from work he would return to England a Greek scholar, a philosopher, and a theologian.[48]

For some time now, his dependence on Winter had been nominal.[49] As early as December 1534 he had become, like Belson, an integral part of Pole's household. There is probably a pun in his remark that Pole had rescued him from winter's cold.[50] In August 1535 he was getting assistance from both Starkey and Cromwell,[51] and in the following March he was writing that Winter "either will not or cannot any longer assist my studies." [52] But by that time, Winter's help was supererogatory; for Cromwell had invited him to come to England, and his career seemed assured. As with Starkey, who actively supported his suit in London, so with Morison, studies had proved their worth. Conscious of the same humanistic ideal, he had written in February offering to come home if Cromwell thought his learning could serve his country; otherwise he would prefer to finish his studies.[53] In May he left Padua for the court, his ears tingling with Cromwell's praise, his services wholly committed to his new patron.[54] "I would not now wish to have been born of rich parents," he confided to Cromwell, "it is almost thought disgraceful in England to be noble and learned." [55] In a way that Wolsey could not have anticipated, his college at Oxford relived in Padua.

Starkey and Morison were not the only members of the young liberal group at Wolsey's college in 1528 who appeared in Pole's household at this time. John Friar had also taken up residence there. Already actively engaged in the service of Edward Fox, Henry's brilliant negotiator with the

[47] L&P, IX, no. 1034; X, no. 321.
[48] L&P, X, no. 320.
[49] L&P, X, no. 661.
[50] L&P, IX, no. 102.
[51] L&P, IX, no. 103.
[52] L&P, X, no. 418.
[53] L&P, X, no. 372.
[54] L&P, X, no. 565.
[55] L&P, X, no. 660.

Germans, Friar had temporarily disengaged himself from his master. Perhaps he is to be identified with the John Frier who was named as one of the servants of the marshal of Calais, Sir Edward Ringeley, at about Easter time, 1534. Since Fox was in Calais at the time,[56] the identification is probably correct.[57] The first record of his association with Pole in Padua is his letters to Starkey from Venice and Padua beginning in October 1535, which indicate that he was already engaged in the medical studies leading to his doctorate.[58] How old this friendship was is unknown. It may have begun five years before when Starkey came to Paris in Pole's company; it is quite possible that they knew each other as early as the period of Friar's residence in Cardinal's College. Now, at any rate, they were close friends, and their letters were frequent, though only Friar's share of the correspondence has survived.

Friar still regarded Fox as his patron, and through Starkey, who as royal chaplain was at this time close to Fox, he kept informed of his patron's movements. These were stirring times for young scholars anxious to make use of their learning in the quickly developing political scene, and at the moment no better opportunity presented itself than service with the man who may have been most responsible for the liberal policy of Cardinal's College. On October 20, Friar was jubilant over Starkey's news that Fox had been made Bishop of Hereford in anticipation of his mission to the Protestant princes in Germany for the purpose of arriving at an agreement on policy and establishing a common

[56] L&P, VIII, no. 823.

[57] An altercation arose from Friar's demand of a bill of money from Robert Garnysshe and resulted in Garnysshe's imprisonment. During the trial before Lord Chancellor Audeley a year later, certain evidence was taken against Friar, though there is no indication that he was there. L&P, VII, no. 585; VIII, no. 516.

[58] L&P, IX, nos. 648, 687.

front of secular princes against papal dominion.[59] In December, Starkey was able to give him the news he was waiting for: Fox wanted him in Saxony. But still there was no word directly from Fox. "See what you can do," he pleaded; "there is nothing I wouldn't do for him." [60] Go to Germany, was Starkey's answer, "and take advantage of [Fox] there." By late February or early March, Friar had taken the advice.[61] With his return to England after the Diet of Schmalkalde, and his career as a man of medicine, his interest as a humanist ceases. Nevertheless, his presence in Padua at the same time as Starkey, Morison, and Cole, all of whom were either observers or active participants in the "Lutheran" upset at Oxford, emphasizes the legacy of tolerance which Pole inherited from Wolsey, and upon which a healthy humanistic activity depends.

The phenomenal success at court of Pole's protégés in 1534 and 1535 undoubtedly established the reputation of Pole's residence as a center of learning in Italy and attracted students of lesser pretensions. There were the two younger scholars with distinguished fathers, George Lily and Richard Shelley, both of whom had taken up residence with Pole before Starkey left Padua. George, the son of William Lily, the grammarian, later to write the first biographies of his father and the preceding generation of English Paduans,[62] had lived under the shadow of his father's fame. The very fact that William Lily was a fellow student of Linacre, Grocyn, Latimer, and Colet at Padua laid a pattern for him, and in boyhood his natural tastes and aptitudes had compelled him in the same direction. He studied with Morison daily, and congratulated Starkey on learning that he had be-

[59] L&P, IX, no. 648.
[60] L&P, IX, no. 917.
[61] L&P, IX, no. 1011; X, nos. 321, 411.
[62] Colet, Grocyn, Linacre, Lupset, Pace, and Latimer.

come "familiar" with the King.[63] But when Starkey urged him to come to England, Lily drew back. Mentioning the importance to England of the current advancement of learned men, he thanked him for his advice "to study higher and greater subjects, such as philosophy and the books of the old lawyers," and assured him that he was studying rhetoric and the most approved authors. Even if Pole returned to England, Lily was uncertain if he should accompany his patron or remain in Padua. Possibly not unaware of Pole's present inclinations, he told Starkey that in spite of the hereditary advantages of his father's reputation and possessions, the best part of which he would inherit as the only living child, he surmised that it would all come to nothing; and he seriously contemplated throwing himself into "this new school of Chieti" (the Theatines).[64] It seems likely that Pole's influence even then was strong; certainly, in the end, to join the Theatines was the course that he found most congenial.

Richard Shelley was the son of William Shelley, Grand Prior of the Knights of St. John in England, a title which Richard would be the last to inherit. William Shelley had close connections with Wolsey. It was his house in Paris, it will be recalled, which Taylor took steps to procure for Thomas Winter in 1526, and as legal advisor to Cardinal's College he was one of those to whom Wolsey appealed at the time of his fall.[65] Richard, the second son, was therefore a "legacy" to the scholarly tradition and acted as might be expected. He arrived in Padua, probably for the first time, in August 1535, with letters from Starkey to Morison, who spoke of him as "young Shelley" in sending his salutations.[66]

[63] L&P, VIII, no. 581.
[64] L&P, IX, no. 292. September 6, 1535.
[65] L&P, IV (2), no. 2545; Original Letters, second series, II, 37.
[66] L&P, IX, no. 103. Shelley was about twenty-two.

He was with Pole, "Don Albano Inglese," possibly until his departure for Constantinople in the train of Edmund Harvel in May 1539, but long before that time he had grown "wearier of this scholastical life than he can express." [67] A man like Morison commanded his respect both for his scholarship and for his continual occupation "in things of great moment," and Shelley reported his progress in studies to him and listened to his advice. But in spite of his linguistic abilities and his mastery of the Ciceronian style, to which Leland testified,[68] "young Shelley" did not take his studies seriously; indeed, he was under no compulsion to do so. One gets closer to the real tastes of Shelley in Leland's description of him as "modestus, candoris nivei, & lepôris almi," and in his remark to Morison that he had been recreating himself after study "with a little music, as I remember . . . (wiselier than I did then understand) you counselled me to do." [69]

IV

Pole's household, it may be inferred, was anything but an isolated retreat. Aside from the daily routine of study, its life was enlivened by the periodic visitations of messengers with news from London and Paris, and of English travelers, who found its gracious hospitality a welcome break for their journeys.

Among the visitors, two old associates of the Paris days were especially welcome. John Mason, King's scholar in Paris since 1530, visited his friends in Padua in July 1534, during the course of a continental tour in preparation for a

[67] A. F. Pollard in *DNB*, "Richard Shelley."

[68] John Leland, *Principum ac illustrium aliquot et eruditorum in Anglia virorum Encomia,* in *De rebus britannicis collectanea* (London, 1774), p. 147.

[69] *L&P*, XIII (2), nos. 724, 847.

diplomatic career.[70] Florentius Volusene, whose house in Paris had been a rendezvous for English scholars five years before, may have visited Padua after a conversation with Starkey in the garden of Anthony Bonvisi, Italian merchant in London. Acting on the same advice, he had then gone to Carpentras, where Sadoleto took him in, greatly impressed by his learning.[71]

Messenger duties seem to have fallen most heavily on Thomas Jones, recently and possibly still the servant of Richard Pate,[72] and on friendly terms with Starkey,[73] Morison,[74] Lily,[75] and Sandro.[76] Michael Throckmorton, Pole's colorful personal messenger, was a family friend of both Starkey[77] and Morison.[78] Morison's quip while he was in dire poverty, "I am his man for I wear his livery," [79] was matched by Throckmorton's some years later, "Where other men get money, you get men's hearts." [80] Throckmorton's later activities as confidential agent of Cromwell while apparently still in the confidence of Pole must be passed

[70] He was apparently on intimate terms with Starkey, and the friendship continued to prosper in correspondence after Starkey had gone to England. In a letter of December 17, 1535, from Naples, Mason addressed Starkey as "my assured friend," then described the antiquities at Baie, Puteoli, and Cumae, reserving his comments on Lipari for "our meeting together." *L&P*, IX, no. 981.

[71] *L&P*, VIII, no. 856 (43); IX, nos. 395, 867; XI, no. 1435.

[72] *L&P*, VII, no. 960. Pate to Starkey, May 31, 1535 (*L&P*, VIII, no. 785): "This messenger, your old friend, is the cause I write no news, as he can tell all."

[73] *L&P*, VIII, nos. 785, 875.

[74] *L&P*, IX, no. 101; X, nos. 417, 419.

[75] *L&P*, IX, no. 673.

[76] *L&P*, IX, nos. 127, 1028.

[77] "They, and I, and our other friends are beholden to you for your good word and loving mind, always ready to the furtherance of young fry." *L&P*, VIII, no. 536. Friar and probably the rest of Pole's circle were acquainted with him. *L&P*, XII, no. 430.

[78] *L&P*, XII, no. 430.

[79] *L&P*, IX, no. 102; X, no. 320.

[80] *L&P*, XII, no. 430.

over here.[81] Likewise irrelevant to the present purpose, and therefore regretfully to be left unsung, is that extraordinary character, Henry Phillips, friend of Morison and erstwhile student at Louvain, reputedly the man who "took" Tyndale and called the King *tyrannum expilatorem reipublicae*.[82] Sometime before October 1538, Phillips turned up in Padua arrayed like a "Svycer" or ruffling man of war, with a pair of Almain boots and a hope for the support of Pole, and with Throckmorton in hot pursuit. Pole, who had just arrived in Padua from Flanders, jumped to the conclusion that Phillips had been suborned by the council to spy on his activities, and thoroughly alarmed by Phillips' warlike costume and suspicious story, forbade him his house and—with what right is not clear—the whole dominion of Venice.[83] It must be said in Phillips' defense that he had some aspirations to the name of a scholar. In 1535 he claimed to have been a student for twenty years,[84] and in 1536 Cromwell had apparently furnished support for him under the same conditions that he had for Richard Morison.[85] This would indicate that Morison and Phillips may have been fellow students in Padua, a relationship confirmed by Morison's hope for his friend's success now that he had taken up his studies once again and proceeded "so far on his journey," since it was by his persuasion that Phillips gave up the court for literature.[86]

Throughout this period of intellectual activity, Pole's circle was under the continual surveillance of that wholly

---

[81] *L&P*, XI, nos. 4, 1297, 1363; XII, nos. 34, 1293.

[82] *L&P*, VIII, no. 1151.

[83] *L&P*, VIII, no. 1151; IX, nos. 1138, 1144; X, nos. 529-530, 796.

[84] *L&P*, IX, nos. 1138, 1143.

[85] *L&P*, X, no. 224.

[86] *L&P*, XI, no. 1482. Morison promised to try to get Cromwell's permission for Wakefield, who held the professorship of Hebrew in Wolsey's college, to help Phillips and others desirous of a knowledge of that language.

sympathetic though non-academic English resident of Venice, Edmund Harvel, whose observations give the clearest insight into the dilemma now facing Pole himself. Harvel had spent some years before Pole came to Italy as a wool merchant in Venice, but Pole's coming apparently meant new friends and a new outlook. It was he who spoke the finest epitaph for Lupset: "There was in him great plenty of wit, much learning, and a great loving mind to his friends." [87] Indeed, there was a magnanimity in the man that moved Starkey to speak of his "imperial mind," to which Harvel responded modestly with the hope that "the Britannical shall appear nothing inferior." [88] Attracted by the serious political objectives of Pole's protégés, he developed a businessman's hankerings for life at court, although his values were broadly humanistic rather than materialistic. Studies, he believed, should be directed toward the betterment of common rather than private wealth. "No man," he declared to Starkey, "can witness better than you of my studious mind for the wealth of our country, by that reasoning I made with you *de lanificio*." [89] On this principle, as we have seen, he had remonstrated with Pole against the cloistered life in 1531, in what is perhaps the finest contemporary definition of the aims of the humanist.[90] And again, in 1535, he regarded Pole's continuance in Italy since 1532 as an inexcusable retirement from public life. In April, when Pole seems to have given the impression that he was going to return to England,[91] Harvel promised that he would not cease to exhort him to choose some other kind of life instead of consuming his

---

[87] *L&P*, V, no. 301.
[88] *L&P*, VIII, no. 535.
[89] *Ibid.*
[90] See above, p. 75.
[91] *L&P*, VIII, nos. 535, 579. Lily, it will be recalled, had the same impression. See *L&P*, VIII, no. 581.

perpetual life in letters, and that the King, his country, and his friends might sometimes have his work.

Nevertheless, when it came to acting on his own advice, Harvel exhibited a singular lack of resolution. He had made overtures to Cromwell early in 1535.[92] But when Cromwell's answer came, advising him to come to England, and Harvel faced the necessity of giving up his business, he began to seek excuse. Over a year later, in spite of repeated encouragement from Starkey, he was still in Italy. On May 26, at just the time that Pole declared his mind to Henry, Harvel wrote to Starkey, "To show you my minde liberally, I have litil pleasure and comfort of myselff considering the perpetual factions and discords of the worldly things wiche makith me cold to come emong men *in publico.* My minde enclinith moche rather to folow a private and quiet liff and give ope the worldly fastidie to them *qui ambiunt honores,* in the wiche number I was never gretely to be rekenid." [93] One might well suspect that Pole's influence was responsible for Harvel's vacillation and final rejection of Cromwell's offer; but it is quite clear from his correspondence with Starkey at this time that he was not in Pole's confidence.

Yet Harvel's money and his house in Venice served the cause of humanism well, and his enthusiasm for the idea of learning applied to contemporary problems in England acted catalytically upon men like Starkey who found in him a man of ideals who could give substantial support to the position from which they would presently discover that their patron, Pole, had been gradually withdrawing since the Charterhouse period. Harvel became their voice, defending their action against the implications of purely material aims.

[92] *L&P*, VIII, no. 373.
[93] *L&P*, VIII, nos. 511, 579, 874; IX, no. 1029; X, no. 803; *Original Letters,* second series, II, 77.

They were not unaware that their sincerity might be called into question. Starkey was anxious to have it known that he was not a "feigned man," that gold and honors might have affected him when he was younger, but "by the benefit of letters" now no longer.[94] But in urging Pole to express himself on the subject of the divorce, they were urging precisely the active role in public affairs which Pole as a humanist espoused; and though they deferred to his learning, in this respect they spoke with complete conviction.

Quite naturally, the government made a special bid for the support of the humanist whose name would give his judgment value above that of the others. But Pole temporized. With that "prodigious taciturnity" which Longueil had earlier observed in him, Pole gave no inkling of his feelings to his own household. Maintaining silence on the nature of his response, he nevertheless contrived to give them the impression that he was favorable to the new policy. There was nothing in his previous conduct inconsistent with this impression. Both Harvel and Starkey had been long enough associated with Pole to feel confident in their judgment of the man; and they were hopeful, in spite of his Socratean disregard for life or glory, that Pole could be persuaded from retirement. Had they entertained any doubt, they would surely not have so endangered their reputation as to assure the King that Pole still supported him. In February 1535 Starkey told Henry that while he did not know Pole's views on the divorce or the supremacy, he could affirm Pole's mind, heart, and desire, "wych I know no other wyse then I know myn owne," to do Henry's service, and that he was of the opinion that Pole would apply all his learning to maintaining "such thyngys as hys gracys wysedome by court of parlyament therin had decred."[95]

[94] *L&P*, VIII, no. 575.   [95] Herrtage, p. xiv.

In June, Harvel wrote Starkey from Venice, assuring him that Pole would satisfy the King, and testifying to his prudence and virtue which Starkey would have better cause to know than he, having been his "domesticall" for so many years;[96] and in March 1536 he expressed his confidence to Starkey that Pole's work would be a "noble monument of his wit and virtue" and a glory to the country and posterity.[97]

Actually, they knew nothing. Through the winter and spring of 1535–36, while Pole's labors were most concentrated and all thought of going to England had been abandoned, he explained merely that he must finish the book "in the quiet life" of Italy, where his attention would not be diverted and where friends and relatives would not interrupt.[98] But his friends in Rome were kept informed; and Contarini in particular read and criticized the book, part by part, as the writing proceeded. Safe in Italy, Pole confided to them his broadened aim: he was not writing for the King alone, but for the English people, who are apt to be led astray by books and edicts.[99] In January 1536 he had finished the portion about the authority of the Pope (Part II),[100] in March, the rebuttal of Sampson (Part I).[101] There were reports that it was completed in April, and late in May he entrusted the finished work to Michael Throckmorton to deliver personally into the hands of the King.

V

Excepting More's, *Pro ecclesiasticae unitatis defensione* is the best statement of conservative opinion in England. Thomas More had said in his own defense that if he differed

---

[96] *L&P*, VIII, no. 874.
[97] *L&P*, VIII, no. 579; X, no. 503.
[98] *L&P*, VIII, no. 579.

[99] *L&P*, X, no. 420.
[100] *L&P*, X, no. 217.
[101] *L&P*, X, no. 619.

from one kingdom, he had all antiquity and all other nations on his side. Pole spoke with the same reverence of that
tradition. While he framed his book, in the fashion of contemporary polemics, as a specific answer to Richard Sampson's *Oratio*,[102] he recognized, as More recognized, that the
strength of his position lay in defense rather than attack,
and that the issue involved was no less than the unity of
Christendom. The King, in Pole's opinion, had required an
answer repugnant to divine law. By assuming the royal
supremacy, he had invaded ecclesiastical prerogatives heretofore unquestioned, by him alone among kings rejected.[103]
Tradition thus flouted, the unity of Christendom would be
broken. For if kings in their realms are heads of churches,
then in effect Henry was proposing many heads in the
church. No change in a state is possible without grave injury
to the commonwealth. But when the rule of a kingdom,
which is the highest form of state, is forcibly transferred to
many, how much greater the injury, how much graver the
danger. This is the kind of injury now inflicted on the
church, whose tradition of rule by one has been confirmed
as the best by many generations. As a matter of fact, it
would be impossible for the English people to bind over the
spiritual supremacy to the King, England being but a part
of the Christian commonwealth constituted by God.[104]

Nevertheless, Henry for certain liberties had chosen to
break this unity, and the results, as Pole viewed them, were
deplorable. Had England, as Sampson alleged, suffered
"servitude" under "the heavy yoke of Rome"? Pole pointed
by contrast to the three years since the establishment of the
royal supremacy as a time during which the church in Eng-

[102] *Oratio qua docet Anglos regiae dignitati ut obediant*, Berthelet
(1535?).
[103] *Pro ecclesiasticae unitatis defensione* [Rome, 1536], sig. A v.
[104] Sig, A iv-A iv[v].

land had suffered more burdens than under all the popes for many centuries past.[105] The so-called head of the church in England had proved rather to be a robber of the church, raising pleasure houses rather than monasteries, destroying the nobles and raising worthless men to power at the expense of the throne, butchering men of the quality of More, Fisher, and Reynolds, even disinheriting his own daughter. What an irony that the nephew of the man (Edward, Earl of Warwick) whom this destroyer's father executed should now be defending the succession! [106]

But the king who has performed all these enormities has assumed that he was answerable to no man. Indeed, there are those who have reached the ear of the king who argue that all is the king's. How much more to his honor had he listened to those who argued more truly that nothing belongs to the king except as he protects and administers for the common good what is common to all.[107]

In protest against this rank assumption of power in disregard of the unity of Christendom and the good of his people, and in particular against those evil counselors, who like Sampson, asserted that the king should not be resisted, Pole advanced a theory of limited obedience. Men should obey an earthly king in those things which pertain to the office of a king, but when that same king orders the worship of a golden statue, thereby plainly exceeding the bounds of royal power, the people should rather be thrown into the fiery furnace than obey that order of the king.[108] Kings are appointed to rule by the people, to whom they are merely servants or instruments.[109] Surely, in bestowing the crown, the English people have not forgotten their ancient liberty to bring kings to account publicly for administering badly the affairs entrusted to them.[110] In the past, the English

[105] Sig. F v^v.   [107] Sig. S iii.   [109] Sig. E i^v.
[106] Sig. O ii^v ff.   [108] Sig. B iii.   [110] Sig. R v^v.

people, when oppressed, have exercised the right of deposition, and Pole quite frankly advocated it now unless Henry should change his course, and of this there seemed very little prospect. In the event of civil war, he expressed confidence that the English people could count on the Emperor and the French king.[111] Pole's final address to Henry, couched in terms of personal appeal, was actually a militant threat. In the name of tradition, he was enunciating no less than a revolutionary manifesto.

VI

The immediate effect of the release of *Pro ecclesiasticae unitatis defensione* was to bring to a sudden, climactic end the household of Pole in Padua and Venice at the time when it had achieved its height of activity. Over thirteen years had elapsed since Lupset had crossed the Alps into Italy and joined Pole there in extended and serious study. In the course of the years, the personnel of Pole's circle had undergone constant change and included the widest variety of personalities and purposes. Enthusiastic young English students had there freely mingled with distinguished cisalpine and transalpine scholars of the quality of Nicolo Leonico, Peter Bembo, and Christopher Longueil. At least seven scholars of rank can be identified as seriously engaged in study there during 1535 and 1536. Others visited them. And all felt the arterial stimulus from the highest sources in England in the person of Reginald Pole. Consequently, as long as Pole remained there, the colony flourished. But nothing could be more indicative of its dependence on him than its rapid decline after he had burned his bridges to England and departed for Rome at the end of May 1536.

Even before Pole had revealed his carefully concealed

[111] Sig. S vi ff.

opinions, John Friar had taken up the practice of medicine in London and Richard Morison was en route to his new duties under Cromwell.[112] Henry Cole was still in Padua on September 30, and his association with Pole at the time of the completion of *Pro ecclesiasticae unitatis defensione* [113] suggests that he may have left when Pole did, presumably for Paris where he had apparently been for some time in June 1537.[114] The last record of George Lily in Padua is in May 1536.[115] William Belson was in England early in 1537, though he continued to act as messenger for the Pole family for several years after.[116] Michael Throckmorton performed similar services. Thomas Jones left for "his own country" soon after Pole's announcement.[117] Edmund Harvel stayed on after Pole left, strongly tempted by the encouragements of Thomas Winter, John Russell, Thomas Starkey, and Richard Morison, all of whom urged Cromwell to employ Harvel's long Venetian experience in England.[118] His decision to remain, however, did not prejudice him in the eyes of Henry and Cromwell, who as a token of their good will remembered him in 1537 with a "licence of wools" in Venice and a stipend,[119] and eventually with the Venetian ambassadorship. Richard Shelley, who had arrived in August 1535, may have remained at Pole's Venetian residence, the house of Donato, after Pole's departure for Rome; he was certainly there in October 1538, when he addressed Pole, then or shortly before in Padua, as "Don Albano Inglese," and reported that "Messere Sigismunde Harvell nostre" had not

[112] *L&P*, X, nos. 961, 970.
[113] *L&P*, XI, no. 402.
[114] *L&P*, XII (2), no. 40.
[115] *L&P*, X, no. 971.
[116] *L&P*, XII (1), no. 430; XIII (2), no. 829.
[117] *L&P*, IX, no. 1028; X, no. 417.
[118] *L&P*, VIII, nos. 579, 874.
[119] *L&P*, XII (2), no. 1127.

yet been made King's secretary there, and that the matter seemed to have cooled.[120] But the rigor of study was not for Shelley, and neither he by disposition nor Harvel because of absorption in business affairs was likely to continue the scholarly tradition maintained by Pole.

And in any event, for Englishmen in Padua, Pole's decision marked the end of a period of fruitful scholarship, and, as he must have known, the beginning of an irremediable schism. The personal stakes were high. Quite deliberately, he had sealed his fate as a political exile. He had thrown his mother and brothers in England into grim jeopardy. He had written a sardonic finis to Starkey's career at court. Henceforth, there could be only recriminations and a tragic separation both physically and intellectually from his dearest friends. These were costs that he could reckon, costs that would be long paid before he should return to England as Archbishop of Canterbury. In the face of Henry's certain reaction, these considerations might well have given him pause. Yet the whirligig of time was to bring in one result that he could not have anticipated. As Archbishop, he may have smiled wryly to find that his theory of the popular origin of kingship served equally well when those whom his answer to Henry had permanently alienated, in their turn, became exiles.

Up to the moment that Pole declared himself, however, the prospect of England from Padua seemed cloudless. Ignorant of their patron's feelings, the circle of humanists around him welcomed unreservedly the good fortune that promoted them by a single leap into the very confidences of the throne, eager with a scholar's anticipation to translate their philosophy into an English idiom. It was with high hopes that one by one they doffed their academic robes and hurried to England and opportunity.

[120] *L&P*, XIII (2), no. 724.

V

A SCHOLAR ON KING'S BUSINESS

When Thomas Cromwell invited members of Pole's circle in
Padua into his official family in England, he was as much in
need of them as, for the most part, they were of him. The
King's declaration of independence from the Pope in 1534
had posed problems of policy the solution of which Cromwell, hardheaded and practical as he was, recognized from
the first as the task of scholars. "What is policy according to
Aristotle?" he demanded of Thomas Starkey soon after their
first meeting, and stayed for an answer. It was no academic
question, and Starkey must have shaken in his shoes, but he
carried out the assignment. Like Wolsey, Cromwell relied
on men of quick wits, "persons of great quickness and abilities," as Strype put it;[1] but the number of his advisors was
larger, and those who had demonstrated their usefulness
had greater rewards. Latimer, looking in retrospect at
Cromwell's record of patronage, wrote with his customary
candor: "And yett thus much now I wyll say, ande natt say
it alone, butt with many, that your lordshype won man have
promotyd many moo honeste men synyste God promotyd
you, then hath many men doon befoore your tyme thowgh

[1] *Ecclesiastical Memorials*, I, 582.

111

in licke authorite with you." [2] Never had the opportunity been greater for men solely on their merits as scholars to influence national policy, and never did scholars live up to their opportunities more brilliantly.

Expediency demanded that where accepted legal precedent was inadequate, acceptable legal precedent had to be found. It was no mean undertaking, and it was complicated by the conservatism of the people on the one hand and the King on the other. Yet it is important to remember the strength of certain popular prejudices, particularly the tendency that had persisted since Wycliffe's time to regard the Pope as a foreigner in England; so that, in a matter of choice between Pope and King, national feelings were strong enough to insure loyalty in the great majority of the people. That the policy makers recognized this fact and counted heavily upon it will be sufficiently evident from the most casual perusal of the documents issuing from the government press during the crucial period. Moreover, the dispossession of the monasteries greatly quickened the flow of wealth already moving into the direct control of Englishmen, and though it worked hardship among rural tenants, who suffered from sharply rising rents,[3] the sale and resale of monastic lands increased and strengthened the new owners to whom the Tudors naturally looked for political backing.[4] Thus social as well as political influences operated in support of the break with Rome.

[2] *Three Chapters of Letters relating to the Suppression of Monasteries*, edited by Thomas Wright, Camden Society, no. 26 (1843), p. 149.

[3] *English Economic History*, edited by Bland, Brown, and Tawney (London, 1925), pp. 251-254.

[4] Baskerville, *English Monks and the Suppression of the Monasteries*, pp. 96-119; S. J. Liljegren, *The Fall of the Monasteries and the Social Changes in England Leading up to the Great Revolution* (Lund, 1924). Liljegren estimated that one-fourth of the nation's wealth shifted hands through the reign of Edward VI.

But if popular appeals to national spirit and personal cupidity tended to strengthen the government's hand, an appeal to tradition was fundamental in justifying the new order. While expediency was the most immediate factor determining the character of political and social theory during the period in which Thomas Cromwell was in power, the establishment of the royal supremacy never involved a serious break with tradition.[5] On the contrary, every effort was made to avoid such an implication by aligning it with traditional policy. Essentially, Henry's problem was to discover theoretic warrant for a *fait accompli* without the sacrifice of catholicity or conformity. A formula deriving its force from national isolationism and its most enthusiastic adherents from the ranks of the radical English Lutherans could hardly be acceptable to the defender of the faith. To create a satisfactory apologetic Cromwell turned to the humanists whose studies in both England and Italy he had actively assisted and whose range of reading among classical and modern authors particularly qualified them to carry out this commission. It was because of their efforts that expediency found justification in theory.

Recent scholarship has recognized the importance of these government apologists in the creation of a rationale for the royal supremacy;[6] but because of their function as

[5] Franklin L. Baumer in *The Early Tudor Theory of Kingship* (New Haven, 1940) has described it as revolutionary in English political thought. But see Roland H. Bainton in *Review of Religion*, V (1941), 239-240, who accepts this view as "essentially sound" but "slightly overdone." One might reasonably question calling a program revolutionary which met with such a large degree of popular support. On this point, see A. F. Pollard in *English Historical Review*, LVI (1941), 311.

[6] Pierre Janelle, *L'Angleterre catholique à la veille du schisme* (Paris, 1935); Gustave Constant, *The Reformation in England: the English Schism* (New York, 1935); A. Passerin d'Entrèves, *The Medieval Contribution to Political Thought* (Oxford, 1939); Baumer, *Early Tudor Theory of Kingship*.

propagandists, it has prejudged their case. Janelle [7] has pictured them as astute Machiavellians, violating their personal convictions to the point of downright dishonesty; and their latest historian,[8] following Janelle's lead, has interpreted their repeated appeal to tradition as a deliberate policy of deception. There can be no doubt that the circumstances of their entry into the government's service and the nature of their activities would make such inferences plausible, and the sycophancy of Morison in particular lends weight to the charge. But such an interpretation not only misrepresents the moderate temper of other members of the group—a temper sometimes described anachronistically as Erastian [9] —but it judges them wholly on personal grounds, ignoring the sense of public duty which animated their return to England from Padua and their approach to the problems of policy facing the government when they arrived. Furthermore, such inferences cast doubt on the legitimacy of the government's case. The establishment of the royal supremacy undeniably meant change, but one need not charge with duplicity those who believed that it was a reversion to a more ancient tradition than the papal supremacy. The humanists' respect for tradition, not as a trick but as an honest effort of liberals to join the past and the living present, informed the Cromwellian polity.

In precisely the same way they approached the chief social change during Cromwell's term of office. The pattern of a fixed social order had been outgrown, and expediency required a new social theory to accommodate the current situation. Here again, the personal interests of the apologists

[7] *L'Angleterre catholique*, pp. 232-319, especially pp. 309-319.

[8] Baumer, *Early Tudor Theory of Kingship*, pp. 38-45, 49-56 (especially p. 52, n. 53), 216.

[9] C. H. Smyth, *Cranmer and the Reformation under Edward VI* (Cambridge, 1926), pp. 29-30; E. A. Whitney, "Erastianism and Divine Right," *Huntington Library Quarterly*, II (1939), 373-398.

were at stake, yet their approach to a solution was on a broad humanistic level, as traditional as the theory it displaced, and in part even detrimental to their self-interest. It would be wise, before stigmatizing them as dishonest, to recall Edmund Harvel's plea to Starkey when he learned of his retirement to the Charterhouse, that he "come forth to teach others, and make all the land know *quam sit humaniter vivendum*," that he "help to take out all barbarous customs, and bring the realm to an antique form of good living." [10] A renaissance of the antique form of good living often appears as the high and unremitting purpose of those who studied with Pole at Padua.

II

Moreover, if the English Paduans would teach England *quam sit humaniter vivendum*, they would also teach her *quam sit liberaliter vivendum*. A liberal point of view, traceable from the youthful days in Cardinal's College when they read in secret the bootlegged Lutheran heresies, and encouraged through the years in Padua while Pole was still friendly with the most enlightened Protestant opinion of Europe, now asserted itself in the creation of English policy. In an authoritarian age, often characterized as despotic, their achievement is the more remarkable. It is an interesting quirk of fortune that this, the most significant and enduring contribution to intellectual history in the Tudor period, should have been largely the work of comparatively obscure men, but it is not surprising in view of the facts. The declaration of the government in 1534 that it had freed itself from papal domination provided the intellectual environment for a parallel theory of official toleration. But in so doing it created a division of allegiance among scholars

[10] *L&P*, V, no. 301.

which proved irreparable. It was inevitable that this division should have appeared in Pole's circle, as it did everywhere else, and that the division here also should have been permanent. Their shock when Pole sent his book to Henry in May 1536 and disclosed his real sentiments is a measure of the distance apart that men of liberal views found themselves on the great question of the day.

Pole's break with Henry did not mean a complete break with liberal thought. His constant association in Padua and at Rome with Gianpetro Caraffa, Bishop of Chieti and founder of the Theatine movement, later Paul IV, and with Gasparo Contarini, Giacomo Sadoleto, Gian Matteo Giberti, and Alvise Priuli, all of whom were closely identified with the Counter Reformation, is proof enough of that. Of these associations, more apparent since October 1534, when he wrote to Sadoleto that he must leave Venice to seek the society of the Bishop of Chieti and Contarini,[11] Starkey was kept duly informed by his friends in Padua. Sandro wrote: "Gasparo and M. Matthio Dandolo are here continually after dinner; Lazaro, Lampridio, Poero Boëmo, and Priuli came to lodge here as if to their own." [12] Lily reported that "Priolus, very friendly with his master, is now at Padua." [13] Starkey saw in these reports no cause for concern; on the contrary, he urged Pole to consult these men on the pressing issues: "Dyrecte your knolege yf you see nede by mastur gaspero, the byschope of chete, wyth other such men of hye lernyng & iugm[ent.]" [14]

Nevertheless, the strong ascetic leanings of the Theatines ran counter to the humanistic ideal of the active use of one's learning for the welfare of the state, and ultimately widened the breach among scholars created by the King's great question. This influence on Pole was observed by Friar in writ-

[11] *L&P*, VII, no. 1159.

[12] *L&P*, IX, no. 512.

[13] *L&P*, IX, no. 1034.

[14] Herrtage, p. xxxi.

ing to Starkey in December 1535: "Pole is studying divinity and *meteorologizei*, despising things merely human and terrestrial. He is undergoing a great change, exchanging man for God." [15]

Others in Pole's household were similarly affected. George Lily, as we have seen,[16] could see no alternative to throwing himself into "this new school of Chieti." [17] There may be a reminiscence of this crisis in Lily's career when, years later, he met Pole in Padua once again. Lily had come as messenger for Vittoria Colonna, Marchioness of Pescara. One can only guess what thoughts may have passed through Pole's mind as he let Lily say what he would for a very long while, waiting, as he wrote to the marchioness afterward, to see if "il nostro Lilio" would tax me with ingratitude "administered with that ingenuousness which I have always liked in him." [18] Lily refrained. For Thomas Goldwell, on the other hand, the attraction of the Theatines proved irresistible. According to Wood,[19] he lived among them with a papal appointment to baptize Jews in Rome and to confer orders on all such Englishmen as fled their country for religion's sake.

Henry Cole's attitude on the vital national issues is less easily analyzed. The fact that in his later career he played with great adroitness the part of a trimmer casts suspicion on his empty correspondence during the crucial years. Like everyone else, he loaned Morison money, and took a chamber for him at Padua when Morison did not know where the next meal was coming from;[20] and when he learned of Morison's immediate employment by Cromwell, he expressed his pleasure that Morison had shown himself fitter for a higher fortune than hitherto, and his hope that he would get it

[15] *L&P*, IX, no. 917.
[16] See above, pp. 97-98.
[17] *L&P*, IX, no. 292.
[18] *Ven. Cal.*, V, no. 409.
[19] *Athenae Oxonienses*, II, 822.
[20] *L&P*, X, nos. 320, 321, 661.

soon.[21] That is as close to a stand as the record shows. Yet
his training in the civil law and the languages is the characteristic pattern for political preferment. Pole found him as
zealous a Catholic under Mary as he had been Protestant
under Edward, and the tempting inference is that his failure to win advancement until Mary came to the throne was
neither for lack of desire nor excess of conscience.

Less equivocal were those who by disposition or training
were not actuated primarily by political ambitions. The
merchant, Harvel, ultimately addressed himself to wool
rather than the woolsack, and remained abroad. Wotton and
Friar, after their return to England trained in medicine, did
not veer from their profession. But though they took no
direct part in the formulation of English policy, their continued intimacy with those who did, gives them an incidental importance. Wotton as King's physician did not
forget his friends nor they him, Cole sending him gifts from
Paris, Starkey in his will bequeathing him his books.[22] Friar,
during his stay in Germany as physician to Bishop Fox,
remained *en rapport* with his more politically minded
friends at home and abroad. His long-standing friendship
with Starkey continued to flourish. Morison addressed a letter to "medico peritissimo" in 1536, sending the compliments
of all his former fellow students in Venice. "I will make
Starkey your colleague," he boasted with mock bravado. "To
resist two such champions is impossible." [23] Yet in spite of
such inducements, Friar turned a deaf ear to the blandish-
ments of public office. As the party lines began to be drawn,
he apparently preferred to remain aloof.

Of much greater significance was the close relation that
now existed between Fox, whose *De vera differentia* was at

[21] *L&P*, XI, no. 513.
[22] *L&P*, XII (2), no. 45; Herrtage, p. viii, n. 4.
[23] *L&P*, X, no. 418.

the time of its publication in 1534 the official defense of the government's position on the question of the supremacy, and Starkey, author of the tracts which removed the question from the status of a polemic to a philosophy of government. Fox's aid in founding Wolsey's college at Oxford in 1525 may have first brought him in contact with Wolsey's studious proctor there. They must certainly have conversed again en route to Paris in 1529 on the matter of the divorce, for Pole put the safe delivery of Fox's books in Starkey's hands. Now, on the eve of another important mission, they appear to have been in contact again, this time, by virtue of Starkey's new dignity of King's chaplain, on much evener terms.

Their acquaintance confirms the impression that at this juncture in English affairs liberal thought was controlling the government policy. The attempt at a settlement with the Protestant German princes, which was the occasion for Fox's present journey (1535), was the sign and symbol of this new liberal outlook. Biased as Froude's account was, he recognized that this ecclesio-political policy had far more general implications. He wrote: "Henry was obliged (as Elizabeth after him) to seek the support of a party from which he had shrunk: he was forced, in spite of himself, to identify his cause with the true cause of freedom, and consequently to admit an enlarged toleration of the Reformed doctrines in his own dominions." [24] Setting aside the irrelevant ecclesiastical question of which was the "true cause," one can still say that Froude laid his finger on the characteristic quality of political thinking for the years immediately following the declaration of the supremacy. Henry's message to the German princes has the sound of one genuinely interested in getting at the truth by free inquiry; in fact, the

[24] J. A. Froude, *The History of England from the Fall of Wolsey to the Defeat of the Spanish Armada* (London, 1862–1870), II, 420.

general policy symbolized by the *rapprochement* with the Schmalkaldic League was unprecedentedly liberal. Ecclesiastical lines of difference had not yet been sharply enough drawn to make implausible an agreement between moderates in Germany and Rome, and this apparently was Henry's objective:

He had known of certainty divers who by their immoderate zeal or the excessive appetite to novelties had from darkness proceeded to much more darkness, wherein the Anabaptists and sacramentarians were guilty; so by secret report he had been advertised, that upon private communications and conferences, the learned men there [in Germany] had in certain points and articles yielded and relented from their first asseveration; by reason whereof it was much doubted whether by other degrees they might be dissuaded in some of the rest.[25]

With this open-minded determination to find a ground for agreement, liberals of all religious parties would not be expected to cavil; certainly not Pole, whose efforts in association with the Theatines were directed toward this end and did not in fact cease until the failure of the congress at Rechensburg in 1541.[26] But it is important to see that the issues at stake involved more than points of doctrine, "a 'midge-madge' of contradictory formularies," as Froude, quoting Burleigh's epithet, described it; they involved new formulations based on a new realization of national independence within an international framework, to which papal supremacy was the only, but insuperable, bar. Contarini at Rechensburg could not hurdle it; and Henry

[25] Instructions to the Bishop of Hereford: Rolls House MS, as reprinted in Froude, *England from the Fall of Wolsey*, II, 422-423.
[26] John Addington Symonds, *Renaissance in Italy* (London, 1900), VI, 59-61.

unequivocally stipulated that it should not enter the discussions in Germany. If they "opened the great gate," he warned them, the Pope would rebuild "the fortresses that were thrown down, and by little and little bring all to the former estate again." [27] Hence, Cromwell's appeal to the English Paduans for aid in narrowing the grounds of disagreement.

The task of creating the theoretic backgrounds of Tudor policy depended in no small degree on the fact that its creators were liberals, willing to bring the spirit of free inquiry which they had enjoyed in Padua to bear on the most important issue of the day. In pursuance of this objective they did not feel restricted by the fact that the royal supremacy was not legally debatable. On the contrary, freedom from papal dominion was the prerequisite of negotiation. The unity of Christendom for which More and Pole looked to Rome might be achieved by mutual consent of sovereign powers. That is why Starkey wrote to Pole that Henry was "much wyllyng to haue your consent in hys grete causys although they be defynyd alredy, in so much that your jugement therto can lytyl avaunce, except perauentur in some parte to the confyrmacyon therof." [28] While Pole recoiled, they accepted the royal supremacy as an established fact and turned their efforts to providing it with a logical and historical *raison d'être*. The question for them was not the morality but the legality of the supremacy.

It is as much an ethical problem as a historical problem to determine which of the parties so created should be called intransigent. But of this there can be no doubt, the King's cause rather than the cause of Rome offered the greater opportunity for speculation. Some hint of the direction that that speculation would take is in the King's in-

[27] Froude, *England from the Fall of Wolsey*, II, 425.
[28] Herrtage, p. xxiii.

structions to Fox before he left for the court of Saxony. Fox was to say that His Majesty would neither "go in any part beyond the said truth, ne for any respect tarry or stay on this side the truth, but would proceed in the right straight mean way." [29] A "right straight mean way" was Starkey's approach to the problem of the shift of authority which must be solved if the royal supremacy was to attain the status of a justifiable polity. It was in essence the Anglican *via media*.

Clearly, it was more than fortuitous circumstance that men of liberal views formulated English policy in this, the most critical period of Henry's reign. One reason for the importance of these men in intellectual history is their proximity and indispensability to Henry in the actual administration of government. They were writing under the direct influence and suggestion, even extending to editorial comment, of both Cromwell and the King. Their books were issued anonymously from the King's press. This close association gave whatever they wrote the weight of royal sanction.

No less important was the mark of authority guaranteed by their long academic training. However pressing their immediate aims, their solutions would be broad enough to insure the permanence of their contribution to English thought. They were dedicated to learning in the best tradition of English humanism in Italy, not for itself but "to take out all barbarous customs, and bring the realm to an antique form of good living." Yet the immediacy of the problems they were facing vitalized their pens as they wrote, and saved them from the anaemia of merely academic solutions. By a singular concatenation of events they were presently to be in a position to exert a direct pressure on the policies of government, the crucial importance of which for their own time they recognized and accepted.

[29] Froude, *England from the Fall of Wolsey*, II, 422.

III

Thomas Starkey's relations with Pole during this period illustrate the breach that was opening between liberals and conservatives. First of the Paduan humanists to be admitted to the King's counsels as an advisor on policy, Starkey exhibited in a high degree the sense of proximation characteristic of those who live at moments of intellectual crisis. Speaking for both the King and Cromwell, he urged Pole to give his opinion on the divorce, contrasting Pole's absorption in "secrete & quyat studys the vncertayne frute, wych hengyth for the most parte of the blynd Judgment of the redar & of the posteryte" with "the wyse & prudent handelyng of controuersys of weyght in thys our present age, to the ordur whereof we in thys tyme specyally be of nature borne & brought forth, as the posteryte to materys of theyr tyme." [30] Once he had fulfilled his obligations to king and country, Pole might conscionably return to his "scholastical studies" if he so desired; as for Starkey, the dedication of his learning to the use of his country was permanent and without reservation, and, from the point of view of classical tradition, normal.

Starkey could urge Pole in good conscience since he had already discharged his obligation to defend the royal supremacy in its first test case, the willfulness of the monks of the Charterhouse and Reynolds of Sion, who were incarcerated in the Tower in April and then subjected to the dissuasions of men especially appointed by Cromwell. Starkey, who was one of these, must have found the duty distasteful. Four years before, it will be recalled, he had found temporary retirement with Pole in the Charterhouse; now to find himself ironically in the position of prosecuting attor-

[30] Herrtage, p. xxii.

ney must have filled him with a regret as keen as he expressed to Pole for Reynolds: "Wyth hym I conferryd gladly, for sory I was for many causys that a man of such fame as he was here notyd both for vertue & lernyng, schold dye in such a blynd & superstycouse opynyon." [31]

Starkey found in Reynolds neither strong argument nor great learning, though he had no more success than the others who were sent in for the same purpose. His own argument on that occasion is briefed in his letter to Pole describing the interview. The legal offense of the Carthusians was to abjure the royal supremacy as established by parliament, and "retorn to theyr old obedyence." Starkey maintained that the grounds for their denial were insufficient: first, because they assumed that papal obedience was necessary to personal salvation, and, second, because they assumed that papal supremacy was necessary to spiritual unity. In Starkey's opinion, the weakness of their argument lay in their failure to discern "the dyuersyte betwyx the vnyte spiritual & the vnyte polytycal, wych they thought schal run to ruyne for lake of thys hede." [32]

The distinction here made was fundamental in Starkey's thought and formed the basis for his more extended utterances on the subject during his first year in Cromwell's service. He did not debate the royal supremacy; he accepted it, *de jure* and *de facto*. As of the date of the Act of Supremacy, the royal supremacy was. The problem thus narrowed, the real question could be asked: Was national unity possible under the royal supremacy? Here papalists believed that the state "schal run to ruyne for lake of thys hede"; Starkey, with remarkable political prescience, insisted on the necessity of separating ecclesiastical from secular government, and thus recognized the possibility of a self-sufficient secular state. His argument was essentially a

[31] Herrtage, p. xxi.   [32] Herrtage, p. xx.

declaration of political independence, and even though it was directed against small men, he was hardly in ignorance of the fact that as he wrote, Fisher and More were standing in the same danger.

Perhaps for this reason, he was interested in testing foreign reaction to the executions of May 5. It was far from reassuring. "To write yow plainly therof," wrote Harvel on June 15 in answer to Starkey's inquiry,

the thinge was notid her of extreme crueltye, and al Venice was in grete murmuracion to her it; and spake long time off the bessines to my grete displesure, for the infaming of our Nacion with the vehementist words they cowde use; for they are perswadid of the dede mennis grete honeste and vertus, and that ther opinion was conforme with the most part of all Cristendome; wherby they stand it was don ayenst al honest lawis of God and men to put soche men to deth, and after that kind wich is novum et inauditum. *I promise yow faithfully I never saw Italians breke not at no matter tofor so vehemently as at this thing it seamid so strange and so moche ayenst ther stomacke.*[33]

This from a friendly source! Very well, then, let the solution be English. A basis for English unity would be found, and found, moreover, within the laws of God and man, not *novum,* not *inauditum.* Furthermore, its most characteristic quality would be sharpened by another adverse opinion which Harvel did not anticipate when he wrote from Venice. The accents of the man who wrote *On the Liberty of Speaking and Writing* are unmistakable in Starkey's first letter to Pole after reading *Pro ecclesiasticae unitatis defensione:*

Thys I haue euer rekenyd, that dyuersyte of opynyon in such thyngys wych perteyne not of necessyte to mannys

[33] *Original Letters,* second series, II, 73-74.

*saluatyon, schold neuer brek loue & amyte betwyx them
wych haue jugement & dyscretyon, no more than doth
dulnes or scharpenes in the syght of the ye, wherin one
frend to be angry wyth a nother bycause he sethe ferther
or not so fer as dothe he, ys veray smal reson, for as the one
schold cause no anger so the other schold brede no enuye;
so that although I varyd from you in the jugement of the
mater, yet your sylence declaryd much ingratytude toward
me.*[34]

The sum of your book, said Starkey, is this: "Because we
are slyppyd from the obedyence of rome, you juge vs to be
separate from the vnyte of the church & to be no membrys
of the catholyke body, but to be worse then Turkys or
Sarasynys."[35] Obviously, Starkey was unwilling to accept
the breach as irreparable. Yet on the moot point, "the things
which pertain not of necessity to man's salvation," Pole and
Starkey had been in disagreement even before Starkey had
left Italy.[36]

Starkey's plea for tolerance on personal grounds clearly
represented a continuing liberal view. It anticipates precisely the theological principle of "indifferent things" which,
as will be seen, he was soon to utilize in a political sense to
create the Anglican theory of the *via media*. His shock on
reading Pole's book, one can be sure, was therefore not
merely chagrin at the discovery that his promises concerning Pole's opinion on the divorce had proved false, but his
disillusion in the man whose house during the years in
Padua had been open to men of wide "diversity of opinion."
It could hardly have been otherwise in a group including
Richard Taverner, John Friar, Henry Cole, and Richard
Morison, all of whom since the "Lutheran" days at Cardi-

[34] Herrtage, pp. xxxiv-xxxv.   [36] *L&P*, XI, no. 73.
[35] Herrtage, p. xxxvi.

nal's College had exhibited at some stage of their diversified experience the same disposition toward new ideas. In the liberal atmosphere of Padua, diversity of opinion had found expression without the breaking of love and amity.

Mere admiration of the Platonic tradition does not wholly account for the fact that the only formal record of the intellectual conversation between these men of ideas, Starkey's *Dialogue between Pole and Lupset,* is Socratic in form and content. It is significant that the radical character of the ideas there attributed to Pole and in a less degree to Lupset has frequently led modern commentators to doubt their authenticity. But one need only recall the friendship existing between the author of *Utopia* and Pole to understand that his questioning of such established institutions as hereditary kingship and his advocacy of the practical adoption of the Roman civil law were no more than the ordinary speculation of liberal minds at Padua. In this light, one may understand the importance of Henry's and Cromwell's persistent efforts to enlist the energies of Pole and his circle at Padua in the actual business of government. Pole held aloof, but the accomplishment of those who accepted the invitation richly vindicated this enlightened policy. The immediate necessity, a working political theory, gave Starkey scope for his powers.

VI

STARKEY AND THE CROM-
WELLIAN POLITY

The Anglican *via media* has been generally accepted as an Elizabethan settlement, defined by the Elizabethan Acts of Supremacy and Uniformity. T. S. Eliot finds in it "the finest spirit of England of the time," and in the work of its representative writers, Hooker and Andrewes, he sees illustrated "that determination to stick to essentials, that awareness of the needs of the time, the desire for clarity and precision in matters of importance, and the indifference to matters indifferent." [1] This is indeed the heart and substance of Anglicanism, but if it is the spirit of Elizabeth it is hers by inheritance. That principle had been clearly established by Thomas Starkey, after he had become chaplain to Henry VIII, in his *Exhortation to Unity and Obedience,* a work written in 1535 and published by the King's printer in 1536. Since this, so far as is known to the writer, was the first official statement of the English *via media,* Starkey may be justly credited with the formulation of the theoretic foundations of Anglican polity. An examination of the manuscript and

[1] "Lancelot Andrewes" in *Essays Ancient and Modern* (New York, 1932), pp. 4-7.

128

printed work heretofore neglected [2] will provide the means for revaluating Starkey's importance in originating a philosophical justification of the new order.

It has often been observed that the civil law and the conciliary theories of Marsilius of Padua were contributing influences in the formulation of an English polity; and Starkey, as will be shown, was well aware of their value. But the importance of another influence, combining classical and Christian tradition in a manner far more congenial to the English temperament, has hitherto remained unnoticed. In the classical tradition, Starkey will be seen to have drawn precedent from the law of nature; in the Christian tradition, he could find authority in Paul's epistles and in Augustine; but, more immediately, he found these traditions mingled in the position of the moderate Lutherans of his own day, more especially in Melanchthon's *Loci communes theologici*, just dedicated to Henry VIII, in which he identified *adiaphora*, or things indifferent for salvation, with human or positive law under the law of nature. Melanchthon's Christian adiaphorism, presented in that work as the philosophical basis for Protestant church unity, became, through Starkey, the direct ideological forbear of the Anglican polity. Starkey was sufficiently perspicacious to see the political implications of the idea; and it was through him that it became anglicized in the form in which it appeared in the Thirty-nine Articles, in Hooker's *Of the Laws of Ecclesiastical Polity*, and in Laud.

The official character of his work should be given its due weight in judging this deference to tradition. Behind his effort to clothe expediency in acceptable garments was the direct and personal suggestion of both Cromwell and the King. Their criticism, as will presently appear, specifically enjoined conformity with the two great sources of tradition,

[2] See above, pp. 3-4.

Aristotle and the Bible. Melanchthon's *Loci communes theologici* provided the means.

Starkey's moderation significantly asserted itself in his unwillingness to naturalize either the Roman civil law or the *Defensor Pacis*. In spite of the fact that his humanistic and legal training had fully awakened him to their value in defending the royal supremacy, he was too good a scholar not to be aware also of their strategic limitations. On occasion, he could cite the civil law to Pole, his former companion in study at Avignon; as when in denying the papal authority to make, abrogate, or dispense with "catholyke lawys & vniuersal groundys of chrystian lyuyng" without written authority of general council, he added, "As to the emperourys we fynd legem regiam qua potestas senatus & populi erat in principem collata." [3] Neither the laws of nature nor the civil law, which as Starkey would have recalled Pole considered in many respects synonymous,[4] were in his opinion ever bound by papal authority. Yet he did not press the Justinian corollary that the prince was his own law.

Like other civilians,[5] Starkey directed Henry's attention to Justinian as a model, but again with reservations. Arguing that the laws of general councils are inoperative until they are received by every nation "by cōmon assent," [6] he looked to the civil law for support: "And this to be true, declareth a lawe made of the emperour Justinian, whereby to suche rytes and customes ecclesiastical, as from the see of Rome

[3] Herrtage, p. xxix.

[4] *Dialogue,* pp. 193-194.

[5] Edward Fox and Stephen Gardiner. See Pierre Janelle, *Obedience in Church and State* (Cambridge, 1930), pp. 116-119; Baumer, *Early Tudor Theory of Kingship,* p. 75 and n. 131.

[6] This is a reversal of Starkey's position in April 1533, when he was rash enough to advise Henry that, even though the marriage to Catherine was against "the law of nature and of God," he should nevertheless submit his case to a general council of the church in order to save his reputation. See Archbold's article on Starkey in *DNB.*

and general assemble, were deriued to many other natiōs, he gyueth power and strength of lawes, settyng them in ful authoritie, the whiche before bounde no man, but were receyued at libertie." [7] Starkey was citing Novella, 131, *De ecclesiasticis titulis,* cap. 1, in which the acts of the Councils of Nicaea, Constantinople, Ephesus, and Chalcedon, commonly recognized as the first four councils of the church, were adopted as law in the empire.[8] Its importance to Starkey was the evidence in the civil law for a tradition of legislative freedom antedating papal authority.

In that same Novella, cap. 3, Starkey found precedent for autonomy among archbishoprics outside of Rome, and hence a precedent for secession from Rome without imputation of heresy or schism, terms that in his opinion could be used rightly only when any man or nation slips from the grounds of scripture necessary for man's salvation, and certainly not for defection from papal authority. As Starkey understood the decree in the civil law, Justinian recognized the ecclesiastical independence of the see of Constantinople, "Gyuynge pryuiledge to Constantynople, openly decreeth, that churche no more to hange of the see of Rome, as it seemed to doo frome the tyme of Constantyne: but that the archebyshoppe there shulde be chosen of his owne churche, hauynge authoritie also to create & institute other byshops vnder the same see, without runnynge to Rome for author-

---

[7] *An exhortation to the people instructynge theym to unitie and obedience* (n. d.), sig. T ii^v. Hereafter referred to as *An Exhortation.*

[8] *Corpus iuris civilis,* edited by Rudolf Schoell (Berlin, 1928), III, 654-655: "Sancimus igitur vicem legum obtinere sanctas ecclesiasticas regulas, quae a sanctis quattuor conciliis expositae sunt aut firmatae, hoc est in Nacaena trecentorum decem et octo et in Constantinopolitana sanctorum centum quinquaginta patrum et in Equeso Prima, in quo Nestorius est damnatus, et in Calcedone, in quo Eutychis cum Nestorio anathematizatus est. Praedictarum enim quattuor synodorum dogmata sicut sanctas scripturas accipimus et regulas sicut leges servamus."

ite." [9] Taken by itself, Caput 3 lends itself partially and in
an ingenious way to such an interpretation. It decrees that
the archbishop shall have under his own jurisdiction for
Justinian the bishoprics of Dacia, Prival, Dardania, Mysia,
and Pannonia, and that in the adjoining provinces, he shall
take the place of the apostolic see of Rome in respect to
those matters defined by Pope Vigilius.[10] But in so interpret-
ing Caput 3, Starkey chose to ignore Caput 2 of the same
Novella which granted unmistakable precedence to the
Pope over the archbishop at Constantinople.[11] That papal
supremacy was freely conceded in Novella 131, Starkey
could not of course have been unaware and did not maintain. What he found of value there was its limitation of
papal authority and its admission of provincial authority
outside the see of Rome, specifically with regard to the independence of the existing authority in those sees. Judged
by the usual standards of controversial literature of the day,
that is substantially all he did assert, and in language that
makes it quite clear that the essential issue was national
freedom. This, in a limited degree, the civil law sustained.
Yet it may be because of this limitation that he stopped short
of receiving it in England. In the *Dialogue* Starkey balances
Reginald Pole's idealistic enthusiasm for a general reception

[9] *Exhortation,* sig. Z i^r-Z ii.

[10] *Corpus iuris civilis,* III, 655-656: "Per tempus autem beatissimum archiepiscopum Primae Iustinianae nostrae patriae habere
semper sub sua iurisdictione episcopos provinciarum Daciae medi-
terraneae et Daciae ripensis, Privalis et Dardaniae et Mysiae superi-
oris atque Pannoniae, et ab eo hos ordinari, ipsum vero a proprio
ordinari concilio, et in subiectis sibi provinciis locum obtinere eum
sedis apostolicae Romae secundum ea quae definita sunt a sanctis-
simo papa Vigilio."

[11] *Corpus iuris civilis,* p. 655: "Ideoque sancimus secundum earum
definitiones sanctissimum senioris Romae papam primum esse omnium
sacerdotum, beatissimum autem archiepiscopum Constantinopoleos
Novae Romae secundum habere locum post sanctam apostolicam
sedem senioris Romae, aliis autem omnibus sedibus praeponatur."

against the more practical rejoinder of Lupset that the long use of the common law would make reception difficult.[12]

An alternative attack on papal jurisdiction lay in the transfer of papal authority to church councils called by lay rulers, the classic statement of which was Marsilius of Padua's *Defensor pacis*. Recent scholarship has shown the importance of this book to the apologists, and Baumer has emphasized Starkey's familiarity with it.[13] That Starkey's was the official view is apparent from the fact that, just four days after the first English edition of the *Defensor pacis* was completed under Cromwell's subsidy, Starkey, acting as Cromwell's agent, sent a copy to Reginald Pole in Padua in an effort to elicit a favorable opinion on the divorce.[14]

But the limits of Starkey's Marsilianism may be measured best in comparison with the attitude of apologists like Richard Sampson and Edward Fox, who were chiefly interested in Marsilius' limitation of the jurisdiction of the Pope's law to his own province.[15] The *Defensor pacis* set up, instead of the international canon law, a national standard, different for each country and determined by its inhabitants. Conceivably, its purview might extend no farther than the common law. For Starkey, on the other hand, the international

[12] Herrtage, pp. 193-196. See also Pollard, *Wolsey*, pp. 95-96.

[13] Baumer, "Thomas Starkey and Marsilius of Padua," and *Early Tudor Theory of Kingship*, pp. 53-56; Janelle, *L'Angleterre catholique*, pp. 258-261; C. W. Previté-Orton, "Marsilius of Padua," *Proceedings of the British Academy*, XXI (1935), 164-166.

[14] *L&P*, VII, no. 423; VIII, no. 1156. Stories to the effect that Marshall, the translator, placed copies of the work in the hands of the Carthusian monks at Shene and that John Fisher was reported to have kept it four or five days and then burned it (*L&P*, IX, no. 523) are incompatible with the date of printing, July 27, 1535. The executions of most of the Carthusians occurred in May, and Fisher was executed on July 6.

[15] Sampson, *Oratio quae docet hortatur admonet omnes potissimum Anglos*, sig. C iv; Fox, *Opus eximium de vera differentia regiae potestatis et ecclesiasticae* (Berthelet, 1534), sig. E iiiᵛ-E ivᵛ, F iv-F ivᵛ.

laws still held. While he took the usual Marsilian position
that general councils can be of no authority until they are
confirmed "by princely power and cōmon coũsell," and that
ecclesiastical ceremonies may vary "accordynge to tyme,
place, and nature of the people," [16] it is notable that he referred continually, not to princely authority, but to "law
established by common authority" (sig. E ii), to the ecclesiastical laws "yet receiued and authorised by cōmon authorite" (sig. F iv), to laws "whiche by common authoritie maye
be remoued . . . and haue their power onely of the consent
of the hole congregation" (sig. L ii^v). Unlike Fox, Starkey
did not regard the canon law as totally dissolved; not all
ceremonies need go by the board. As in the case of the civil
law, his disposition was to conserve tradition, not to break
with it.

That Starkey's attitude grew in part from Marsilius, however, we have his own word. In a letter to Pole, accompany-
ing a copy of the newly published English edition of the
Defensor pacis, Starkey suggested the channels into which
the reading of Marsilius had directed his thought. Those
Carthusian monks who were recently executed, he wrote,
who maintained "long custome, and vsage of many yerys,
and auncyent opynyonys wherein theyr fatherys haue dyed"
against the authority of the law "lake the true jugement of
polytyke thyngys—wych be of thys nature that of necessyte
in processe of tyme & in many yerys euer by lytyl & lytyl
grow to iniuste extremyte, non other wyse than the body of
man by the course of nature euer in tyme fallyth in dekay
& natural debylyte." On the other hand, a perusal of "storys
& scripture" in these matters will show that "chrystys doc-
tryne determ[yn]yth no one kynd of pollycye but in al
statys may be stablyschyd & groundyd, so that thys supe-

[16] *Exhortation*, sig. C i^v, G iii^v, T ii^v.

ryoryte & vnyte of God, ys not to be requyryd of necessyte, but hangyth only apon mere polycy." As Christ denied that his kingdom was of this earth or that he set himself up as a judge, so Starkey inferred that such matters were better left "to the gouernance of men and worldly pollycy." "Thes thyngys I thynke schalbe somewhat in your mynd confermyd by the redyng of Marsilius, whome I take, though he were in style rude, yet to be of a grete iugement, & wel to set out thys mater, both by the authoryte of scripture & gud reysonsys groundyd in phylosophy." [17] Through Marsilius, Starkey had moved from the position of attack on papal jurisdiction to a constructive search for an English polity. Since Marsilius acknowledged a constant debt to Aristotle, the direction of that search is clear. It was an effort, as will presently appear, immeasurably expedited by the direct encouragement of Thomas Cromwell.

II

Yet the humanist attack on the canon law, however essential in the building of a national polity, could be successful only by appeal to a law of equal international validity. The interest which Tudor political theorists showed at the time in secular general councils reflects their effort to create an English polity with an acceptance as universal as the canon law. Although it is not a coincidence, of course, that their interest should coincide with Henry's moves to call a general council free of papal jurisdiction, there is no reason for assuming that the effort to find a common doctrine with the Schmalkaldic League was solely a matter of expediency. In actual fact, English theorists had moved closer to the conciliar theories of the German Protestants in 1535 and

[17] Herrtage, pp. xxiv-xxv.

1536 than they were ever to do again.[18] In 1535 Melanchthon had dedicated a new edition of *Loci communes theologici* to Henry and was contemplating accepting the royal invitation to come to England. Henry was sending some of his best minds to Germany in search of a common ground of policy.[19] For the moment, a confederation of Protestant states seemed possible.

The precedent for a conciliary plan was in the *Defensor pacis;* but Marsilius was writing in a time of universal empire, and the apologists did not sense the problem of authority inevitable if such a plan were applied to a union of the independent heterogeneous nations that composed sixteenth-century Europe. This confusion of mind may be conveniently illustrated in Gardiner's *De vera obedientia.* In defining Henry's power over the church, Gardiner made use of a Marsilian argument: "Seinge the churche of Englande consisteth of the same sortes of people at this daye that are comprised in this worde realme of whom the kinge his called the headde: shall he not beinge called the headde of the realme of Englande be also the headde of the same men whan they are named the churche of Englande?" [20] At the same time, he maintained that God's church is not only Anglican but also Gallican, Spanish, even Roman. Obviously, Gardiner was thinking of the church in two quite different senses, which he did not attempt to reconcile. If the church meant a community of believers in a

[18] Constant, *Reformation in England,* pp. 402-407, points out that the Ten Articles of 1536 were based on the sixteen Wittenberg Articles except in points of dispute and that they were "the least explicitly Catholic."

[19] Though Melanchthon spoke highly of them to Henry (*L&P,* VIII, no. 384), he apparently had a mean opinion of all except Heath (Strype, *Ecclesiastical Memorials* [1816 ed.], I, 364).

[20] "Roane" translation in Janelle, *Obedience in Church and State,* p. 93. Cf. *Defensor pacis,* II, xvii.

common creed which was finally determined by the prince who had no authority outside his province, it could not exist outside that province. If the church crossed national boundaries, its control could not come under any prince's jurisdiction. Gardiner did not face clearly the problem of authority. He was, in fact, straddling the issue with one leg on the side of political authoritarianism, the other on the side of a loose doctrinal confederation. When the German princes offered a set of articles to Henry as a basis for doctrinal uniformity, Gardiner hedged.[21] None of Henry's apologists were, in the Catholic sense, internationalists.[22] Tied to an English church, they looked to a general council, called by princes, to formulate a common polity. But they never faced the real problem under those circumstances: Whose authority shall be accepted in council? Henry could be pope, but not outside England.

A higher authority than prince or council must be found, and it was Starkey among the apologists who found it in Melanchthon's application of the Thomist law of nature to the current minimal theology as a basis for church unity. In *Loci communes theologici*, Melanchthon laid down the traditional view that natural law embraces all other laws—human and divine—the Roman civil law being the most perfect and most illustrious of human laws founded on nature, divine law as represented in the decalogue being identical with it.[23] Then he broadened the base for the theological distinction between the greater and less in

---

[21] *L&P*, X, no. 256, pp. 93-94.

[22] W. K. Jordan, *Development of Religious Toleration in England from the Beginning of the English Reformation to the Death of Queen Elizabeth* (London, 1932), p. 80.

[23] *Corpus reformatorum*, XXI, 390, 392, and especially p. 403: "Nam cum ius naturae sit totum naturale iudicium, multa continet, in quibus alia sunt praecepta summa, quae gubernant omnes leges, aliae sunt leges inferiores, quae interdum cedunt superioribus."

creedal requirements for salvation (Matt. 6:31-33) by associating the essential in theology with natural or divine law and the nonessential with human law. Inasmuch as the law of nature transcends the authority of any merely human or positive law by virtue of its universality and immutability within the stricture of God's will, the one takes on the character of unchangeable authority, the other depends on custom, which varies according to the variety of existing circumstances. The custom of things changes; the jurisdiction of nature does not change. Consequently, when reference is made to the law of nature as immutable, the whole jurisdiction of nature is meant, not merely custom in those things which by their very nature are indifferent ("indifferentes").[24] Thus, within the scope of natural or divine law, Melanchthon was able to establish a dichotomy between immutable law and that vast range of human or positive laws which he called significantly *adiaphora*.

The distinction here drawn between necessary (immutable) and indifferent (mutable) things was fundamental in Melanchthon's thought. It allowed him to classify ecclesiastical traditions, such as holidays, fasts, and apparel as of their own nature *adiaphora*, or things indifferent. In such matters, the end ought to be considered; for, if the end is political, *adiaphora* may be either permitted or omitted.[25] Hence, in traditions, Melanchthon recognized that a kind of equity (*epieikeia*) is necessary for church government. On the one hand, traditions must not become overloaded with superstition; on the other, a principle of liberty must be retained, because the mere observance of traditions is not uprightness in the eyes of God, nor does their omission constitute a cause for scandal. Generally, there is need of great discretion in order that traditions be neither despised

[24] *Ibid.*, p. 403.   [25] *Ibid*, pp. 511, 512.

barbarously nor observed superstitiously.[26] Although ceremonies presuppose neither reverence nor the necessity for
observance, it is fitting to preserve *adiaphora*, since they
conduce to good order and tranquillity in the church.[27]

The adiaphoristic conception, as it appeared in various
forms throughout his writings during this period,[28] was
reinforced from his arsenal of Christian learning. "Adiaphorism" as a term appeared first in Stoic philosophy used
in a purely moral sense;[29] but Melanchthon preferred to
ground his argument in scripture, especially Paul,[30] and in
Augustine's letter to Januarius,[31] which was popularized in

[26] *Ibid.*, pp. 512-513.

[27] *Enarratio libri V. Ethicorum Aristotelis, Corpus reformatorum*,
XVI, 406. First edition, 1532; the second edition was published in the
crucial year 1535.

[28] *Philosophiae moralis epitome* (1538): "Semper in Ecclesia exor-
tae sunt rixae, ut de tempore paschatis, et de similibus *adiaphorois*
quae non habent mandatum Dei. Haec etsi re vera sunt libera, tamen
Paulus ita moderatus est, ut ritibus Iudaicis apud Iudaeos plerumque
usus sit, apud Ethnicos non sit usus, ne alteris petulans, alteris super-
stitiosus videretur" (*Corpus reformatorum*, XVI, 77).

[29] Cicero's use of the term (*De finibus*, iii, 16) has been pointed out
by Janelle, *Obedience in Church and State*, pp. 178-180, and by Edward F. Meylan, "The Stoic Doctrine of Indifferent Things and the
Conception of Christian Liberty in Calvin's *Institutio religionis Christianae,*" *Romanic Review*, XXVIII (1937), 135-145. While suggesting
a Stoic influence, Meylan emphasizes the importance of Melanchthon's *Loci communes theologici* in the formulation of Calvin's adiaphorism.

[30] Matt. 6:31-33; 15:3-11; Rom. 16:17; Col. 2:16-20; I Tim. 4:1-3;
Gal. 2:3; 5:13.

[31] Augustine distinguishes (1) such things as Christ has bound us
to; (2) such things as are held on authority, not of scripture, but of
tradition, and which are observed throughout the world and are held
as approved by the apostles themselves or by plenary councils; (3)
other things, which are different in different places and countries
(e.g., Saturday fast, daily communion), with which one is at liberty
to comply as he chooses. If such a thing is not contrary to faith or
sound morality, it is to be held as a thing indifferent (*A Select Library
of the Nicene and Post-Nicene Fathers*, edited by Phillip Schaff [New
York, 1886-1900], I, 300).

Protestant thought through John Gerson and the Brethren of the Common Life. It is to these authorities that Melanchthon appealed in insisting that, although the gradual accumulation of ecclesiastical traditions had sometimes superseded God's word and made it impossible to fulfill them all, a certain number were necessary to good order in the church:

> *If any man shall imagine any thing in such mean and indifferent things, with the good counsel of them that ought to rule the Church, which should serve for more uniformity and good and mannerly order, we will gladly help to uphold it . . . We care not whether men eat flesh or fish. And yet we may not let the learning of the difference of meats and of the true godsservice, in such mean unneady things be quenched out, as they were almost before these days clean quenched out. As S. Austen at his time, and an C. year agone Gerson, yea and fifty year agone Wessalus at Basil, Wesell, and Meyntz, and certain other, have sore complained.*[32]

On this adiaphoristic basis Melanchthon hoped for a church unity which would take the place of the usurped papal dominion, and it was with this hope that he dedicated his new edition of the *Loci communes theologici* to Henry

[32] *A waying and considering of the Interim,* translated by John Rogers (1548), sig. C viii^v-D i. Melanchthon also leaned on the authority of Augustine and Gerson for his adiaphoristic position in his *Enarratio libri V. Ethicorum Aristotelis, Corpus reformatorum,* XVI, 406; and in his confession of faith to Charles V (contemporary translation by Robert Syngylton, sig. D iv-E ii).

Professor Roland H. Bainton has stressed the influence of Erasmus and the *Devotio moderna* on English adiaphoristic thought in *Castellio Concerning Heretics* (New York, 1935), pp. 31-33; and in "The Struggle for Religious Liberty," *Church History,* X (1941), 11-14, he has traced the idea through Castellio and Acontius to Whitgift, Laud, and Locke.

in August 1535. In the dedicatory letter he advocated a general council, rather than one man (the Pope), composed of the most learned men and including both bishops and princes, to settle old controversies and set up a complete church polity. Authority would rest in general council for interpretation but in rulers for execution.[33] In his desire to preserve "necessary" doctrine of the Catholic church and in his scorn of Anabaptists, the conservative temper of his appeal is most apparent.[34]

III

It was out of Melanchthon's plan for unity among Protestant nations on an adiaphoristic basis that Thomas Starkey built the English *via media*. Its international aspect, though it had been publicly enunciated by Thomas Cranmer soon after the Act of Supremacy,[35] was destined not to be realized; in fact, it is doubtful whether Henry's interest outlasted the Schmalkaldic negotiations.[36] But Starkey saw that what Melanchthon conceived as an international ecclesiastical polity was capable of a political application in England.

Starkey's two tracts, *A dialogue between Pole and Lupset* and *An exhortation to the people, instructynge theym to unitie and obedience,* are the chief product of his thinking on the subject; and the record Starkey has left of the circumstances in which they were created is of the greatest

[33] *Corpus reformatorum,* XXI, 335.

[34] *Ibid,* pp. 334, 338, 340.

[35] In arguing that general councils had no power over princes, Cranmer maintained that "the determination of councils ought to be well considered and examined by the scriptures; and in matters indifferent, men ought to be left to their freedom" (Burnet, *History of the Reformation,* I, 287).

[36] James Gairdner, *Lollardy and the Reformation in England* (London, 1908), II, 176-177.

interest in the history of English political thought, not least
because it reveals the closest possible coöperation with both
Cromwell and Henry.

Starkey had good excuse for making overtures to Cromwell almost as soon as he arrived in England in December
1534.[37] As a member of the commission to notify Catherine
of the divorce decision, he was probably known to Henry
as early as May 1533. It will be recalled, however, that he
came not by invitation of either Henry or Cromwell, but as
chaplain to Pole's mother, Lady Salisbury, and for the time
being lived at Howgate, Lady Salisbury's residence, ostensibly to recover from the illness that forced him to leave Italy
and that may originally have suggested the semi-retirement
such a post would imply. "I bere the ayre bettur then I dyd
wyth you in Italy," he reported to Pole soon after his
arrival.[38] In fact, the move may have been unexpected and
only temporary, since he did not take his books with him
but left them with Harvel, who in turn entrusted them to
Bernardino Sandro after Starkey had departed.[39]

Once installed at Howgate, however, Starkey set out at
once to make good his opportunities by obtaining an audience with Cromwell, which he followed up with a letter.
Apologizing for his boldness, "beyng to you a straunger &
almost vnknowne," and reminding Cromwell of his "synguler hymanyte schowyd un to me at your fyrst communy-
catyon," he outlined his training and qualifications as a
scholar and suggested that, since the King was "so sett to
the restitutyon of the true commyn wele, that . . . yf hyt
plesyd hys grace to use me therein, I coude in some parte
helpe ther unto." [40] In a second letter he renewed his offer
to apply his learning in the service of his prince and, as a
token of his intention, sent a scroll which he was bold

[37] L&P, VIII, nos. 132, 218.   [39] L&P, VIII, no. 117.
[38] Herrtage, p. xiii.   [40] Herrtage, pp. lxvii-lxviii.

enough to trouble Cromwell with reading. This scroll, the nature of which has not been hitherto examined, is extant in Starkey's hand and is entitled "What ys pollycy aftur the sētēce of Arystotyl." [41] From the prefatory letter it is clear that Starkey wrote the piece at Cromwell's request:

Syr for as much as of late, aftur a cōmunycatyon of your synguler gētylnes instytute wyth me, & by your wysedome set forth to the grete admyratyon of al such as then were wyth you present, hyt plesyd you to demāde of me, what thyng hyt ys aftur the sentēce of aristotyl & the ancyent perypatetykys, that cōmynly among them ys callyd, pollycy, I haue ryght gladly now at thys tyme apon thys occasyon accordyng to your pleasure exercysed myselfe in thys argumēt and breuely geddryd a descryptyon thereof.[42]

At the close Starkey hinted that, if this work were well received, he would be "ryght glad to bryng therby gud currage & mynd to the deuyse of some other thyng here aftur." [43]

The body of the tract is in the form of an imaginary address to "a rude multytude & ignorant, desyrynge to lyue in true pollycy." The germ of much of the argument of the *Dialogue* appeared here for the first time,[44] and a passage of considerable length describing the origins of civil order (fols. 223-227) was carried over with only minor changes

[41] PRO, SP 1/89, fol. 219-230 (*L&P*, VIII, no. 216 [iii]). One recalls that it was the Aristotelian Marsilius who had led Starkey to identify the papal supremacy as "mere policy," that is, within man's dispensation. See above, pp. 134-135.

[42] PRO, SP 1/89, fol. 220.

[43] *Ibid.*, fol. 230.

[44] Civil order is natural to man; but, since man is corruptible, laws are necessary (fols. 221-222); good policy, in the state as well as in the individual, requires health, strength, and beauty (fols. 228-229). See the *Dialogue*, pp. 12-13, 34-39, 46-51.

into the *Dialogue,* word for word.[45] There was a time, said Starkey, when man "waueryd abrode in the wyld feldys & woodys" like brute beasts,[46] till men of great wisdom, virtue, and eloquence began to persuade the people to forsake their rude and uncivil life, to build towns, and to make laws. Thus arose various kinds of policy, each of which, so long as the rulers of the state look not to their own profit but to the general, is acceptable "in dyuerse natyonys & cũtreys accordyng to the dyuersyte of the nature of the pepul in eũy cõmynalty." Policy is "but a certayn ordur, goũnãce, & rule, wher by the multytude & the hole cõmynalty in eũy cũtrey cyte & towne, whether they be goũnyd by a prỹce or cõmyn cõseyl ys euer dyrectyd, formyd, & inducyd to the ryght trade of vertue & honestye." [47]

As Starkey emphasized, the conception of society here described is Aristotelian; it must be perfected by Christian polity (fols. 229-230). This he proceeded to do immediately thereafter in the *Dialogue between Pole and Lupset,*[48] tak-

[45] *Dialogue,* pp. 52-54.

[46] For the primitivistic aspects of the corresponding passage in the *Dialogue,* see below, pp. 251-253.

[47] Fol. 226. "Gud pollycy," said Starkey in fol. 229, "ys no thyng els, but the ordur and rule of a multytude of men as hyt were cõspyryng togyddur, to lyue in al vertue & honesty." With which, compare Thomas More, *Utopia,* edited by J. C. Collins (Oxford, 1904), p. 140: "Therefore when I consider and way in my mind all thies commen wealthes which now a dayes any where do florish, so god helpe me, I can perceiue nothing but a certein conspiracy of riche men, procuringe theire owne commodities vnder the name and title of the commen wealth." There are other parallels which indicate that Starkey had read *Utopia.*

[48] The date can be set before February 15, 1535, when Starkey wrote to Pole that he had received an appointment as royal chaplain, which we know was a reward for the *Dialogue.* It could not have been written much earlier, since he mentions Erasmus' "Boke of the Precher" (*Ecclesiastes, sive de ratione concionandi* [1st ed., 1535]), as appearing "now a late" (p. 210). Starkey must therefore have set to work on the *Dialogue* soon after his arrival in England in late De-

ing his bearings from Melanchthon. It is "bettur to know the lawys that nature hath set in mannys hart surely, then the lawys wych mannys wyt hath deuysyd by pollycy," [49] following Melanchthon's distinction between natural and positive law. Rooted in man's heart, he wrote, is a rule called by philosophers the "law of nature," invariable, not a matter of opinion. It may be distinguished from the laws of civil life, which vary in every country according to its customs, though all good civil laws, like the Roman law, spring also from natural law. Obedience to the civil laws is certainly proper within the country; "yet to thys law or that law, al men are not bounden, but only such as receyue them, and be vnder the domynyon of them, wych haue authoryte of makyng therof." As for such matters as abstention from eating flesh on Friday, chastity among priests, and monogamy, though they are with us a virtue, with others they are not so; hence, they must be laws of custom. "And thus in infynyte other hyt ys euydent to se, how that to be obedyent to the lawys in euery cuntrey hyt ys a certayn vertue, but of that sort wych hath hys strenghth and powar holly of the opynyon and consent of man." [50]

This distinction between mutable and immutable natural law was extended and applied to the current political situation in *An Exhortation*. The circumstances leading to its composition again offer clues to the course of Starkey's thought and to its identity with that of his royal master. As Henry's chaplain and as the personal friend of Reginald Pole, he had been commissioned "by the King's

---

cember and must have completed it before February 15, while he was still leading a quiet life at Howgate as Lady Salisbury's chaplain. Note in confirmation of this, in the dedication to the King (p. lxxiv): "I have now alate in leyser and quietnes geddrid certayn thinges by long observation."

[49] *Dialogue*, p. 4.
[50] *Ibid.*, pp. 14-17.

express commandment" and with the recommendation of Cromwell to convince Pole of the validity of the royal supremacy.[51] Furthermore, conversations with Cromwell "of god, of nature, & of other polytyke & wordly thyngys" had encouraged him to express his ideas "in thes lately defynyd causys." Starkey therefore seized upon the occasion of the return of a book of Cromwell's to touch on certain things "wherof I haue long fancyd wyth myselfe," with a promise to "stabyl hyt more sure in my mind, & in my fãcy therin delyte so much the more" if it should meet with Cromwell's approval.[52] What followed (fols. 136-137) was a discussion of the two polities, "the one cyuyle polytyke & wordly, the other, heuēly supernãl & godly." Except for minor changes, it became the core of *An Exhortation*.[53] As in the *Dialogue*, the foundation of civil laws is the law of nature. "The cyuyle lyfe," he argued, "ys to mã natural & by nature cõuenyent." Truth and honesty are by nature so planted and rooted in his heart that if he were not "ouercũ wyth vayn affectys, they wold bryng hym to such dygnyte as to the excellēcy of hys nature, by nature ys cõuenyent." It is only man's frailty that makes civil polity necessary. Similarly, Starkey discovered a natural basis in certain ecclesiastical laws. The sacraments, for example, are grounded on "the cõmyn & most general groundys" necessary to the conservation of civil order. Thus matrimony is founded on a natural desire of procreation, baptism and penance on natural purity, and the sacrament of the altar on religious faith of the presence of God's divinity. But abuse by papal authority has made it necessary that ecclesiastical polity be "foundyd by mere pollycy"—and this is for the prince to do, being the "only hed polytyke of thys

---

[51] *L&P*, VIII, no. 220, 87, and Gairdner's note.
[52] PRO, SP 1/89, fol. 138.   [53] Sig. K iii[v]-L ii.

hys cõmynalty." [54] On this naturalistic basis it was possible to deny the necessity for considering ecclesiastical polity as originating within the church, and thereby to make room for a theory of human prerogative independent of clerical control.

IV

In May, while reporting his attempt to persuade Reynolds, the Carthusian monk, to acknowledge the royal supremacy, Starkey showed his work on the two polities to the King, who "dyd not gretely approve hyt, saying hyt was not drawn out of scrypture." [55] This news he learned from Cromwell only after the interview was over. But the King must have offered him encouragement, for, shortly after, Starkey submitted a corrected form of the "lytyl scrole," now become a "lytyl oratyon," which he assured Cromwell now rested on scripture and on "the depenes of phylosophy." [56] In this form Cromwell read it and was sufficiently impressed to pass it on to others for their judgment. Their reaction reveals its adiaphoristic character. What Starkey considered its chief virtue, the others criticized as its greatest defect, namely, that he appeared to be "ouer vehement agayn the one extremyte, & to be of nother parte, but betwyx both indyfferent." Cromwell, on the contrary, felt that the mean position which he had suggested that Starkey take had not received sufficient emphasis.[57] Not without misgivings, "for this mean in al thyng ys a strange stryng, hard to stryke apon & wysely to touch," Starkey set out at once to reshape it in the form of a popular exhortation to obedience. For popular consumption he tempered his discussion of the

[54] PRO, SP 1/89, fol. 138.
[55] *Nine Historical Letters of the Reign of Henry VIII,* edited by J. P. Collier (London, 1871), p. 46.
[56] Herrtage, p. lxxi.
[57] *Ibid.,* p. lxxi.

mean, "for as to the pepul thys partycular mean fully to presente I thynke hyt shold not nede, to whome you know obedyence ys more necessary to thyngys decred by commyn authoryte then scrupulose knolege & exacte dysquysytyon." At the same time, he was confident that, if he could induce "such obedience as I have there touched, showing also the manner how they should thereto be induced, I would not doubt, I say, but that in concord and unity they should agree without scruple of conscience to all such things as here be decreed by common authority."[58]

How closely the revision approximated the printed *Exhortation* can only be conjectured. Certainly the theme had taken final form by the time Starkey wrote Cromwell informing him of his plan for revision, for that letter contains a passage extolling the middle way, which was retained without material change as a peroration of the printed work.[59] What is established without question is the official inspiration of Starkey's work and, further, that Cromwell, in spite of extreme advisers, appears as an advocate of moderation.[60]

Starkey's revision of the *Exhortation* was completed during the summer of 1535 and presented to the King between September 11 and September 15 at Winchester in the course of a progress from Windsor to Bristow.[61] At the

[58] *Ibid.*, pp. lxxi-lxxii.

[59] *Ibid.* In *Exhortation*, the passage occurs at sig. Y iv.

[60] Cromwell's interest at just this time in the adiaphoristic position of Melanchthon is confirmed by his commission to Richard Taverner to translate Melanchthon's *Confession of the Faith* and *Apology*. Taverner's translation was published in London in 1536.

[61] Preface to the King in *Exhortation*, sig. a iii^v: "I presented this my writing unto your grace at Winchester in sõmer last past." For itinerary of the progress of 1535 see *L&P*, VIII, no. 989, 391-392. While Henry was at Winchester, he summoned his bishops to order them "to preach up the regal authority" in their respective dioceses (Strype, *Cranmer*, p. 30; Thomas Cranmer, *Miscellaneous Writings and Letters*, edited by J. E. Cox, Parker Society publications, vol. XVI [Cambridge, 1846], pp. 314, 325-327).

time, Starkey had no notion, so he said, that the work would be printed. But references in the letters of his friends in Italy during the winter of 1535–36 make it clear that publication was imminent. In December, Harvel heard that Starkey was planning "some great work," and in March he wrote again: "You put us in great expectation of your work, which I doubt not will be profitable by persuading men to unity and obedience." [62] About the middle of April, Pole received a copy.[63]

In *An Exhortation* Starkey set out to trace the occasion for "all this controuersie & disobedience lately shewid here among us"; but he did far more than this. What he actually succeeded in doing, with the weight of scriptural and classical authority, was to raise the whole controversy over the royal supremacy to a philosophic level. The Aristotelian theory of variable positive law operating within the law of nature was now reinforced by Christian adiaphorism, and one cannot doubt that the alembic was Melanchthon. Starkey distinguished between things good, things ill, and things indifferent. Things good are those things defined by God's word; things bad are those prohibited by God's word; things indifferent are neither prohibited nor commanded but are left to worldly policy, "whereof they take their ful authoritie, by the whiche as tyme and place requireth, they are some-tymes good, sometymes yll." Like Melanchthon, Starkey regarded as "things indifferent" such ecclesiastical traditions as eating flesh on Friday, keeping holy day "after the cus-tomed maner," going on pilgrimages, and praying to saints. None of these are necessary to salvation, "though they may be well used, and after a good fashyon." Like Melanchthon, also, Starkey held that papal authority becomes a matter

[62] *L&P*, IX, no. 927; X, no. 398.
[63] *L&P*, X, no. 600. Not dated, but Harvel's reference to a letter from Starkey as "yours of the 7 passed" and to the death of Ibrahim Pache, which occurred in April, allow an approximation.

of indifference, since it is not expressly commanded in scripture.

Shall general church councils, the only Protestant instrument for unity, be rejected? Starkey labeled them as not necessary, on the grounds that church polity was preserved for over five hundred years without them. Yet, since men of political wisdom established councils to avoid schism and to create Christian unity, Starkey did not reject them. "For as it is gret superstition and playn foly, to iudge it necessarie to mans saluation, so it is a tokē of great arrogancye . . . hit vtterly to refuse, whan so euer hit is taken as a collation . . . of lerned men for the inuention and trialle of the truthe." Again, Starkey followed Melanchthon's view: "Though the truth of goddis worde dependethe nothynge vppon the iugement of man, yet the declaration thereof, to the face of the world, hangeth moche theron." General councils, in Starkey's opinion, serve a useful purpose as international supreme courts: "In so moche that if dyuers nations shulde dissente in the groundes of scripture, and in the interpretation therof, refuge shoulde we haue none conuenient to chrystian policie, and mete to conserue the polyticall vnitie, yf frome generalle counsayle we shoulde take away all order and direction." [64] But conciliar powers are judicial, not administrative; their laws are of no authority in any country until they are confirmed by princely power and common council.[65] "So that this remayneth a sure truth, that to al suche thinges as be decreed by princely authoritie, to goddis worde nothynge contrarye, we are by goddis worde bound, after they be receyued and stablyshed: to the whiche we muste gladdely be obedient with humilite, ye though they be contrary to such thynges, as be pro-

[64] *Exhortation*, sig. H i^v.
[65] *Ibid*, sig. C i^v, T ii^v.

powned by generall counsell and assemble."[66] The same authority may also reject conciliar decisions, especially in indifferent matters, "the whiche at the fyrste counsels were euer omytted and left to the order of worldly policie." In fact, had they remained aloof from such matters, Starkey doubted if any prince would have made any constitution contrary to them.

Having thus established a field of jurisdiction distinct from the laws of God and nature, though growing out of them, Starkey preëmpted it for positive law as it was laid down in the King's statutes. He had thus placed the whole apparatus of the new polity in the only tenable ground upon which man can legislate. From this position he became a moderator between those who would condemn all ceremonies and those who would "stycke in the olde custometomes."[67] By placing the ceremonies and institutions of

[66] *Ibid.*, C i-C iᵛ. Baumer's assumption from such passages that government apologists at the end of Henry's reign were taking a "radical" view of church councils in contrast to a "conservative" view at the beginning (*Early Tudor Theory of Kingship*, p. 49), or that, in so doing, they were "discarding the mask" which in 1532 or 1533 they refrained from doing because they did not wish to "appear too radical all at once" (p. 50), seems to me to be a debatable interpretation. The shift from papal to royal supremacy was, of course, fundamental; but to charge that it disregarded "tradition" is merely to force the question "What tradition?" just as the charge that the repudiation of canon law was "illegal" (pp. 34, 62) invites the question "By what law?" Starkey did not deny the judiciary powers of councils; he denied the powers of councils called by the Pope. Take away the the jurisdiction of councils and, as Starkey says, there would be no court of appeals for Christian policy or political unity. When Starkey calls councils "indifferent," he is using the term in a technical sense (see pp. 55-56). As in other human institutions, the adiaphoristic principle holds: general councils are not to be regarded as necessary or useless but as convenient.

[67] In *De vera differentia* (sig. B iᵛ-B iiᵛ) Edward Fox described a similar range of opinion, as Janelle, *L'Angleterre catholique*, pp. 273-275, has noticed; but it is notable that the philosophic justification in adiaphorism is absent.

greatest controversy within the sphere of things indifferent, he could portray both parties as creators of disorder. The trouble in Germany arose

of thinges in no poynt necessary to mās saluation, but about ceremonies and traditions, to the which many men blynded by superstition, leaned none other wyse, thanne to Christis worde and gospel, they dydde not discerne with ryght iugement, betwixt thinges of themself good & necessary, & other, which ar only for the time conuenient to a certayne policie, but all thinges of longe tyme receyued, by custome, & generall decree, some of them toke as goddis lawe indifferently, & som all turned up so downe vndiscretely . . . but now by the prouidence of god eche one spyeng the foly of other, they begynne to fall vnto the meane, that is to say to Christis true religion, gyuinge to goddis worde the full authoritie . . . And as for ceremonies and traditions, they suffre as thynges conueniente to maynteyne vnitie, where as they repugne nother to goddis worde, nor to good ciuiltie.[68]

The mean which Starkey here hit upon was the real stronghold of the Cromwellian polity, the *via media,* which would lead directly to Richard Hooker.[69]

[68] *Exhortation,* sig. A iv-A iv[v].

[69] After Starkey, adiaphorism became an integral part of the Anglican polity. Thus Henry, in offering the Ten Articles in the following year (1536), urged the clergy "to preach God's word sincerely, to declare abuses plainly, and in no wise contentiously to treat matters indifferent." In 1538, Berthelet published Richard Morison's translation of *The Epistle that Iohan Sturmius . . . sent to the Cardynalles and prelates . . . to serche out the abuses of the churche,* in which Sturmius pleaded for moderation in ceremonies and cited Augustine's letter to Januarius. In translating Erasmus' *Adagiorum Chiliades* (1539), sig. C iiii[v], Richard Taverner distinguished between those who "wyll runne to farre & quyte and cleane take away al honest ceremonies, tradicions, and lawes," and those who "woll wythout choyse styffely defēde yea and kepe styll in theyr churches al cus-

Both parties are blind—the one from superstition, the other from arrogance. The one is disobedient to common authority; the other has contempt for religion. What of those who would condemn all ceremonies? They abrogate all ecclesiastical laws, "though they be yet amōge vs receiued and authorised by cōmon authorite." They condemn all councils as tyranny. They call pilgrimages and veneration of saints idolatry. Purgatory to them is foolish simplicity. They will have no fasting, holy days, sacraments, unless the King had not allowed them. They will have nothing but scripture, which they will understand after their own fancy. "For these men vnder the pretence of libertie, couertly purpose to distroye all christen policie, and soo in conclusion bringe al to manyfest ruine and vtter con-

---

tomes, ceremonies, and traditiōs be they neuer so detestably abused and gone from the fyrst institutiō. So harde it is," he concluded, "to kepe the golden mediocritie whych the sayd Poete Horace full wyttely describeth" (Olive B. White in *PMLA*, LIX, 941). The idea was incorporated in the Thirty-nine Articles (XX, XXXIV) and in Hooker, *Of the Laws of Ecclesiastical Polity*, II, chap. iv, §§ 4, 5; V, chap. lxxxi, § 4. Janelle, *Obedience in Church and State*, pp. 178-179, has noticed its use in Gardiner's answer to Bucer in 1541. Reference to it is much more frequent, of course, after the Interim (1548), as a glance at the citations in the *New English Dictionary* will show. At the accession of Elizabeth the newly returned Marian exiles (Cox, Grindal, Horne, Sandys, Jewel, Parkhurst, Bentham), on the advice of their Protestant friends on the continent, decided to accept certain ceremonies "few, and not evil in themselves," so that they would be in a position to circumvent both Lutherans and suspected papists (Strype, *Annals of the Reformation*, I, 264). Typical Elizabethan statements of the adiaphoristic settlement will be found in Strype's *Annals*, II, appendices XIV, XVI, 459-460, 466-487; Jewel, *Works*, pp. 65, 86; John Whitgift, *Works*, edited by John Ayre (Parker Society, 1841), pp. 175-295, all of which quote the letters of Augustine to Januarius. Passerin d'Entrèves, *Medieval Contribution to Political Thought*, pp. 109-110, 117-125, has noted it in Matthew Hutton, Archbishop of York (1573) and in Thomas Cooper, Bishop of Lincoln (1589) in his important discussion of adiaphorism in relation to Hooker's political thought.

fusion." [70] Don't presume, he warned them, that because
new truth has been opened to us in this age, we should
discard all antiquity and suppose all our forefathers in hell.[71]
To Catholics he was more sympathetic. They "sommewhat
styffely stycke in the olde ceremonies, and rytes of the
Churche, wherein they have benne of youthe broughte
vppe, and taken of their fathers the same customes, not
condemnynge lightly the constitutions ecclesiasticall." [72]
The consequence is that each party endeavors to maintain
"the trewe and catholike faithe, the which some by new
faction pretende to bring in: and some by the old study to
defende," while at the same time each judges the other to
be either a pharisee, a heretic, a papist, or a schismatic.[73]
Starkey's tone was highly conciliatory. He was sure that
each party misjudged the other, that each would support
the government's program. Meanwhile those who "stande
in the olde . . . are not to be blamed as pharisees, but rather
deserue prayse." [74] "For this is suer, that rites, ceremonies,
and customes of the churche, accordynge to tyme, place,
and nature of the people may be varied, as thinges of themselfe nother sure nor stable, ye and necessite it doth require.
For euen as al dyet to al men for bodily helth, is not agreable nor conuenient, so all ceremonies to all nations for good
religion be nother mete nor expedient." [75] Keep the mean,
he advised; let one party "auoyde al blynde supersticion";
the other "eschewe all arrogant opinion."

*For by a certain meane the armonie of this hole worlde
is conteyned in this natural order & beautie: by a meane
al ciuile order and polycye is mayntayned in cities and
townes with good ciuilitie: by a meane mannes mynde with*

[70] *Exhortation*, sig. F iv-F iv[v].
[71] *Ibid.*, sig. E i.
[72] *Ibid.*, sig. H ii-H ii[v].

[73] *Ibid.*, sig. G iii[v], H iii.
[74] *Ibid.*, sig. H ii[v].
[75] *Ibid.*, sig. G iii[v]-G iv.

all kynde of vertue garnysshed, is broughte to his naturall
perfection and lyght: And by a meane all trewe religion
without impyetye or superstytion, is stablysshed and sette
forthe to goddis honour and glorye in all chrystian natyons
and countreyes: ye and soo by a meane we shall, mooste
christyan people, chiefely auoyde this daungerous diuisyon
growen in amonge us, by the reason wherof, somme are
iudged to be of the newe fashyon, and somme of the olde.[76]

Starkey offered no basis of agreement between the two
parties, but that did not concern him. In indifferent matters,
he blandly asserted, the learned have never agreed. His
approach to the question was typically English—expedient
and legalistic.[77] Faced with a strong party of the left and
right, the duty of the government was constitutional and
primarily involved setting up a program which would com-
pose their differences. He was content to leave the whole
problem of a workable polity in the hands of parliament,
"the common authority," through whom, he had no doubt,
"some remedies will shortly be provided."[78] The voice of
parliament had become the voice of God.

Whether such a legal settlement constituted a solution
need not be argued here. One would hesitate to describe
the Church of England as a compromise. Yet, as he con-
templates its inception, one cannot doubt that the moving
force behind the Cromwellian polity, however sincere, was
constitutional—was, in fact, Cromwell himself, whose depth
of religious feeling no one has ever defended. "But Syr,"
Starkey wrote to Cromwell while he was revising *An Ex-*

[76] *Ibid.*, sig. Y iii^v-Y iv.

[77] So Christopher St. German, *A treatise concernynge the diuision*
betwene the spiritualtie and temporaltie (Berthelet, 1532?), sig. C 4^v,
who proposed "the king's grace and his parliament" as arbiters to set
a mean way between spiritual and temporal extremes.

[78] *Exhortation*, sig. B iv, G i.

hortation, "I trust that the gudnes of hym who hathe in-spyryd in to the hart of our prynce thys alteratyon of pol-lycy schal also gyue hym grace to fynd out the most con-uenyent mean to set hyt forward wyth a commyn quyetnes, to hys honowre & glory, for the wych I wyll not cesse to pray, for to other thyng lytyl seruyth my power & capac-yte." [79] A year later Starkey still felt that to establish a "conuenyent mean" was his appointed task: "Yf I may in thys rest of my lyfe be in any parte a mynystur to set forthe thys ordur approuyd by the jugement of my cuntre, wyth concord & vnyte, I schal thynke myselfe not to be borne vtturly in vayne." [80] "Setting forth this order" precisely de-fines Starkey's importance in the history of English thought.

[79] Herrtage, p. lxxii.   [80] *Ibid.,* p. xliv.

VII

A SHOE FOR CAPTAIN COBLER

To the group of humanists remaining in Padua, Starkey's success in applying his learning to the immediate uses of government was a stimulating example of the precise aims they were envisaging. Almost as soon as Starkey arrived in London, his reports began to stream back: he was being consulted publicly by Cromwell on matters of national policy; he was enjoying the confidence of the King himself; his work, "great" to his admirers, was being published by the King's press. They had not yet discovered Pole's real mind, and in the meantime, he gave the impression that he would shortly follow Starkey into the King's service.

None of the group was more roused to emulation of Starkey's bright career than Richard Morison. Long in Italy, so long that he felt Italian, long also in want, he saw in the rise of the King's chaplain an opportunity for himself. Like Starkey, he had spent many years in study of the humanities. From very childhood, according to Bale, he had preferred a knowledge of good letters to all the commodities of this life.[1] During the summer of 1535 the two met again in London, Morison quite possibly acting as messenger during

[1] *Scriptorum illustriũ maioris Brytannie* (Basle, 1559), p. 693.

157

Starkey's correspondence with Pole on the divorce.[2] To Starkey, therefore, the young aspirant addressed an appeal for advancement, referring to himself rather too self-consciously as an "unlettered" man [3]—he wrote the letter in Latin, Greek, and Italian. And it may have been through Starkey's help that he struck almost at once his first opportunity to use his learning in the service of his country.

Cromwell's concern at the moment was an answer to Johann Cochlaeus' attack on the divorce and the royal supremacy.[4] The late John Fisher's books had been confiscated for the purpose and sent to Cranmer "to be seen and weighted by him and others." On July 28, 1535, Thomas Bedyll wrote to Cromwell that my lord of London had given an admirable declaration of the King's title of supreme head. "And," he continued, "Master M . . . hath used himself like a faithful and true man to his Prince, and I woll ye would write him some commendations or thanks to recomfort him." [5] The manuscript of Bedyll's letter is mutilated in such a way as to make the name illegible,[6] but there can be little doubt that Morison's answer to Cochlaeus marks the beginning of his writing career under Cromwell, although the work was not published until 1537, when it appeared under the title *Apomaxis calumniarum, convitio-*

[2] Morison's presence in London is verified by Lily's letter to Starkey on September 6, 1535, asking to be remembered to Morison. He was in Padua on August 27, and again on October 26, an indication of the shortness of his stay there (*L&P*, IX, nos. 198, 292, 687). In June 1524 Leonico in Padua reported that "Richard, the messenger (they say) has come back from Britain" (Gasquet, *Pole*, p. 70), but identification with Morison at such an early date is purely conjectural.

[3] *L&P*, IX, no. 101.

[4] *De matrimonio serenissimi regis Angliae Henrici octavi congratulatio disputatoria.*

[5] *L&P*, VIII, no. 1125.

[6] James Gairdner, editing this volume of *Letters and Papers of Henry VIII*, significantly conjectured "Mores."

rumque.[7] After a fulsome dedication to Cromwell, Morison reviewed the events in the Elizabeth Barton case, seeking to discredit Cochlaeus' account of the conduct of More and Fisher and defending Latimer, Fox, and Gardiner. He denied that *Apomaxis* was a personal attack, insisted that he took up the cudgels less against Cochlaeus than against "the universal agitation of papists."[8] Apparently Cromwell was sufficiently impressed with Morison's ability as a propagandist to invite him to come to England.

Then came delays. Starkey held out hope to him,[9] but Cromwell, while he gave him some support, showed no further interest. Not to be discouraged, Morison offered Cromwell further proof of his potentialities by translating into English *The answer that the Germans assembled in Smalcha made to Petrus Paulus Vergerius, the bishop of Rome hys ambasciatour, the yere of our Lord 1536,*[10] a document which he probably obtained through his friend, John Friar. Friar was with him in Venice at the time, preparing to join his patron, Edward Fox, at the moment head of the mission to the German Protestants. Friar's interest in Morison's welfare was demonstrated in his letter to Starkey four days after Morison had completed the translation, urging him to help the indigent scholar.[11] In February Morison was still in Italy, offering to come to England if Cromwell thought his learning could serve his country; otherwise he would prefer to finish his studies abroad.[12] Not until the spring did Cromwell underwrite his invitation by an offer to pay his passage.[13]

[7] The date of the colophon. Morison, however, dated the dedicatory epistle July 12, 1538.

[8] *Apomaxis*, sig. A iv.

[9] *L&P*, IX, no. 102.

[10] Dated December 21, 1535. *L&P*, IX, no. 1016.

[11] *L&P*, IX, no. 1011.

[12] *L&P*, X, no. 372.

[13] *L&P*, X, nos. 417, 418.

Morison was delighted with the prospect of a literary career under Henry's chief minister. Even before the invitation was issued, he was full of plans. If Cromwell recalls me to England, he wrote Starkey, see that he provides funds for the journey and "for the purchase of those Greek books, which you know are either not procurable or very dear in England." [14] To Cromwell, he paid a deft compliment with significant social overtones: he would not now wish to be born of rich parents since in England it was thought almost disgraceful to be both noble of blood and learned.[15] Two more months passed by, however, before Starkey was able to procure for him the funds for his journey. Not until May 21 did he finally leave Italy bound to Cromwell's service.[16]

II

Morison could not have known then that his career was being moulded while he was yet in passage. On May 27, six days after his departure for England, Pole sent the long-awaited answer to Henry's request for an opinion on the divorce. The fact that Pole had kept the contents secret even from his associates in Padua makes it almost certain that Morison shared Starkey's surprise, though hardly his embarrassment, at the sharpness of the criticism. Both Starkey and Morison had been placed in an equivocal position by Pole's declaration; indeed, their careers were jeopardized. But Morison, forthright, realistic, self-assured, whose relations with Pole had never been more than superficial and whose opportunism had already asserted itself, could be expected to land on his feet, whereas Starkey's long

[14] *L&P*, X, no. 565.
[15] *L&P*, X, no. 660.
[16] *L&P*, X, nos. 801, 961, 970. Archbold in *DNB* dates his departure a year early.

association with Pole and with Pole's family bound him in a far more personal way to his former companion in study. Moreover, he had staked his personal reputation so completely on the presumption that Pole would support the King that he found it impossible to dissociate himself from the obloquy of Pole's surprising revelation. Both men reacted characteristically, Starkey by admonitory letter after three careful readings, the last with Tunstal;[17] Morison, by abstracting Pole's treatise under the caption "Abbreviations of a certain evill willyd man or wryt ayenst the Kynges doinges."[18]

For a while Starkey's standing remained precarious. Cromwell accused him of "popish" leanings and of dissembling; even his family and his friends were under suspicion.[19] Smarting under Henry's reported displeasure, he retired to a small benefice at Bosham near Chichester, whence he directed letters to the King, Cromwell, and Wriothesley to clarify his attitude. On the whole, his defense was dignified and courageous, with every indication that he retained his independence of judgment.

In his letter to the King, he expressed sorrow without indignation at "the perpetual losse of the conuersatyon of so faythful a frend, wyth whome I haue byn so many yerys brought vp in cumpany & contynual study."[20] Then setting personal issues aside, he wrote a frank and comprehensive critical analysis of the King's new policy. Against the background of Pole's fiery indictment of it and his prediction of its early failure, Starkey's levelheaded defense, together with "the hopys wych I haue of thys present state & kynd of pollycy," represented a worthy complement to *An Exhortation.*

[17] Herrtage, pp. xxxiv-xxxviii.
[18] *L&P*, X, no. 975.

[19] *L&P*, XI, no. 169.
[20] Herrtage, p. xlix.

Turning first to the execution of Anne, Starkey expressed the hope that with this source of sedition removed, Henry might settle the succession. He proposed the appointment of the Princess Mary as heir, in the hope that "other fruit" would obviate her succession, and that in the meantime unfavorable sentiment incident to the establishment of the supremacy would be thus allayed. "Herin lyth a grete ground & stabylyte, a grete stey & knott, of al your gracys actys in thys new pollycy." Consistent with his policy of moderation, he advocated strict control of those over-zealous members of the reforming clergy who were in the habit of expounding the dark places of scripture after their own fancies, and who "vnder the colowre of dryuyng away mannys tradycyon & popyschnes, had almost dryuen away al vertue & holynes." He was certain that "they wych babyl so much of the popys popyschnes abhorre no more hys vsurpyd powar & domynyon then doo they whome they note yet to be papystys & ful of superstycyon." [21]

In surveying the consequences of the suppressions, he did not share the opinion of some who believed that poverty in the realm would be increased; but he was concerned about the disposition of the ecclesiastical riches now made available to the crown. In 1533 he had urged poor relief from ecclesiastical first fruits. Now, knowing that "penury euer bredyth sedytyon," he hoped that revenues so acquired would be applied to the relief of the poor and to the support of the two sorts of men necessary to the maintenance of common policy, men of learning and men of war, and that the suppressed religious establishments would not be leased to lords and gentlemen of great possessions but to younger sons living in service and to the lower classes. As for the monastics released by the suppressions, it was his opinion that they would help not only to increase the

[21] Herrtage, p. liii.

wealth which at present, in spite of the number of people unemployed, lay unexploited in the natural resources of the country, but to repopulate the towns now reduced in numbers, especially if the vow of celibacy was set aside.

Starkey found particular satisfaction in the official sanction which the King had now given to the *via media* as outlined in *An Exhortation*. He recalled the fears and suspicions of "many honest hartys & relygyouse" at the time of the establishment of the supremacy that "we schold haue fallen & slyppyd also from al old rytes & rulys of our relygyon." "But now sythen hyt hathe pleasyd your grace by your authoryte to stablysch the gud & auncyent custumys vsyd in chrystys church from the begynnyng, and to set forth the indyfferent mean betwyx the old & blynd superstycyon and thys lyght & arrogant opynyon lately entryng here among vs" Starkey could even look forward to the time when "al other chrystian pryncys schal take therof lyght of true iugement." [22]

To Cromwell, Starkey appealed for intercession with the King in his behalf, protesting his innocency of collusion with Pole, and reminding Cromwell that he had been convinced of the undesirability of the papal supremacy "before thys mater was mouyd here in our cuntre," an opinion for which he had then often been criticized, and which he "onys declaryd vn-to the kyng." [23] As a matter of practical policy, the suppressions and the establishment of the supremacy would not, in his opinion, have caused such shock if the world "might see these great monasteries which yet stand converted and turned into little universities." [24] Yet again, as with the King, in spite of his personal crisis, Starkey did not lose sight of the broad and liberal policy which he had formulated in *An Exhortation*. Preachers, he insisted,

[22] Herrtage, pp. lx-lxi.
[23] Herrtage, p. xli.
[24] *L&P*, XI, no. 73.

should set forth the truth, "& aftur the conseyl of sayn Poule in thyngys indyfferent schold haue consyderatyon of the wekenes of men & infyrmyte, wherby they schold promote & avaunce the truthe with charyte, & not exasperat[e] & styr one parte to the hate of the other by lyght suspycyon & folysch contentyon mouyd apon such thyngys wych be indyfferent, & no thyng necessary to mannys saluatyon." [25]

Here Starkey clearly reaffirmed his desire to formulate English policy on philosophical levels above the heat of current controversy. In this spirit he accepted Cromwell's judgment, as he had accepted that of the King when he was writing *An Exhortation,* that he was "more traynyd in phylosophye than in the trade of scripture & in the wrytarys therapon." [26] For he sought truth, whether it lay within or without accepted tradition; and in so doing, he represented the most enlightened humanism of his day. It was a fine answer to Cromwell's humiliating charge that he was "studying a mean doctrine for his own glory":

I forge no mean but that wych I fynd wryten in goddys worde, and approuyd by the iugement of our clergy. Trothe hyt ys that I can not frame my iugement to plese al men, beyng in such varyety of sentence & controuersye, for some perauenture yet thynke truthe to be treyson, & some perauenture that hyt ys heresye, betwyx whome I stond, & wyl so long as I schal stond in thys lyfe. from thys truthe you schal fynd me my lord to be no sterter, wauerar, nor hengar in the wynd. [27]

While Starkey thus sought to defend himself from the implications of Pole's letter, Morison found in it new opportunity. Pole's letter had arrived at a time when Morison was tasting his first success. Berthelet had begun printing *Apo-*

---

[25] Herrtage, p. xlii.
[26] Herrtage, p. xliii.
[27] Herrtage, p. xxxix.

maxis, and Morison's friends in Italy were eager to see it. Edmund Harvel, writing from Italy on August 18, congratulated Morison on being "set a work which will doubtless be for your preferment by your wit and learning." [28] By the end of September, Henry Cole in Padua observed that Morison had shown himself fitter for a higher fortune than heretofore, prayed that he might soon obtain it, and expressed a desire to see the book when it was printed.[29] In England, too, his reputation as a writer was becoming known.[30] Morison's comment to Cromwell after he had seen Pole's letter reveals his ill-disguised elation and new-found confidence: "I am a graft of your Lordship's own setting, and will stand in no other's ground . . . Other men have but tickled the Pope, I have so pricked him that men shall say I know how to anger popes. Would it were the answer to Mr. Traitor Pole's book; if I thought he would be so mad as to put forth his, I would stop mine and 'turn Cochleus in Polum.' " [31] Thus cavalierly could Morison dismiss "an evil-willed man."

It is easy though not necessary to interpret Morison's repudiation of Pole as crass time-serving. Pole thought so when some years later Damianus a Goes accused Morison of returning contumelies for benefits. While accepting Damianus' judgment that Morison was ungrateful, Pole professed to read Morison's writings more with pity than with anger, "as they show the miserable servitude of his mind." [32] Morison is less to be blamed for his subservience—he now

[28] *L&P*, XI, no. 328.
[29] *L&P*, XI, no. 513.
[30] Thomas Swinnerton, alias Robertes, in dedicating *The Tropes and Figures of Scripture* to Cromwell remarked that a person of "more rype lerninge than I, as for good Master Moryson," might have done the book. *L&P*, XI, no. 1422.
[31] *L&P*, XI, no. 1481.
[32] *L&P*, XVI, nos. 154, 155.

had a job and his debts were paid—than for the glee with which he waved Pole's scalp after the recent hospitality shown him in Padua. Even when the splenetic tone of Pole's diatribe is considered, Morison's brag is inexcusable. One recalls by contrast Starkey's temperate comment to Pole that he had little desire to continue to correspond with one "who hathe so lytyl regard of hys masturys honowre & so lytyl respecte of hys frendys & cuntrey." [33] And Starkey had lost a friend, Morison merely a patron. Yet ignoring the swagger, Morison made the same accusation of Pole: he was a traitor. Judged on political grounds, that accusation was true. On personal grounds, Pole's charge of ingratitude in Morison was defensible in the same degree as Starkey's charge of ingratitude in Pole toward his prince and country. The fact that Pole's answer to Henry may have served Morison's personal ambitions does not make less justifiable his attack on it as a national danger. Furthermore, if Morison's conduct was servile, his fellow students in Pole's household did not recognize it as such. Rather, they praised his good fortune and his learning.

Morison's boast that he would stop publication of *Apomaxis* was unexpectedly fulfilled, first by his illness and later by Cromwell's order.[34] It was not destined to be published until the following year. For on October 1, 1536, Captain Cobler rang the church bells in Louth and the Pilgrimage of Grace began. Both Starkey and Morison were plunged immediately into new and major roles as propagandists for the government.

III

The Pilgrimage of Grace was the most dangerous challenge to Tudor policy that Henry had to meet. It was a

---

[33] Herrtage, p. xxxv.   [34] *L&P*, XI, no. 1481.

minority opposition, at cross purposes with itself, and consequently doomed to failure; but for a short period in the fall of 1536 the danger seemed critical. The revolt was essentially a popular uprising, but its popular character was somewhat obscured by ecclesiastical and large land-holding interests, which found in the Pilgrimage a means of expression. This confusion of interests hamstrung the revolt in Lincolnshire,[35] and eventually vitiated the whole effort. As a class, the northern commons were far more conservative than the commoners in the South, but the seeds of class discontent were there. That condition of society which Thomas More had ascribed in 1516 to a conspiracy of rich men, had even further deteriorated two decades later. From an economic point of view, the commons in the North were depressed and poverty-stricken in contrast to the yeoman class in the country as a whole. Enclosures, irresistibly profitable for the gentlemen, nevertheless involved the pulling down of the small villages and farms which were economically self-sufficient and which constituted the basis of the economic system in the North. The consequent rise in rents and scarcity of food, augmented by a series of bad harvests,[36] had reduced the commons to an acute state of want. Poverty stalked the North. This disturbance of the economic and social equilibrium was aggravated by the suppressions, which at one end of the social ladder cut away the chief support of the pauper classes, and at the other end opened enticing compensations to those northern nobles who chose to exchange loyalty for a share of the ecclesiastical wealth already beginning to flow into secular channels. Such an opposition of interests could breed nothing but distrust; it

[35] Confession of Thos. Mayne: *Rolls House MS,* first series, 432. Froude, *History of England from the Fall of Wolsey,* III, 116-118.
[36] W. J. Ashley, *English Economic History and Theory* (London, 1925), p. 355.

boded ill for united action against the recent ecclesiastical changes on which as traditional conservatives, northern nobles and commons could be expected to agree. Even here, the inertia of the lords of the North, to whom the commons customarily looked to present their case to London, caused resentment, and resentment undoubtedly sharpened the perennial and radical cleavages between the estates.[37] Thus, while working unanimity of all classes existed on ecclesiastical grievances, on social issues a division of interests was inevitable.

For the most part, the voice of the commons remained inarticulate. One could hardly expect it to appear in such public declarations as the Pilgrims' manifesto to the King, which was dominated by aristocratic sentiment and hence conservative in tone, the commons apparently deferring to the other estates in its formulation. Of the six demands, three—the restoration of religious houses, the cessation of payment of tenths and first fruits to the crown, and the deprivation of heretic bishops—appear to have been clerically inspired; the other three—the remission of the subsidy, the repeal of the Statute of Uses, and the removal of villein blood from the King's council—were of noble origin. None,

[37] Not resentment on the part of the commons at the success of individuals among their own number, as in M. H. and R. Dodds, *The Pilgrimage of Grace and the Exeter Conspiracy* (Cambridge, 1915), I, 177. Likewise open to question is Kenneth Pickthorn's belief, in *Early Tudor Government: Henry VIII* (Cambridge, 1934), p. 306, that the Pilgrimage "showed from the outset, what remained true and decisive to the end, the common people's intimate and ineradicable persuasion that they must have at any cost the leadership of their betters." As will presently be shown, the latter view had appeared by 1549; but in 1536, the evidence makes it clear that although the rank and file suspected their noble leaders from the first—and that their suspicion was well founded was borne out by events—they felt incapable and unwilling to proceed without the help of their social superiors. See R. H. Tawney, *The Agrarian Problem in the Sixteenth Century* (London, 1912), p. 322; *L&P*, XII (1), no. 70 (x).

in spite of the overwhelmingly popular character of the Pilgrimage, hinted at the economic hardships of the northern commonalty.

It was rather in rumor riding on the wings of the wind that the authentic popular voice became distinguishable. Ominously, ubiquitously, "Master Poverty" sprang up throughout the North as "conductor, protector, and maintainer of the whole commonalty";[38] and in less ambiguous language Robert Aske accused the temporal lords of not properly providing for the poverty of the realm, so that of necessity, the North country should "either patyssh with the Skotes,[39] or for of very pouertie, enforced to make comocions or rebellions; and that the lordes knew the same to be trew and had not down ther dewtie, for that they had not declared the said pouertie of the said contrey to the kinges highnes, and the dangers that otherwise to his grace wold insew, alleging the holl blame to them the nobilite therin, with other lyke reasons." [40]

Of this incompatibility the government was thoroughly aware, and staged its campaign of propaganda accordingly. "I need not encourage the nobles against them," says a personified England in one of Morison's tracts. "Lay my wealth apart, what is he that will not fight for his own." [41] No document issued from the King's press during the Pilgrimage hints at the collusion of either gentry or clergy. The government recognized it for what it was, a popular uprising, and addressed itself invariably to "the rude and ignorant" commons.

[38] *L&P*, XI, no. 892 (1) and (2); XII (1), nos. 411, 467, 687 (1), and (2), 786 (18), 849 (27), 914.

[39] Froude read the manuscript: "perish with skaith." *England from the Fall of Wolsey,* III, 137.

[40] Mary Bateson, "Robert Aske's Narrative of the Pilgrimage of Grace," *EHR,* V (1890), 336.

[41] PRO, SP 6/13, fol. 39.

The astuteness of this move is apparent at once. On this basis, most of the program of reform advocated by the Pilgrims could be dismissed categorically as impertinent or presumptuous, and the commons could thereby be deprived of a basis for complaint. One of the most widespread causes of discontent in the North was the collection of the second part of the subsidy commission of 1534, which had just come due and which would levy 2½ per cent on incomes above £20. Rumor had it that the money would be used to bear the costs of the war in Ireland, a cause unpopular in the North; the fact that the lower income groups were excused from the tax was lost sight of in the general cry against "a shilling a pound." Government propaganda stressed the building up of northern defenses like Berwick as bulwarks against the Scots, and of the southern coastal defenses against France; but it also took particular pains to remind the commons of their exemptions. As for their demand for repeal of the Act of Uses, Henry dismissed consideration of it as beyond their understanding.

The same technique was employed in reverse against the nobles. In the military campaign the insurgent northern lords, having advocated the removal of villein blood from the King's council, found themselves facing Norfolk and Shrewsbury of the council on the field of battle at the head of the King's forces.

Government strategy is here clear enough. Without leadership from their traditional lords, the commons could hardly offer a serious threat to the government. Robert Aske might have had popular support for such an undertaking, but he was obviously not a Jack Cade, and the rebel lords, confronted with their peers, hesitated, as Henry hoped they would, just long enough to raise the suspicion of the embattled commons on the north bank of the Don, just long enough for Henry to release a barrage of propaganda on the sin of rebellion and the rewards of obedience. Suppose you have the upper hand, one writer for the King insinuated to the commons at this ticklish stage in the uprising, whom would you choose for leaders? Will ungentles treat you gently when there is neither man nor law to prevent them? "How lyghtly wolde suche as you chose to be yō capitaynes, fall to gether by the eares to trie whiche shuld be chiefe? how coude they chose, seinge there is no goūnour nor policy to kepe them in order, namely sith they be rude rusticalles, and villaynes vnexpert in comely order and ciuile policy, that you ryse & rebelle with?" [42]

But beyond the immediate military strategy of creating a split between "gentles" and "rude rusticals" was an awareness of latent historic malcontentism, the gravity of which the government did not underestimate. The presence of an armed force in the northern counties led by disgruntled Yorkists with the avowed purpose of changing basic policy by coercion was a potent reminder that the wounds of civil war were still green. Behind the divorce of Catherine and the break with Rome lurked the poisonous serpent, Sedition. What possibilities of disruption might grow out of a coalition of the group favorable to Catherine, the disaffected clergy, and the remnants of the party of the White Rose could be illustrated in the recent affair of Elizabeth Barton, the Nun of Kent. Reginald Pole had now moved into a definite position of opposition, and government intelligence brought continual confirmation of his secret overtures to the rebels and to the Emperor.

Government propaganda must make certain that any such coalition did not obtain popular support. Hence, the press was flooded with tracts on obedience to the sovereign and the benefits that accrue therefrom, and with the misfortunes of disobedience or civil war. This theme, played in various

[42] PRO, SP 1/113, fols. 253ᵛ-254.

tempos and keys, formed the leitmotiv of political propaganda, larded with a roll of citations from sacred and profane history. Obedience to the King is obedience to God since God has given the authority to kings to rule. Even bad kings should be obeyed; but Henry is a good king, defending us from invasion, invading France, and delivering us from "the claws of the bishop of Rome." The advantages of obedience are riches, good order, quiet, strength; civil war brings only destruction from within, while the country is laid open to foreign invasion.

This, with varying degrees of condescension, constituted the backbone of the attack. Its result was to thwart the disgruntled nobility and to pillory the commons as traitors, that is, political criminals, under which classification they were undoubtedly guilty. Once this political crime had been fixed, the way was cleared to enforce established policy on the controversial issues. As Starkey told Pole, the King was very willing to have Pole's consent in his great causes, "although they be defynyd alredy." [43] And Starkey was in a position to know.

But the urgent social grievances could not be so forestalled, and here the government was forced to yield. The Poor Relief Law of 1536 was the first important legislative attempt to solve the fundamental problem, and it could hardly be a coincidence that it was enacted in the year of the Pilgrimage. Furthermore, while Henry in his answer to the Pilgrims confined himself to denunciation of their announced demands, his propagandists revealed official sensitivity to the problem of poverty in the North. And since the issue arose from a policy of the government itself, Henry's advancement of commoners to high office, they were forced, temporarily at least, to adopt a theory of social equality.

[43] Herrtage, p. xxiii.

It is a strange quirk of circumstance that an authoritarian regime should in effect have sponsored such a program of social reform. It is understandable to a degree at least in the light of the national emergency which made the propaganda necessary. The Pilgrims had publicly announced their determination to destroy Cromwell. Obviously they must be shown the rashness and lack of understanding of such an action. They must be convinced that destroying Cromwell was destroying the most outstanding example of what they themselves might be. However unwillingly arrived at, the implications in social history were incalculable. In what earlier time in English history would such a position have been possible? Interpreted literally, it meant that no longer would poverty or humble birth deny a person of talent the highest place next to the King in the kingdom.

Such a revolution in thought will not be wholly understood without consideration of the social revolution that was occurring within Henry's own household. It had a personal meaning for that man on Cromwell's writing staff who on being called from abject poverty in Italy had asserted that in England it was now almost disgraceful to have noble blood. This at least is not strange: that Richard Morison, the most prolific writer of propaganda during the Pilgrimage, should also have been the most class-conscious and the most outspoken proponent of social equalitarianism in Cromwell's employ.

At the height of the Pilgrimage, a rapid succession of vigorous counterattacks of official propaganda issued from the press of Berthelet, the King's printer. From mid-October to early November he printed five and possibly six tracts. Three of them were official government statements. Before October 12, Henry "devised" his *Answere to the petitions of the traytours and rebelles in Lyncolneshyre*. It was dispatched to the rebels, perhaps in manuscript, on October 15, though it was certainly in print three days later.[44] *Articles to stablish Christian quietness* appeared before October 23,[45] the answer to the Yorkshire rebels before November 5.[46] In addition to these official pronouncements, two anonymous tracts were published to bolster the government's case, *A lamentation in whiche is shewed what Ruyne and destruction cometh of seditious rebellyon*, and *A Remedy for sedition, wherein are conteyned many thynges, concernynge the true and loyall obeysance, that commẽs owe unto their prince and soveraygne lorde the kynge*. C. R. Baskervill's identification of Morison as the author[47] is confirmed by John Bale's earliest catalogue of Morison's works. After referring to *Apomaxis*, Bale listed *Pro suo rege defensionem* (*Exhortation?*), *De ruinis ex rebellione* (*Lamentation*), *Remedium erga seditionem* (*Remedy*), and *Stratagemata* (Morison's translation of Frontinus).[48]

[44] *L&P*, XI, nos. 672, 717, 1406.

[45] On October 23 Henry sent a copy of his articles "which before I had ready." *L&P*, XI, no. 842 (1). Lord Herbert of Cherbury's *The life and raigne of king Henry the eighth* (1649), p. 415, says that "certain Books the King sent down, which were, as I take it, the Articles of Religion, devised by himself, being received by them, took much misunderstanding and ill impression."

[46] Pickthorn, *Early Tudor Government*, p. 340. It was delayed until November 6 because of the news of fresh insurrection. *L&P*, XI, nos. 985-986, 995. On November 14 (?) Henry informed Norfolk that "certayne bookes on His Hieghnes aunswere" to the Yorkshire rebels were forwarded with "a proclamation implieng a pardon, copies of the same . . . and all suche other writinges, escriptes, and mynumentes, as be prepared for their dispeche." *State Papers Published Under the Authority of His Majesty's Commission, King Henry VIII* (London, 1830–1852), I, 499; *L&P*, XI, no. 1064.

[47] "Sir Richard Morison as the author of two anonymous tracts on sedition," *Library*, fourth series (1936), no. 1, pp. 83-87. The article was published posthumously "without his final revision."

[48] *Illustrium Maioris Britanniae scriptorum* (1548), enlarged and printed as *Scriptorum illustrium maioris Britanniae Catalogus* (1557-1559). Bale added "Atque alia in patrio sermone plura." In his

A *Lamentation* was written during a critical moment of the uprising in Lincolnshire, certainly before October 15, when the King dispatched his acceptance of the rebels' surrender; before it could be published, Yorkshire was up,[49] and again Morison's literary talent was enlisted to appeal to the rebels. Sometime after October 26,[50] A *Remedy* was in print. One or both of Morison's tracts were probably referred to in the King's proclamation of pardon on November 2. Excusing their offenses as proceeding from ignorance, it announced that "his Highness has caused certain books to be sent them, by which they may see and acknowledge their errors." [51] There may also be an oblique reference to A *Remedy* in Henry's retort to Norfolk's gloomy report on the situation in the North at a critical stage: "We could be as well content to bestow some time in the reading of an honest remedy as of so many extreme and desperate mischiefs." [52]

autograph notebook (probably begun in 1549 or 1550 and finished after September 1557) printed by R. L. Poole under the title *Index Britanniae Scriptorum* (Oxford, 1902), Bale mentioned *Invective, Exhortation,* and a *Historiam de rebus gestis ab Henrico octauo,* with the note "Ex Bibliotheca regis." The Folger Shakespeare Library, Washington, D. C., possesses a single sheet in manuscript (MS. 1283-1) headed "Ex oratione Cardinalis Campagii ad Henricum octavum Anno regni decimo habetur in Libro morisoni de rebus gestis Hy: 8." Bale may reasonably have known Morison during the years of their service under Cromwell and later as Morison's associate during their exile under Mary.

[49] PRO, SP 6/13, fol. 39: "I cõplayned of Lincolne, but to late, I felt an other parte of mỹ busy with me, or ever my Lamentacon cowd ever a brode." See Pickthorn, *Early Tudor Government,* pp. 323, 327.

[50] The date of the overflow of the Don (Herbert's *Henry VIII,* p. 414), mentioned in A *Remedy* as a providential act of God to prevent bloodshed (sig. C ii). Starkey's *Induction to Concord* contains a strikingly similar reference to the same episode (PRO, SP 6/9, fols. 220-221).

[51] *L&P,* XI, no. 955.

[52] *State Papers, Henry VIII,* I, 511.

These tracts comprise only the printed output of propaganda during the brief period when the Pilgrimage was a serious threat. Three tracts in manuscript are also extant to indicate the pressure exerted on writers for copy. "A Letter sent to the commons that rebell, wherin louyngely is shewed to them, how they every way ryse to they owne extreme ruine and distruction," [53] labeled also "Admonicõn to the Rebells in the North to desiste" and "A book of Rebellyon agaynste it," is apparently a draft of "a certain oration lately made by some of our subjects touching the malice and iniquity of this rebellion." It was written shortly after publication of the King's *Answer,* and together with a proclamation by the council, was sent to all parts of the realm on October 21, "to induce the traitors to submit and [encourage] your soldiers to the greater detestation of this abominable rebellion attempted by them of Yorkshire." [54] Though it is not in Morison's hand, the style strongly suggests that Morison was one of the authors. Another tract, an untitled oration with the pompous beginning, "The prynce of Oratores Marius Tullius Cicero whose facundious eloquence was dailie exercised in makyng orations," and a closing legend, "This boke entreateth of obedience to Princes," [55] written while the rebellion was still in progress bears no hint of its author. The third tract, "An Inductyon to Concord to the pepul of Englond," [56] with the alternative title, "A cõfyrmacyon of concord," written after the rebels had laid down their arms at Doncaster on December 2, is the work of Thomas Starkey.

The evidence indicates that Cromwell enlisted all the writing talent he could muster against the rebels. Tunstal

[53] PRO, SP 1/113, fols. 250-255ᵛ (*L&P,* XI, App. no. 12).

[54] *L&P,* XI, no. 816.

[55] PRO, SP 6/9, fols. 173-210 (*L&P,* XI, no. 1420).

[56] PRO, SP 6/9, fols. 219-221 (*L&P,* XI, no. 936).

was probably active in the King's cause in 1536 as he was in 1535 and again in 1539, possibly as one of the authors of "A Letter to the Commons." [57] There can be no doubt, however, that Starkey and Morison both wrote propaganda, and that Morison not only played a major part in the campaign but discovered in it the fullness of his writing powers.

The oration on obedience to princes is a stiff and formal disquisition under the following heads: what obedience is, what advantages come therefrom, how pleasing it is to God, how subjects should obey, and what disadvantages follow from disobedience. The author's learning is displayed in a beadroll from the classics and scriptures, beginning with an extended exegesis of the sacrifice of Isaac as an illustration of God's approbation of obedience. On the whole, it is a highly abstract and bloodless approach toward the sharp realities he was facing, too impersonal, probably, to serve the purposes of active polemics, though none the less valuable, as will appear, in evolving a foundation in theory for a position already taken toward the Pilgrimage.

The other writers, whether deliberately or because of haste, hit a lower style. Starkey's "Induction to Concord" is unpretentious and unaffected, joyful at the cessation of hostilities. It is written in the first person, and on the last sheet is a memorandum to ask Henry whether in his opinion the people will be affected by this approach,[58] and in view of the blindness of the commons "whether they persuasyonys in theyr hedes may be plukkyd up aftur thys manor" (fol. 221). "Induction to Concord" may have been by way of experiment for Starkey. Only the beginning and the end are extant, and the interlined and hatched condition of the remainder identifies it as a rough draft. In view of its in-

[57] Baskervill rightly rejected the headnote of one manuscript draft of A Remedy (PRO, SP 6/13, fol. 16) attributing it to Tunstal.
[58] "hoc ratio modēde [medendi?] affectibus populi conducat."

tended popular appeal, it is significant that a passage complimentary to Norfolk has been canceled.[59]

The collaborative "Letter to the Commons" is a spirited and astute attempt to meet the Pilgrims on their own ground. You seek a commonwealth? it queries. Good. But is rebellion the way to attain it? You insist that you do not want to break order. Yet you would choose rather to hazard putting all England in ruin "than you wolde suffre a small thynge, that justly of you was demanded."[60] You insist that you don't rebel against the King, but against his council. But isn't it rebellion if you raise an army to compel him, and continue to rebel after he has ordered you to desist?[61] Meanwhile, you lay the country open to foreign invasion, and our reputation abroad as a noble wealthy England is destroyed. You will be called fanes, weathercocks. Supposing you should win, what leaders will you choose? And once chosen, how can you expect that they won't fall into altercation among themselves? You had better desist, for if you continue, every man's hand will be raised against you. The authors of the "Letter" knew well where the weaknesses of popular revolts lay. On the whole, it is easily the most telling propaganda of the campaign except for the work of Morison, and indeed it may be partly his handiwork.

IV

On Morison, in fact, was laid the chief responsibility for the literary offensive against the rebels. Henry and Crom-

[59] "For of thys infynyte gudnes hyt cam that hys grace sent to quyet & pacyfye you such men of greate nobylyte, who no thyng les desyryd then the shedyng of your bloode, but such as euer folowyng the steppys of theyr old annceturys haue byn prompt & redy to the shedyng of theyr owne for the welthe of you & theyr cutre." Fol. 220.

[60] Fol. 251ᵛ.

[61] Fols. 252ᵛ-253.

well directed his pen as he wrote, and his success may be measured by the fact that his tracts were the only ones printed aside from the royal admonitions, and the only ones issued from the King's press with the King's imprimatur. Morison gained no public recognition for them, since there is no indication of authorship in either *A Lamentation* or *A Remedy;* but they were a personal triumph, and through them Morison's future was secure.

A Lamentation echoed the official attitude toward the rebels' demands as expressed in Henry's *Answer,* but with a strong sense of the social issues at stake in the Pilgrimage. Morison defended the appointment of commoners in the King's council,[62] the putting down of abbeys, the tax of a shilling a pound.[63] In earlier drafts he accused both monks and nuns of immorality, even homosexuality, charges which he maintained, in spite of criticism, on the strength of the King's and Cromwell's concurrence;[64] and though he canceled these passages in the printed version, he reminded the rebels of their own complaint that monks and priests had too much.[65] In *A Remedy* Morison passed over the immediate and more superficial aspects of discontent and partisan bias to strike at the basic social causes of the rebellion and to suggest a solution for them which completely transcended the ideological exigencies of the current crisis.

[62] The rebels' attacks, leveled mainly at Cromwell, also named Cranmer and Latimer (Pickthorn, *Early Tudor Government,* pp. 306, 318), who, it will be recalled, had known Morison since his college days.

[63] Sig. A iv, B iii, C-C^v.

[64] PRO, SP 6/13, fol. 27^v: "Sõ wer angry wth me, but I truste none but such as few owght to estyme ther anger. They sayd, I shold haue left owght the nouices. I thowght, & so did other, at whose cõmãdmẽt I wrote it, in such a tyme, trowthe myght haue bẽ spoken." (Punctuation revised.)

[65] Sig. B iii, B iv.

Such speed was necessary in composing these tracts that Morison afterward felt apologetic for their literary form. To Henry Phillips in Padua, he wrote: "As for my lamentacion, I dyd it in my botes as my lord and the king also doth know in a after none and a nyght. Thought it be not done as it myght have ben done, yet the litel tyme, marketh my great scuse. I made a reamedy of sedition, I am compelled to do thynges in such haste, that I am ashamed to thynke they be myn when I se them a brode." [66] Berthelet, working likewise under pressure, used the same border for both title pages.

Morison's disclaimer to his admirers in Padua should not, however, be taken too literally. In spite of his haste, the immense responsibility of royal scrutiny goaded Morison to extensive revision. One draft of A Lamentation [67] and two long drafts and several fragments of A Remedy,[68] each extensively interlined and modified by insertions, are extant to testify to his painstaking. Through them, it is possible to look over Morison's shoulder, as we may be sure the King did, and watch him mould his ideas into an acceptable shape for publication. These revisions were in part political. In the course of them, he eliminated much of the specific reference to the rebellion, and, whether by the King's order or not, softened conspicuously the harshness of the manuscript drafts. But Morison was a literary craftsman as well. As if the King as critic were not enough, he kept in mind an expectant audience among the English Paduans, who well knew his linguistic abilities and his learning. In an

[66] PRO, SP 1/113, fol. 212ʳ (L&P, XI, no. 1482), as transcribed by Baskervill, "Richard Morison," pp. 84-85. For further indications of royal supervision, see Lamentation, B ii; Remedy, D i-D iʳ, F iii.

[67] PRO, SP 6/13, fols. 25-34 (L&P, XI, no. 1409).

[68] PRO, SP 6/13, fols. 16-24 (L&P, XI, no. 1409); SP 6/8, fols. 303-304 (L&P, XII (2), no. 405); SP 240, fol. 192 (L&P, XI, Addendum 1143).

afternoon and a night, how could he hope to perfect the Ciceronian phrase, how marshal the weight of literary authority which they had every reason to find in his work? Small wonder that he felt compelled to apologize for writing in such haste. Yet haste may have been a fortunate accident; for it brought out, just as More's controversial writing brought out, an ease with the vernacular and a rich vein of colorful illustration and personal reminiscence.

Most pretentious and least effective was his persistent effort to sharpen the descriptive effect. In a first draft of *A Remedy*, he wrote: "In sedition, who cã gyue ear to lawes?" This was expanded in a later draft to: "In sedition, laws leseth ther voices or to say better, men in such noyse of sodiars, horse, gonnes, and other trasshe waxe thycke of herỹg." It finally became in print: "Surely in tyme of sedition, lawes lese their voyces, or to say better, in suche ragious outcries of souldiours, noyse and brayeng of horses, clutterynge and ienglynge of harneys, men waxe thicke of herynge." [69] In a manuscript draft, Morison wrote: "On pore mã, that hath bẽ, well trauayld, shal ever be good inowghe for too rich, and fatte, and delicate soldiars." In print this became: "One poore soudiour, is good inoughe for two ryche in batayle. He is quycke, these are dulle, he leane and lusty, these fatte and foggy, he made to hunger thurst, and hardness, these delycate and deed, if they be a nyght or two out of theyr nestes." [70]

Much more striking than these dubious flourishes was his mastery of rhetorical argument, most effective when he shifted from heavy-handed oratory to homely ridicule. Every man to his degree, he argued: "A payre of shoes of viii. d. dothe better seruice to the fete, than a cappe of .v. s. though ye put thereon a fether of forty pẽce: a payre of

[69] SP 240, fol. 192; SP 6/13, fol. 16; *Remedy*, sig. A ii.
[70] SP 6/13, fol. 21ᵛ; *Remedy*, sig. F iiᵛ.

gloues of lamme skynne, dothe moche better fytte the
handes, than a payre of breches of right satyn: a frese cote
dothe better on his backe, that hath to do at the carte, or at
the plowe, than a gowne of veluet, furred with sables." [71]
To the Lincolnshire rebels he exclaimed, "What foly, what
madness is this, to make an hole in the shyppe that thou
saylest in? What wylful frowardness is this, to lese both
thyn eies, that thyn ennemy may lese one?" [72] To urge the
eradication of fundamental evils, he cited the boatman who
"lacketh moche wyt, and loseth moche labour, that standeth
all daye with a disshe ladinge out water, that nedes muste
come in agayne, oneles the bote be amended. The faut is in
the breache of the bote, and not in the water." [73] Scathing,
with a threatening undertone, was his ridicule of the clergy:
"It was no lesse then a lerned kynges act, to sende the popes
bulles into theyr owne pasture . . . He is gone, but to many
of his lyuerey tarieth styll. I dare say, if it be proued, this
sedition to come of them, they wylle not tarye euer. I
speake neuer ayenste the good, bycause I knowe not where
they dwelle. This I knowe wel, the kynges grace, for a fewe
good, hath suffered an abbomynable sorte of the yuell
reigne to longe." [74] Citing Socrates on the abandonment of
incurable members of the commonwealth, he said, "This I
do not brynge in, bycause I wolde any man shuld lacke
cherishing, when he is sycke, thoughe there be no hope of
his recouerie: but that I wolde well shewe, howe all good
ordred comune welthes, in tyme past abhorred these belyes,
that haue no handes: these flyes, that fede upon other mens
labours: these that being ydle, without any occupation,
without landes, fees, wages, doo nothynge but complayne of
theym that be gouernours of the realme.[75]

[71] *Remedy*, sig. B iv.
[72] *Lamentation*, sig. B ii.
[73] *Remedy*, sig. D ii.
[74] *Lamentation*, sig. B ii[v].
[75] *Remedy*, sig. C iv.

Morison's literary knowledge was extensive, perhaps wider than that of any of his fellow humanists. That he should be familiar with biblical and classical literature, with a special preference for the Greeks, might be expected from his studies in Padua. And in view of Pole's assertion that Cromwell scorned the opinions of the pious and learned men as themes good enough for sermons or the discussions of the schools but of little use in practical politics, it is also worthy of note that Morison should quote sparingly from the church fathers. He cited only Jerome in *A Remedy*, and then by way of taunting the monks whom he accused of not reading him.[76] As testimony for the "lightness and lewd judgment" of the commons, he inserted in the printed text of *A Remedy* a quotation from Chaucer.[77] On the subject of philosopher-kings, he called on "those that have been the princes of eloquence in our time" to speak for him: Vives, whom he "might bring in" but didn't;[78] and Erasmus, "the greattest lerned man of our tyme," whose praise of Henry VIII he quoted at length.[79]

[76] SP 6/13, fol. 36. The passage is deleted in the printed text.
[77] Sig. B i[v]:

> O sterne people uniuste and untrewe
> Ay undiscrete, and chaungynge as a fane
> Delytynge euer in rumours that be newe
> For lyke the mone euer waxe ye and wane
> Your reason halteth, your iugement is lame
> Your dome is false, your constance euyll preuith
> A full great foole is he that on you leueth.

Speght (1532), fols. lviii[v]-lix:

> O sterne people unsad and untrewe
> Aye undiscrete and chaungynge as a fane.
> Delyting euer in rumer that is newe
> For lyke the moone euer waxe ye & wane
> Euer ful of clappyng dere ynough a iane
> Your dome is false your cõstauce iuel preueth
> A ful great foole is he that on you leueth.

[78] *Remedy*, sig. F iv[v].
[79] *Remedy*, sig. F iii-iv[v].

But the quality of Morison's mind is best represented by his familiarity with the works of another contemporary, Niccolò Machiavelli. Of the impact of that powerful mind on Morison, and through him on the political policy of Cromwell, there is no longer room for doubt. The fact is that Morison made use of Machiavelli in government propaganda written in 1535, 1536, and 1539. But since this evidence invalidates the current opinion that the influence of Machiavelli on Cromwell's policy was negligible or nonexistent, the subject deserves further consideration.

The traditional view, held through the nineteenth century, that Cromwell modeled his policy of statecraft on the political theories of Machiavelli has been based largely on Pole's highly colored letter to Charles V describing Cromwell's outspoken preference for the practicalities of Machiavelli to the idealisms of Plato.[80] Such a conclusion unduly simplifies the eclecticism of the creators of Tudor theory, and presumes on the evidence by emphasizing the necessity rather than the convenience of Machiavelli's doctrines. But it is far closer to the truth than a more recent school of critics, who, having disposed of Pole's letter as insincere and inaccurate, concluded that Machiavelli had no influence whatsoever. In 1905 Paul Van Dyke asserted that the book to which Pole referred was not Machiavelli's *Prince* but Castiglione's *Courtier*.[81] Some years later, L. Arnold

[80] John R. Green, for example, in *Short History of the English People,* concluded that Cromwell's statesmanship was "closely modelled on the ideal of the Florentine thinker whose book was constantly in his hand," and Lewis Einstein in *The Italian Renaissance in England* (London, 1902) described Cromwell as "the first great English disciple of Machiavelli." Literary critics like Edward Meyer, *Machiavelli and the Elizabethan Drama* (Weimar, 1897), and Mario Praz, "Machiavelli and the Elizabethans," *Proceedings of the British Academy,* vol. XIV (1928), principally interested in discovering the origin of Elizabethan distortions of Machiavelli, have ignored this early influence altogether.

[81] *Renascence Portraits,* pp. 401 ff.

Weissberger took up Van Dyke's assertion as a part of a more sweeping thesis that Machiavelli exercised "no appreciable influence in the thought or policy of Tudor England." [82] It is true that in the *Apologia* Pole fails to mention the name of the book he is attacking, and his description at one point, though it is relevant enough, has no counterpart anywhere in Machiavelli. But these observations may be disregarded in the face of the general effect of his description, which, as most critics agree, can hardly be applied to any other than Machiavelli, and certainly not to Castiglione's *Courtier*. Nor do the facts warrant Weissberger's assumption that Cromwell was too obscure in 1528 for Pole to search out Cromwell's *vade mecum* or to leave England in 1531 on Cromwell's account. As early as 1525 Cromwell had begun the suppression of the smaller religious houses, a policy most distasteful to Pole,[83] and in 1527 he was well acquainted with Pole in London. Weissberger doubts both the sincerity and accuracy of Pole's *Apologia*. But it is useless to argue that papal sanction of the publication of Machiavelli's works by Pole's own publisher would indicate his sentiments toward Machiavelli when his antipathy is so unmistakably confirmed by John Leigh's testimony.[84] Max Lerner has categorically summarized present opinion: "So far, at least, as the English-speaking world is concerned, Machiavelli entered our consciousness largely through the Elizabethan drama . . . Tudor England had scarcely read Machiavelli at all." [85]

[82] "Machiavelli and Tudor England," *Political Science Quarterly*, XLII (1927), 605.

[83] See above, p. 15.

[84] See above, p. 14.

[85] Introduction to *Machiavelli's Prince and the Discourses of Livy* (New York, 1940), p. xxxix. For an extreme example, see George T. Buckley, *Atheism in the English Renaissance* (1937), p. 33: "Weissberger has recently labored to maintain a thesis, which I think will be readily accepted, that for all the talk about Machiavelli in England dur-

Yet since the publication of the *Letters and Papers of Henry VIII*, in the middle of the last century, there has been no lack of concrete evidence that all the political works of Machiavelli were being read and his doctrines being weighed in terms of princely conduct while Cromwell was in power. Liberals at once detected its relevance to current policy. Early in 1537 Henry Parker, Lord Morley, called Cromwell's attention to a passage in the *Florentine History*, urging him "to shew the very words unto the Kyng. For I do thinke his Majestie shall take great pleasure to see them . . . And ffurthermore, this Boke of Machiavelle de Principe ys surely a very speciall good thing for youre Lordschip, whiche are so ny abought oure Soueraigne Lorde in Counsell to like upon for many causys, as I suppose youre self schall judge when ye have sene the same." [86] Again, an anonymous correspondent from Antwerp in reporting the state of affairs on the continent in 1540 referred knowingly to Machiavelli's *Discourses on the Decades of Livy*: ". . . and my thynkyth that that proverbe of Makiavelly, which seyth that when the dawnger of a warre is over oon it is better to prevene it than to deeffarre it were verey salutiffer for the Fraunche kynge." [87] And Pole's warning in the same year that Machiavelli "had already poisoned England and would poison all Christendom" was also printed in the *Letters and Papers*.[88]

When these casual instances are augmented by evidence

---

ing the period, Tudor statecraft and policy cannot be shown to have been influenced by him at a single point, and further, where they appear to have been so influenced Machiavellianism was inherent in the nature of the situation."

[86] *L&P*, XIV (1), no. 285. Henry Ellis (*Original Letters*, third series, III, 63) dates this letter February 13, 1537. So also Sidney Lee in his article on the eighth Baron Morley in *DNB*.

[87] *L&P*, XV, no. 356. *Discourses*, Bk. II, ch. xii.

[88] *L&P*, XV, no. 721.

of Morison's habitual use of Machiavelli, the labors of the
critics to purge Tudor England of the maligned Florentine
may be said to be over. Not only do Morison's references
substantiate the opinion of the nineteenth century that
Machiavelli influenced the thought of those who made
policy under Henry VIII, but they also establish the earliest
known date for his appearance in England.[89]

Morison's first reference to Machiavelli was in *Apomaxis*,
completed, as previously noted, shortly after his arrival in
England. To illustrate the prerogatives of monarchs in state
affairs involving interference with things ecclesiastical, he
cited the *Discourses*:

*Imo q̃ despicatui dicebatur, si Nicholao Macchauello, qui
diligētissime res gestas in Italia, Italorum sermone per-
scripsit, credimus, eiiectus a populo Romano ĩ Tusculo,
uitam agebat, neq; redire in urbem permissum est, tametsi
pollicebatur, se non nisi in rebus ecclesiasticis, quiq̃ iuris
sibi uēdicaturum. Usq; adeo inquit ille, quae apparent
potius q̃ re ipsa sũt, multo magis, procul q̃ prope formidātur.
Nobis quē non terrorem exhibuit?* [90]

It is pure coincidence that this passage was not the first of
Morison's citations of Machiavelli to get into print. The Pilgrimage of Grace began just after the copy had been sent
to Berthelet, and it was shelved to make way for government propaganda against the rebels. Not surprisingly, Morison, commissioned to justify the government's conduct of
the affair, again found support in the *Discourses*. Machiavelli had cited Dante's *On Monarchy* for the observation

---

[89] J. W. Allen, *Political Thought in the Sixteenth Century,* p. 249,
n. 3, writes: "The earliest reference to Machiavelli in English writing
appears to occur in a letter written from Padua in 1525 to Cromwell.
See J. W. Horrocks, *Machiavelli in Tudor Opinion and Discussion,*
1908." Allen is citing an unpublished dissertation, University of London.
His reference may be to a letter to the Vicar General in August, 1535
(*L&P,* IX, no. 198).

[90] Sig. X ii[v].

that the people are often hoodwinked by an apparent good into desiring what really amounts to their own ruin as well as that of the state, shouting "Life to our death, and death to our life." [91] Morison also cited the passage as from Dante, "that good Italyane poet," without acknowledging his immediate source, Machiavelli.[92] Scanning the following pages of the *Discourses*, his eyes fell on the next chapter head: "How much influence a great man has in restraining an excited multitude." Nothing is so apt to bring a mob under control, Machiavelli observed, as reverence inspired by some dignified man of authority, and he illustrated this maxim with an episode in the history of Florence. Morison saw in the episode a parallel to the state in which "we were latelye here in Englande," and concluded: "This Machiauellus wryteth, as a thynge wonderfull, howe be it, if people were as obedient as they ought to be, and byshops in suche reuerence as they haue ben in tymes past, for their good lyfe and lernynge, this wolde be no wonder." [93] This, so far as I know, is the first printed reference to Machiavelli in England.[94] Three years later, when the Exeter Conspiracy brought Morison's abilities as a propagandist once more into play, Machiavelli was again among his references, on this occasion, *The Florentine History*.[95] There is no direct reference to *The Prince* in Morison's writings, but that is

[91] *Discourses*, Bk. I, ch. 53.

[92] *Remedy*, sig. B i[v]: "It is seldome sene, that the people crie not, *Viva la mia morte, muoia la mia vita*, That is, Let lyue my dethe, lette dye my lyfe, lette that go forthe, that bryngeth my distruction, lette that be banyshed, that is my welthe and safegarde."

[93] *Remedy*, sig. E ii[v]. The reference is to Wolsey. See p. 193 below.

[94] Meyer and Praz mention no earlier direct references to Machiavelli than the Sempill ballads (1568).

[95] *An Invective against Treason*, sig. a iiii[v]. *The Historical, Political, and Diplomatic Writings of Niccolo Machiavelli*, edited by C. E. Detmold (Boston, 1882), I, 375.

probably mere accident; the important fact is that over a period of years Cromwell's secretary, writing propaganda under the surveillance of both Cromwell and the King and publishing from the King's press, knew and made habitual use of his knowledge of Machiavelli's political works in the practical business of politics. There is no sign in Morison's tracts or in the letters of John Leigh, Lord Morley, or the anonymous Antwerp correspondent that these English contemporaries of Machiavelli shared Pole's abhorrence of him as a menace to Christendom, or that they anticipated the fascinated horror of Elizabethans, who saw him, through Gentillet's prejudiced eyes, as the devil's advocate.

Too much can be made of the Machiavellian influence in Tudor political theory; but it cannot be ignored. It would even be possible to say that had Machiavelli not been known in England during the reign of Henry VIII, Tudor policy would have been much the same. Nevertheless, the forces that were activating English thought came into play because of political and social exigencies for which traditional patterns no longer sufficed. And among these forces, Machiavelli was one. In the same way that moderate Lutheran thought as represented in Melanchthon served the purpose of adapting existing political theory to the current political situation, Machiavelli served to justify the social changes now brought to sharp focus by the Pilgrimage of Grace, and Richard Morison was the chief agent of this justification.

VIII

THE PILGRIMS AND SOCIAL EQUALITY

Intellectual historians have quite properly emphasized the general acceptance in the sixteenth century of the classical concept of a fixed social order as a basis for Tudor authoritarianism;[1] but it is equally true that this order was being inevitably and permanently destroyed even while Tudor theorists praised with one voice the traditional principle of degree. The event had outrun theory. Yet if the historian of ideas is to account for the theories of social leveling of the Puritan Revolution, he must be prepared to find equalitarian notions in formulation at least in the sixteenth century.[2]

[1] See Allen, *History of Political Thought in the Sixteenth Century*, Part II, ch. iii, and James E. Phillips' elaborate citations of the idea in *The State in Shakespeare's Greek and Roman Plays* (New York, 1940), pp. 76-92. Its *locus classicus* is Ulysses' speech on degree (*Troilus and Cressida*, I. iii. 75-137). J. H. Hanford has traced the idea to Plato in "A Platonic Passage in 'Troilus and Cressida,'" *Studies in Philology*, XIII (1916), 105, but it is, of course, a far more general inheritance. Aristotle found the principle of degree in a law of nature (*Politics*, II, 2; VII, 8, 9); Aquinas in the order of the universe as originally established by God (*On the Governance of Rulers*, ch. xiii).

[2] G. P. Gooch, *English Democratic Ideas in the Seventeenth Century*, with supplementary notes and appendices by H. Laski (Cam-

Troeltsch understood the importance of the problem of equality in the development of European society,[3] though his influence may be the reason for its being overlooked in sixteenth-century England. Since Troeltsch, it has been customary to associate the first burgeoning of the democratic spirit with socially radical movements of the Reformation such as the Peasants' War and the rising of the Anabaptists on the continent and the Lollard movement in England, in which the rebels were the spokesmen for democracy. But in the most important social revolt of the Tudor period, the Pilgrimage of Grace of 1536, the fact is clear that paradoxically, principles of social equality were voiced, not by the "outs" but by the "ins," not by the Pilgrims but by Henry VIII's own apologists in tracts issued from the King's press. Such an inconsistency, superficially an act of expediency in a crisis, is significant not merely as a revelation of democratic modes of thought not far below the surface of a nominally authoritarian regime, but as the earliest official application in England of an equalitarian formula in a purely secular context. There was nothing new in the principle in and of itself. As an ecclesiastical conception, equalitarianism was as old as the church. But it is characteristic of a point of view eager to clothe a policy of expediency in the language of tradition that the supporters

---

bridge, 1927), passes over the sixteenth century with a brief mention of More and Ponet. So far as I know, the only discussion of the subject is by Professor Helen C. White in an important recent book, *Social Criticism in Popular Religious Literature of the Sixteenth Century* (New York, 1944), with which the present analysis will be found to be in substantial agreement. Professor White does not emphasize the Pilgrimage of Grace, however, when the idea was forced into the open for the first time in the Tudor period.

[3] "The history of the problem of equality would be one of the most important contributions which could be made to the understanding of the development of European Society." *The Social Teaching of the Christian Churches* (London, 1931), p. 902.

of Henry's new program made it serve their own purposes. Confronted by the hard and dangerous fact of the Pilgrimage of Grace, they sought the refuge of the old patterns in order to legitimize novelty in practice, and thus evolved —almost, it would seem, against their will—a theory whose general application and ultimate implications they would certainly have rejected.[4]

It would be strange, in fact, if the loosening of class distinctions, which has often been observed as characteristic of the Tudor period, did not find expression in theory. The ground was being prepared, not merely by the increasing independence of the yeoman class,[5] but by the policy of the government itself. The absorption by the crown of powers of administration over courts of law, the great shift of landed wealth from the church into the hands of a new class of royal servants, the depressing of the traditional aristocracy in favor of a newly created and prospering middle class—all are too familiar aspects of social change to be stressed here,[6] but all tended to cut across the established social barriers and to assist the rise of the lower classes. What does need emphasis is the fact that most of these changes were accelerated by commoners whom Henry VIII had elevated to the highest offices in the kingdom. Wolsey, Cranmer, and Cromwell were obscure men until the King chose to disregard class distinctions and employ their serv-

[4] On this characteristic of reformist thought, see White, *Social Criticism*, pp. 1-2, 132 ff.

[5] Tawney, *Agrarian Problem in the Sixteenth Century*, p. 325, and the cases cited by I. S. Leadam, *Select Cases in the Court of Requests* (Selden Society, 1898), p. lv.

[6] W. S. Holdsworth, *A History of English Law* (London, 1937), IV, 402-407; Rachel R. Reid, *The King's Council in the North* (London, 1921), pp. 48, 90-97; Edward P. Cheyney, *Social Changes in England in the Sixteenth Century* (University of Pennsylvania, 1895), pp. 105-106; Liljegren, *Fall of the Monasteries and the Social Changes in England*.

ices. Social equalitarianism may thus be regarded as sanctioned, however unintentionally, by the crown itself.

There is every reason to believe that this break with tradition was recognized by Henry's lowborn officers. A. F. Pollard doubts Leadam's thesis that Wolsey created the policy of relying on the people against the aristocracy,[7] but the truth remains that through Wolsey's efforts, particularly in establishing the Court of Requests for the arguing of poor men's causes,[8] the position of the common man in court was greatly strengthened. And the personal testimony of Morison, Wolsey's former servant and petty canon,[9] reveals Wolsey's similar disregard of social position, in his diocese of York as advocate of the commons [10] and in his college as a patron of letters. Learning, Richard Pace wrote in 1517, was now better than ignorance and noble blood.[11]

[7] *Wolsey*, pp. 78-79.

[8] Pollard, *Wolsey*, pp. 79 and the references there cited, 81-87; Reid, *King's Council*, p. 97.

[9] An office, it will be recalled, created for poor commoners. See above, p. 23.

[10] Morison testified in *A Remedy*, sig. E ii^v-iii: "Who was lesse beloued in the northe, than my lorde Cardynall, god haue his sowle, before he was amonges them? Who better beloued, after he had ben there a whyle? we hate oft times, whom we haue good cause to loue. It is a wonder, to see how they were turned, howe of vtter ennemyes, they becam his dere frendes. He gaue byshops a right good ensample, how they might wyn mens hartis. There was fewe holy dayes, but he wolde ride. v. or. vi. myle from his howse, nowe to this paryshe churche, nowe to that, and ther cause one or other of his doctours, to make a sermone vnto the people. He sat amonges them, and sayd masse before al the paryshe . . . He broughte his dinner with hym, and bad dyuers of the parish to it. He enquired, whether there was any debate or grudge betwene any of them, yf there were, after dinner he sente for the parties to the church, and made them at one." Note also a northern criticism of Wolsey's appointment of Thomas Donyngton as his steward that "he never had staff in his hand." *L&P*, IV (3), no. 6447.

[11] *L&P*, II, no. 3765, cited by Pollard, *Wolsey*, p. 79; Strype, *Ecclesiastical Memorials*, I, 199-200.

This democratic policy of advancement, begun by Wolsey, was continued by Archbishop Cranmer. On the occasion of the secularization of the cathedral church of Canterbury, he was able to override those who argued that only the sons of gentlemen should be put to school there, on the grounds that "pore mennys children arr many tymes enduyd with more synguler giftes of nature, which are also the giftes of God, as with eloquence, memorie, apte pronunciacion, sobrietie, with suche like, and also commonly more gyven to applie thair studie, than ys the gentilmannys sonne delicatelie educated." To exclude the plowman's son and the poor man's son from the benefits of learning is as much as to say that "almightie God sholde not be at libertie to bestowe his greate giftes of grace apon any person, nor no where els but as we and other men shall appoynte them to be enployed according to our fansey, and not according to his most godlie will and pleasure: who gyveth his giftes both of lernyng and other perfections in all sciences, unto all kinde and states of people indifferentelie." It was satisfying for one who, having been scorned as an hostler, was now establishing a place of learning, to hew a new line for the founders of the King's School: "I take it that none of us all here being gentilmen borne (as I thincke) [12] but hadd our begynnyng that wey from a lowe and base parentage; and thorough the benefite of lernyng and other civile knowlege for the moste parte all gentil ascende to thair estate." [13] Cranmer's point of view is reflected in Cromwell's injunction to the clergy in 1536 that fathers and mothers, masters and governors avoid the social con-

[12] None of the commissioners was highborn, according to W. F. Hook, *Archbishops of Canterbury*, VII, 24.

[13] Ralph Morice, servant of Cranmer, in *Narratives of the Days of the Reformation*, edited by J. G. Nichols, Camden Society, no. 77 (1859), pp. 273-275.

sequences of idleness by bestowing their children and servants either in learning or in some other honest exercise,
occupation, or husbandry,

and to the intent that learned men may hereafter spring the
more . . . every parson, vicar, clerk, or beneficed man within
this deanery, having yearly to dispend in benefices or other
promotions of the church, an hundred pounds, shall give
competent exhibition to one scholar, and for as many hun-
dred pounds more as he may dispend, to so many scholars
more shall give like exhibition in the university of Oxford,
or Cambridge, or some grammar-school, which after they
have profited in good learning, may be partners of their
patrons' cure and charge, as well in preaching as otherwise
in the execution of their offices, or may, when need shall
be, otherwise profit the common wealth with their counsel
and wisdom.[14]

It is clear that the principle of ignoring rank in discovering and encouraging able commoners to service in the state
was being generally put in practice when Cromwell took it
up. With him, it became known policy. Indigent university
students like Richard Besiley of Oxford and William Byr-
lyngham of Cambridge recognized in Cromwell a benefactor "especially of poor men, whom you are always glad
to help." [15] And Richard Morison, while he was a student
in Padua, dared to close one of his frequent appeals to
Cromwell's generosity with the acid remark that the Cardinal, had he been living, would never have suffered him to
remain in such mean circumstances.[16] Such policies account
for Roger Ascham's nostalgic complaint to Cranmer four

[14] David Wilkins, *Concilia Magnae Britanniae et Hiberniae* (London, 1737), pp. 814-815.
[15] *L&P*, VIII, nos. 68, 828; IV (2), no. 5069. For Besiley's later
career, see Garrett, *The Marian Exiles*, p. 85.
[16] *L&P*, IX, no. 198.

years after Cromwell's fall that new students at Cambridge
"were for the most part only the sons of rich men, and such
as never intended to pursue their studies to that degree as
to arrive at any eminent proficiency and perfection in learning, but only the better to qualify themselves for some
places in the state, by a slighter and more superficial
knowledge." [17]

The breakdown of the traditional social stratifications
implicit in Tudor policy was presently to be illustrated in
Ascham's own career. In 1550 he realized his ambition to
travel abroad as secretary to an ambassador; his superior
was Sir Richard Morison, newly knighted and appointed
to the Emperor's court, he who fifteen years earlier had
been relieved from penury by Cromwell to employ his
learning in defense of the policy which had made his rise
possible.

II

That this democratization of social classes, deliberately
fostered by those who had themselves risen from low to
high degree, was being felt in some quarters as a serious
menace to the stability of the social structure may be inferred from the demands of the Pilgrims, voiced during the
Pilgrimage of Grace, when for the first time the policy of
the government was publicly challenged. The outcry in the
North against Cromwell and the King's other lowborn officers arose from commonalty as well as nobility, a circumstance not unnaturally perplexing to the King's lowborn
officers.[18] Indeed, it was not as radicals but as conservatives
that the Pilgrims seemed most threatening. A challenge to

[17] *The Whole Works of Roger Ascham* . . . , edited by Rev. Dr.
Giles, I, 69; translated in Strype's *Cranmer*, p. 242.

[18] And to modern scholars as well. See Tawney, *Agrarian Problem,*
pp. 333-337.

the existing order as clearly radical as Robert Aske's could be met, and was met, with an easy conscience; but when in the name of tradition Pilgrims of all ranks proposed to remove radicalism in the existing order, they became both united and embarrassing to the government. For however far apart they might drift on the issue of poverty, in restoring and conserving traditions which they felt were endangered by current governmental policy, noble and villein had discovered a genuinely common objective. No small part of their strength derived from the conviction that ecclesiastical traditions were being destroyed by radical reformers who had won the ear of the King. It is indicative of the Pilgrims' conservative temper on ecclesiastical issues that they viewed the revolutionary Anabaptist uprising in Germany with alarm, determined that neither Reformation nor reformers should gain a foothold in England. At home, all ranks recognized the monastic suppressions as a blow at the very foundations of the social structure as they had known it,[19] and also recognized Thomas Cromwell as the chief perpetrator of these reforms.[20]

[19] "Wherfor the said statut of subpression was greatly to the decay of the comynwelth of that contrei, & al those partes of al degreys greatly groged ayenst the same." Bateson, "Robert Aske's Narrative of the Pilgrimage of Grace," *EHR*, V (1890), 562.

[20] "Cromwell is in such errour and hatred with the peple in thos partes [*second version:* "in all partes"] that in maner they wold eat him . . . And ther especiall great groge is ayenst the Lord Cromwell, being reputed the distrewer of the comynwelth, as well emonges most parte of the lordes, as all other the worshipfull and comyns." *Ibid.*, pp. 340, 342-343. Cromwell's reputation in the North should be balanced against a southern view: "He perswaded the king by maintteininge of *equum jus,* and by holdinge-downe the over-emminent power of soche great ones as in time paste, like bell-wethers, had led the sheppeshe flockes of England against their prince, to knett fast to him the love of his commons and specially of his cittie of London." According to this report, Cromwell sold much monastic property "to many men four reasonable prises, exchaiinging many of them with the nobilitie and other for their auncient possession to

This community of interest against Cromwell, the suppressor of monasteries, could not be expected to obtain against Cromwell, the upstart, where the interests of the aristocracy were primarily at stake. The fact that the northern nobles made common cause with the lower classes was in itself a tacit acknowledgment of the jeopardy to their caste in the rise of Cromwell. Already their dignities had been superseded by the parvenu Wolsey, and were passing further into eclipse with the appointment of Wolsey's and later of the King's servants.[21] And now Cromwell, inordinately ambitious like his master, had catapulted into office and was misguiding the King.[22] To the feudal lords of the North, the presence of men of such humble and ignoble origins as Cranmer and Cromwell in the King's council was an open challenge to the traditional principle of degree exactly in the quarter where it should have been most scrupulously observed.[23] The records in the *Letters and Papers of Henry*

their greate gaine with whome he exchainged, preferring many sufficient persons to the kinges servis who were sone raised to nobilitie and to worshipe and good calling, and all indewed with maintenaunce out of the revenewes of abbyes." *Three Chapters of Letters,* pp. 114-115.

[21] Holdsworth, *History of English Law,* IV, 39; Reid, *King's Council,* pp. 92, 102-114. For the possible enlistment of Skelton's pen on the side of the aggrieved Howards, see William Nelson, *John Skelton, Laureate* (New York, 1939), pp. 210-211.

[22] Darcy, on trial for his part in the Pilgrimage, accused Cromwell directly: "Cromwell, it is thou that art the very original and chief causer of the apprehension of us that be noblemen, and dost daily earnestly travail to bring us to our end and to strike off our heads, and I trust that or thou die, though thou wouldst procure all the noblemen's heads within the realm to be stricken off, yet shall there one head remain that shall strike off thy head." Dodds, *Pilgrimage of Grace,* II, 186-187, quoting *L&P,* XII (1), no. 976.

[23] "The nobility despised him [Cromwell], and thought it lessened the greatness of their titles, to see the son of a blacksmith raised so many degrees above them." Burnet, *History of the Reformation,* I, 441. See also *The Correspondence of Edward, Third Earl of Derby,* edited by T. N. Toller, Chetham Society (1890), pp. 50, 52.

VIII leave little doubt that the Pilgrimage of Grace was precipitated in part by the increasing apprehensions of the older nobility that their accustomed world was falling about their ears, and that the traditional social ranks were being dangerously invaded.

It is even conceivable that the plea of northern aristocrats for ousting Cromwell and Cranmer and substituting noble blood in the King's council might not have prevailed with the commons had not all classes been united by a deep-rooted respect for social degree. On this ground, the Pilgrims unanimously took their stand as spokesmen and guardians of the commonwealth. Under an oath to be true to King, Church, and Commonwealth, they would expel "all villain blood from the King's grace and his privy council for the common wealth, and restoring of Christ's church." [24] The King's council must be composed of virtuous men "as would regard the commonwealth above their princis lo[ve]," and the King in turn must be counseled by nobles, baronage, and commons for the said commonwealth. They warned Henry's commander, Norfolk, "and such noble folks as are of ancient blood with baronage of the sowth and commonalty also" to recall how Suffolk dealt with Lincolnshire men in 1525, "for their part is not unlike to be in after this." Not that they insisted on a fixed social order at the expense of their responsibility as human beings. There is a striking family likeness in the candid independence of Shakespeare's common soldier, Williams, and in the Pilgrims' blunt reminder to the King that "when he has killed a man he [cannot] make a man alive again." [25] Henry's position was vexing. Were the "subverters of the good laws

---

[24] *L&P*, XI, no. 622, p. 249; no. 705 (i, ii, iv); no. 892 (ii), p. 356; no. 902 (ii), p. 358.

[25] *L&P*, XI, no. 1244; *Henry V*, IV. i.

of the realm" [26] the rebels or Henry's agents? In 1536 the charge against the new men was serious enough and the government's case vulnerable enough to make justification necessary, and the process of justification forced government apology into a premature but unmistakable expression of democratic social theory.

Official apologists found themselves in the uncomfortable and ironic dilemma of justifying a government whose chief officer was regarded by the Pilgrims as a flagrant violator of the traditional order. Under these circumstances it was tactically safe to ignore the nobles who had joined the Pilgrimage and to confront the rest of the Pilgrims with their audacious disruption of political unity; it was undoubtedly good politics to compare their act of rebellion with that of the Münster Anabaptists, the infiltration of whose beliefs they had specifically decried in their petition to the King. But how could the attack on Cromwell and his officers be answered in terms of conventional social theory? This was the embarrassing question that government apologists were called upon to answer; the manner in which it was answered betrays their grave anxiety over an alarmingly widespread social discontent during the very years sometimes referred to as the "Henrician tyranny."

III

Henry's personal response, as a matter of fact, was truculent and inflexible. At first he answered force with force; only when he felt that the rebellion was definitely under control did he reply to the Pilgrims' criticism of the new social order. Then, in contemptuous and minatory language, he categorically denied the right of "common and inferior

[26] The eighth demand of the Pilgrims at Doncaster: L&P, XI, no. 1246.

subjects," of "rude and ignorant common people," to question his appointments to the council: "How presumptuous then are ye the rude commons of one shire, and that one of the most beastly of the whole realm, and of least experience to find fault with your prince for the electing of his councillors and prelates; and to take upon you, contrary to God's and man's law to rule your prince." [27] This was mere bluster. But later, in answering the Pilgrims' petition at Doncaster, he denied that the principle of degree had been violated, inasmuch as now there were more noblemen in his council than at the beginning of his reign. Of his first councilors, only two, Surrey and Shrewsbury, were "worthie calling noble"; Marney and Darcy were "scant well borne gentilmen, and yet of no grete landes, till they were promoted by Us." [28] The fact that he named nine temporal lords in his present council was cold comfort to the northern nobility. They were only too painfully aware that he had discreetly omitted mentioning Cromwell, Cranmer, Audeley, and Rich, the objects of their protests. As a matter of fact, he had consistently flouted the principle of degree by appointing no one to the council in the North above the rank of knight.[29] Consequently, when the Duke of Norfolk dared to suggest that only noblemen were fitted to keep order in the West Marches after the Pilgrimage of Grace, the Privy Council sent the curt rebuff: "If it shal please his Majesty to appoynt the meanest man . . . to rule & govern in that place; is not his Graces aucthoritie sufficient to cause al men to serve his Grace under him without respect of the very estate of the personage?" Significantly, Cromwell and Cranmer were among the signers of that statement. To it,

[27] *Answer to the Petitions of the traitors and rebels in Lincolnshire,* in *State Papers, Henry VIII,* I, 463.

[28] *Ibid.,* pp. 507-508.

[29] Reid, *King's Council,* p. 103.

the King added his own comment: "For surely we woll not be bounde of a necessitie to be serued there with lordes. But we wolbe serued with such men what degre soeuer they be of as we shall appointe to the same." [30]

Insofar as Henry undertook to defend his position at all, he addressed himself to the Pilgrims of high rather than low degree. But as he must have known, the feudal nobility as a class were no longer a serious threat. While there is ample evidence that they felt their danger, they were timid and inclined to acceptance and collaboration.[31] One finds Norfolk, for example, currying the favor of his hypothetical enemy Cromwell and sharing the spoils incident to the dissolution of the monasteries; Shrewsbury, a member of the council at the King's accession, profiting from transactions involving the alienation of ecclesiastical property; and the Marquis of Exeter accepting a grant of priory lands and property in November 1536, while the North was still seething.[32] In the end, they capitulated to the spirit as well as the fact of the new order. Thomas, Lord Darcy, admitted to Thomas Treheyron, Somerset herald of arms, that he was sorry he had spoken foolishly of Cromwell at Doncaster, "for to say truth every man had a begynnyng and he that the kyng will have honored wee must all honor and god forbyde that any subject shuld goo about to rule the kyng in his owne realme." [33]

The real social problem behind the Pilgrimage of Grace, the new independence of the commons, Henry chose to ignore. Having sown the dragon's teeth, he preferred to leave the rationalization of his policy to his official apologists. They approached it in precisely the manner in which

[30] *L&P*, XII (1), nos. 636, 1118.

[31] Baskerville, *English Monks and the Suppression of the Monasteries*, pp. 161-163.

[32] Liljegren, *Fall of the Monasteries*, pp. 33, 110.

[33] Dodds, *Pilgrimage of Grace*, I, 305; *L&P*, XI, no. 1086, p. 437.

they approached the political problem, as traditionalists rather than as innovators, as supporters of a tradition as venerable as the principle which their practice apparently violated. And they arrived at a theoretic justification of current social policy quite as novel if not quite as unassailable. Since they were responsible only and directly to Henry, they could, of course, take the position that the King on his mere prerogative might advance whom he pleased, regardless of his birth or his riches. We must obey the rulers constituted by the King, said one propagandist writing against a background of the Ten Articles of July 11, 1536,[34] and the rebellion,

not hauyng respecte to ther richesse, to ther nobilite, to ther honour to ther birthe but as his cõmyssioners because god cõmanndeth us so to do. A kyng in his Realme maye promote whom he liketh whom he thynketh meete to be his deputie or Connsailor, be he neũ so pore and so beyng promoted we ought to haue hym in as high honour in as high reverence in as high reputacon, as though he beside wer borne to enherit by the Lawes of the Realme the greatest Dukedome of the same, not for hymselfe, but because god cõmanndeth us so to do; as one that is advannced by the kyng that is goddes mynyster.[35]

This was no more than Henry's argument for unrestricted appointive power, supported by the usual biblical citations,[36] and the author was conscious that so stated and without qualification, it meant the overthrow of degree—and hence of the traditional social system—without offering anything in its place. He therefore sought to temper its naked and arbitrary character by grounding it in principles

[34] PRO, SP 6/4, fol. 197.
[35] *Ibid.*, fols. 192-193.
[36] Romans, 13:1-7; Titus, 3:1-2; I Peter, 2:13-15, 18; 5:5.

just as traditional. The crux of the matter is in the phrase, "not for himself." Granted full honor and reverence and reputation to the King's commoner-appointee because God commanded it, could not that same honor and reverence and reputation be granted also for himself? And if this wer? granted, did it not abrogate the whole artificial set of distinctions represented in the principle of degree? The only logical answer must admit a theory of equality, and the new social theory is stated boldly. The concept of degree, the writer argued, was a violation of the natural order of society. Originally, all men had been created equal; ever since, virtue, not birth, had been the measure of true nobility: "At the begynnyng of the wordle [sic] ther was no difference of persones but afterward dyuers for ther holynes and gode qualitees wer ordeyned and constituted by god to be Rulers, dyuers also afterward which wer but of base byrthe and cam not of that stocke lyneally that were first ordeyned by god to be rulers beyng but poore men for ther vertue wisedome and qualitees and by the favour of noble Emperours and kynges wer constituted and put in high auctorite." [37] The Pilgrims themselves had demanded virtue as the qualification of the King's officers; Henry's propagandist merely substituted a principle of equality for a principle of degree as a basis for social relations. But by that simple substitution, he had acclimatized the radicalism of John Ball's

> When Adam delved, and Eve span,
> Who was then a Gentleman?

and at the same time forged a link between the social thinking of the middle ages and the seventeenth century.

[37] PRO, SP 6/4, fol. 193. Cf. William Marshall's gloss on "universal multitude" in his translation of Marsilius of Padua's *Defensor Pacis* (1534), sig. f 4ᵛ-f 5: "He meaneth suche offyces as yᵉ prynce or kynge wyll haue instytuted by acte of parlyament els all other officers & degres it lyeth ĩ yᵉ kynges absolute power to appõite at all tymes."

What is at once apparent is the eclecticism of his position. The formula he proposed was derivable from both classic and Christian thought and traditional enough to appeal to all sorts and conditions of men. Aristotle placed political virtue above either birth or wealth (*Politics*, III. 9) and maintained that those superior in virtue and in power of performing the best actions should be obeyed (*Politics*, VII. 3), but the construction of Aristotle's state did not allow for a free access to political office of all social ranks (*Politics*, III. 12) nor for social equality except in a very limited sense (*Politics*, II. 7; III. 9, 13). In Cicero, however, a natural and historical principle of equality, the Stoic *omnes homines natura aequales sunt*, was explicit.[38] It is a provision of nature, he said, that only those superior in virtue and in spirit should rule the weaker, and that the weaker should be willing to obey the stronger. Indeed, only ignorance of virtue leads men to think of the rich, prosperous, or wellborn as the best men; for riches, names, and power, when they lack wisdom and the knowledge of how to live and to rule over others, are full of dishonour and insolent pride (*Republic*, I. xxxiv. 51). Cicero observed this principle in use among the early Romans, who, rustic though they were, saw even then that kingly virtue and wisdom, not royal ancestry, were the qualities to be sought (*Republic*, II. xii. 24).

Christian ideology, likewise, offered a limited authority for a theory of social equality. It admitted an original equality among men, but inequality after the Fall. It accepted a spiritual equality among all men, but limited it to the

[38] For the significance of this development in political thought, see R. W. and A. J. Carlyle, *A History of Mediaeval Political Theory in the West* (Edinburgh, 1928–1936), I, 8. C. H. McIlwain, *The Growth of Political Thought in the West* (New York, 1932), p. 115, calls it "the profoundest contribution of the Stoics to political thought."

spiritual realm. And though the present state of the church hardly conformed to the pattern, the first ecclesiastical government as established by Christ ignored degrees.

But while there was ready at hand both classical and Christian support for advancing a doctrine of equality to meet a current situation, and while the apologists were anxious to align the government position with traditional thought on the subject, they were alive to the danger of its literal adoption as a social program, and their use of it was consequently defensive, not doctrinaire. They thought within the framework of the present regime. With the more radical forms of equalitarianism, the communism of either More or the sects, they would have nothing to do. For pressed to its logical conclusions, equalitarianism led either to the fanciful land of Utopia or to the real and bloody insurrections of Münster.

Nor did they have any intention of surrendering to God the things that belonged to Caesar. Tradition in the form of man's law must prevent the anarchic excesses of equalitarianism implicit both in the law of Christ and the Stoic law of nature. According to Starkey, a plowman is ideally as dear to God as the most royal king or prince in his high majesty, a cobbler as the greatest philosopher, a merchant abroad in the world as the monk in his cloister. In spite of the diversity among men, "before God . . . there is no regarde of person nor degree." [39] On the other hand, there are men of arrogant blindness who

if hit were not for feare of mannes lawe, wolde brynge to ruyne all order and policye, they wolde haue all thynges whyche nature hathe broughte forth to the common comforte of manne, to be in common, iudgynge this inequalitie in possession of thynges, where as somme have to lyttell,

[39] *An Exhortation,* sig. D.

and some ouer moche, to be playne agaynste Nature, and
manyfeste iniurye. They wolde in all thinges serue their
owne fantasye, they wolde in harte be subiecte to no cere-
monie, lawe, nor mannes tradition: for that they saye
agreethe not to the libertie of a Chrystian manne, who is
free frome all bondage of lawe, and subiecte to no cere-
monye, the whiche they say be only snares and stayes vnto
weke myndes, nothynge agreing vnto theyr dignitie.[40]

Indeed, an ideal of equality based solely on classical virtue
and Christian humility was far from compatible with the
practical exigencies of the present crisis. Cuthbert Tunstal,
the King's appointee to the office of President of the Council in 1530, could cite Christ's warning to the apostles that
the first among them would be servant of all (St. Mark,
10:44): "Here we doo see, that Chryste wolde haue the
mekeste and moste humble to be chiefe in his flocke, by
humilitie and by seruyce done to other." [41] But obviously,
ambition rather than humility, active ability rather than
passive virtue, were the more immediate motives of the
royal servants. And viewed externally for its uses as propaganda, with how good grace could they recount illustrations
of the advancement of poor men "for ther vertue wisedome
and qualitees" when the complaint of the Pilgrims against
Henry's lowborn officers lay precisely in their lack of virtue?

Redefinition of the concept of nobility in terms of practical politics was necessary, and Richard Morison, writing at
a critical moment during the insurrection, recognized the
need. For a man who was familiar with the works of
Machiavelli, the transposition of values was easy. In Morison's addresses to the Pilgrims, Aristotelian virtue has been

[40] *Ibid.*, sig. [F iii^v]. A comma after *iniurye* has been changed to a
period to clarify the thought.
[41] *A sermon . . . made upon Palme sondaye* (Berthelet, 1539), sig.
C iii.

replaced by Machiavellian *virtù*, Christian humility by ambition, theoretical by practical motives as a basis for social equality. "Who can justly blame him," he asked arrogantly in defending Henry's advancement of commoners, "for making them great, that indeed have all those things which at the beginning of nobility only made them noble?" [42] In so doing, the King was putting in practice the Platonic principle of the ἄριστοι: "An order muste be hadde and a waye founde, that they rule that beste can, they be ruled, that mooste it becommeth so to be." [43] But who are those that can rule best? The question was crucial, and Morison deliberated, wrote first, "those that nature hathe other indewd wth greater giftes or fortune sette in higher degree thā other," then qualified significantly to "those that nature hath endewed with synguler vertues, and fortune without breache of lawe, sette in hygh dignitie," [44] and finally added in the printed version a revealing clarification: "They only ought to be officers, that are known to be discreet, politic, wise, and of such stomach that if need be, they can set little the hatred and malice of them that seldom love such as are in greatest authority." [45]

"Wherever virtue is, there is nobility," Dante had said, speaking in the Aristotelian tradition;[46] and Chaucer's Wife of Bath put it just as simply: "He is gentil that doth gentil dedis." But nobility is also what we make of ourselves since we are all by nature equal; Machiavelli makes the demagogue Ciompi say, to stir the commons to revolt, "Nor must you let yourselves be cowed by that nobility of blood of which they make boast to us; for all men, having had the

[42] *A Lamentation*, sig. A iv.

[43] *Remedy*, sig. A ii[v].

[44] PRO, SP 6/13, fol. 16; *Remedy*, sig. A ii[v].

[45] *Remedy*, sig. A iv[v].

[46] *Convivio*, IV, xvi. The statement is made in an extended passage showing true nobility as determined by moral and intellectual virtues.

same beginning, are of equally ancient birth, and nature has made them all in the same fashion. Were we all stripped naked you would find us alike; dress us in their clothes and they in ours, without doubt we should seem noble and they mean, forasmuch as it is only poverty and riches that make us inequal." [47] Morison, familiar with both points of view, paraphrased and integrated them with a prudential twist of his own. Henry, he claimed, had set up a new definition of nobility: "True nobility is never but where virtue is . . . this only to be the way of promotion, and here nobility to consist. In all other things, it little availeth whose son a man be . . . What shall we need to endeavor ourselves unto, when whatsoever we do, we must be tryed by our birth and not by our qualities?" [48] It is stated with even greater clarity in his translation of Vives' *Introduction to Wisdom* (Berthelet, 1540):

What other thynge is nobylite nowe, but a chaunce, to be borne of this or that gentyll bloud, and an opinion grafte vppon the foolishness of rude and vnlerned people, whiche oftentymes is gotten by robberie and lyke wyaes.

True and perfect nobilite, springeth of vertue, wherfore it is gret madnesse for any man, to crake of his parentes, beinge naught him selfe, dishonourynge theyr noble actes, with his lewed doinges.[49]

[47] *Florentine History* (Everyman edition), p. 118. Cf. Edmund Dudley, *Tree of Commonwealth* (1509), pp. 45-46: "Looke when our glorious garmentes be done of [off] and we be naked, what difference is then betwene vs and the poore laborers? Peradventure a more fowle and shamfull carcase."

[48] *Remedy*, sig. A iv^v-B ii.

[49] Cf. Dante's view in *Convivio* that nobility is a broader term than virtue, including other kinds of excellence (IV, xix). No one, because he is able to say, "I am of such and such a stock," is entitled to believe that he is possessed of nobility, if the seed of blessedness placed by God in the soul is not in him (IV, xx). So Agapetus declared to

Trewely we be all made of lyke elementes, and haue all oone god, father to vs all, yet to contempne the byrthe or stocke of any man, is vnder a color to reproue god, whiche is the autoure of euery mans natiuitie.[50]

Will the commons have no one rule but noblemen born? Morison's shrewd answer was an admission that the caste of the old nobility had gone forever: "Let them have that they require, whom toucheth this so sore as themself, and all their posterity? What doo they leave unto theirs, when they also take away the possibility of better fortune?" [51]

Morison's question, a frank appeal to ambition, is quite to be expected of the obscure but talented authors of Henry's new order, who having been trained in the classics, philosophy, scriptures, and the civil law, were now eager to use their learning in a society in which the old barriers had been broken down and new opportunities opened to them through the benevolence of their prince.[52] It shows how far they were from lending theoretic support to a classless society. For them, social rank would continue to exist, limited only by a man's abilities. As beneficiaries of the new

---

Justinian: "No man shulde glorifie or delite in the nobilite of his kindrede. For why both riche and poure be ingendred of erthe. Therfore no mã ought to exalte and prayse his vile & erthly kyndrede but onely glorifie and reioyce in good and godly maners." *The preceptes teachyng a prynce or a noble estate his duetie,* translated by Thomas Paynell, sig. a. v. For a similar expression of opinion in fifteenth-century Florence, see Hans Baron, "The Historical Background of the Florentine Renaissance," *History,* new series, XXII (1938), 318.

[50] Sig. B vii^v-B viii (Juan Luis Vives, *Introducción á la Sabiduría,* Madrid, 1918, pp. 23-24). Morison's preface, addressed to Cromwell's son, Gregory, makes it clear that in such a passage he had Cromwell in mind: "Folowe your leader, goo on with your guyde, you shall fynde all the steppes and grices, wherby not only my lord clymed to nobilitie, but all other, that in ded are or were atte any tyme noble." Sig. A v^v.

[51] *Remedy,* sig. A iv^v-B ii.

[52] For Starkey's offer of his services to the state, see above, pp. 46-47.

order, they wanted to legalize their own rise, and they were anxious to maintain the privilege.

But Morison had struck a vein of social thinking which justified far more than his own advancement. By unfixing rank and opening to all classes the possibility of better fortune, he was anticipating a new social freedom for Pilgrims and Puritans alike, the "career open to talents" of a later era. "Lordes must be lordes, comunes must be comunes, euery man acceptynge his degree," he stated flatly; and then, as if to open the door wide for the ambitious climber on the social ladder: "Euery man contente to haue that, that he laufully maye come by." [53] That all men were equal in the sight of God would not be contested in the sixteenth century; anything resembling equality of possessions would continue to be just as vehemently and universally denounced; but liberty to choose one's occupation—that was another matter, born of a new age of enterprise.

IV

The establishment of this new concept of equality was not possible without a fundamental revision of the vocabulary of social relations, chiefly with regard to the continuing function of labor in a free society. If society as presently constituted would admit the possibility of better fortune, as Morison had asserted, then provision must be made so that the commonwealth would not suffer for lack of common labor. Again, this meant bringing current modes of conduct into conformity with traditional modes of thought. Augustine summed up the Christian ideal of labor in the early years of the church when he advised the Carthaginian monks, who had preferred to consider the lilies

[53] *Remedy,* sig. B iii, B iv. See also Morison's *Invective Against Treason* (Berthelet, 1539), sig. a ii[v].

and scorn work, that they should "labor with their hands for the common good, and submit to their superiors without murmer." [54] The world being what it is, however, labor for the most part has always been a matter of self rather than public interest. "All men studyeth on euery syde howe they may waxe rych," complained a fourteenth-century plowman, "and euerych man almost is ashamed to ben holden a poore man." [55] In any other place than Utopia, said More, they speak always of the common wealth when as a matter of fact "euerye man procureth hys owne pryuate wealthe." [56] The anonymous author of *Howe to Reforme the Realme in settyng them to werke*, written about 1536, leveled similar criticism at the non-productive labor of London merchants,

commonly pore mens sones naturall borne to labour for their lyving, which after they be bounde prentises to be merchauntes, all their labour, stody and policy is be [by] bying and selling to get singler richis frome the communaltie, and never workith to gete their lyving nother by workes of husbandry nor artificialite, but lyveth by other menes workes and of naught risith to grete richis, entending no thing elles but only to gete richis, which knowith no common weale.[57]

And Robert Crowley found fault with craftsmen who "applye an occupacion to get theyr lyuynge uppon, and not to the intent to profite the common weale . . . The craftes man

[54] *Select Library of the Nicene and Post-Nicene Fathers* (ed. Schaff), III, 514.

[55] *Praier and complaynt of the Ploweman vnto Christ*, sig. E[v].

[56] *Utopia* (ed. Collins), p. 138.

[57] *Tudor Economic Documents*, edited by R. H. Tawney and Eileen Power (London, 1924), III, 126. Reprinted from Reinhold Pauli's *Drei volkwirthschaftlicke Denkschriften aus der Zeit Heinrichs VIII. von England* (1878).

sueth for the fredom of a Citie, not because he intendeth
to be a maintainer of the Citie, but because he hopeth that
he shall lyue so muche the more welthyly hym selfe." [58]

From every direction, the customary principle of fixed
degree was being undermined by the new spirit of enterprise and worldly ambition. Even Thomasian doctrine, as
one critic has recently observed,[59] made its compromises
with current social practice. In Question 118 of the *Summa,*
Aquinas had condemned covetousness on the grounds that
a man's riches are good only insofar as they are necessary
for him to live in keeping with his condition of life, and
that it would be a sin for him to exceed this measure by
wishing to acquire or keep them immoderately. With this
point of view, the Renaissance commentator, Cardinal Caje-
tano de Vio (d. 1534), took issue, on the grounds that no
one would then be able to change his state (*statum*) without sin. Thus a peasant must always remain a peasant, an
artisan always an artisan, a citizen always a citizen, and
never will he be able to acquire any rule of his own. This,
in the opinion of the commentator, was manifestly absurd,
since we see daily many remarkable persons especially
gifted with a certain wisdom either inspired by nature, or
developed in practice, so that they are either born or made
masters of men. And since their rule over others is owing
to them by natural right, if they seek rule, if, moreover,
they accumulate wealth in order to acquire temporal
dominion, they do not thereby depart from the path of right
reason.

Partly because of this transposition of the value of labor
from a mere function in a closed and rigid social system to

[58] *An informacion and Peticion agaynst the oppressours of the pore
Commons of this Realme* [1548], sig. A iii.
[59] Alfred von Martin, *Sociology of the Renaissance* (New York,
1944), pp. 86-87.

a means of personal aggrandizement, idleness is one of the social ills most persistently attacked in the sixteenth century. Laziness, Vives insisted, was not to be tolerated, whether in a well-ordered household or a well-ordered city.[60] Thomas More likewise pictured as a fault common to all nations a rout of idle gentlemen and erstwhile servants of gentlemen who, after their release from employment, turn to thievery.[61] He was at the heart of the problem in declaring that men cannot be kept from stealing "whych haue no other crafte wherby to get their liuing." [62] As another contemporary critic put it: "All the same idull people havyng lyff in theym must nedys have lyving." [63]

But it was not until the apologists faced the problem of poverty in the North that the expediential plea of social equality was expanded into a positive social program. Even before the outbreak of the rebellion Starkey had called the attention of the King to the relation between poverty and social unrest in terms of the secularization of ecclesiastical wealth. As in 1533 he had urged the distribution of all ecclesiastical first fruits among the poor "in order that former inequalities might be more duly proportioned";[64] so, shortly before the insurrection, he advised the King that since "penury euer bredyth sedytyon," the revenue from the suppressions should in part provide support for the poor. But the Pilgrimage had the effect within the circle of Henry's advisers of sharpening and intensifying the dangers of an exasperated and class-conscious poverty, and

[60] *De subventione pauperum,* in *Some Early Tracts on Poor Relief,* edited by F. R. Salter (London, 1926), p. 12.

[61] *Utopia,* pp. 13-14.

[62] *Utopia,* p. 12.

[63] *Howe to Reforme the Realme,* p. 117.

[64] PRO, SP 1/75, fol. 241 [*L&P,* VI, no. 414 (ii)]: "Primi fructus distribuendi pauperibus ecclesiae cuiuslibet, ut inequalites illa olim quae fuit aequitate temperetur."

of provoking a remedy within the new social framework.

As in the political realm, order—but the present order—was a first consideration. Morison's concern over the social instability underlying the Pilgrimage of Grace becomes apparent by comparison with Henry Parker's *Dives and Pauper,* which Berthelet was reprinting at the same time as Morison's *A Remedy for Sedition* was rushed through his press. *Dives and Pauper* is a defense of holy poverty in the medieval manner, the conclusion of which is the Augustinian doctrine that rich man and poor man are necessary to each other. Otherwise, says the poor man, "Who shulde tyll your londe, holde your plough, repe your corne, and kepe your beastes? who shuld shape your clothes or sewe them? what myllar wolde than grynde your corne? what baker bake your breade? what brewer brewe your ale? what coke dyght your mete? what smith or carpenter amẽde your house and other thinges necessarie? ye shulde go showles and clothles, and go to your bedde meateles, all muste ye than do alone." [65] Significantly, the issue of disturbance of degree is not raised. Morison's argument, following similar lines but loaded with poignant sarcasm for "Captain Poverty," betrays his consciousness of the class tensions now racking the social structure:

We thinke it is very euyll, that soo many of us be poore, we thynke it were a good worlde, if we were al ryche. I pray you for a season, let it be as we desire, let us imagine, we be al ryche, doth it not streight folow, I as good as he, why gothe he before, I behynde? I as ryche as he, what nedeth me to labour? The mayde as prowde as her dame, who mylketh the cowe? The fermour hauing no more cause to toyle than he that loketh for the rentes, who shall tyl the

[65] Sig. A iii^v-A iiii. There is a similar passage in Dudley's *Tree of Commonwealth,* pp. 19-20.

*groundeP His meny ye say. How soP why they more than
he, if they be ryche toP What were more to be wayled, than
suche welthe, that shuld bring either euery man, or the
mooste parte of men, to extreme confusyon.*[66]

Clearly, Morison, like Starkey, thought of poverty as the
underlying cause of sedition; his consciousness of a class
struggle crops out in a manuscript version of *A Remedy*,
only to be expunged in print: "In time of peace, be not all
men almost at war with them that be rich?"[67] To Morison,
that war had become an actuality in the Pilgrimage. And
he echoed More's asseveration that the ultimate cause of
poverty was idleness: "Euery mā must haue an honest
occupation, wherby in trouth he may get his lyuyng, without doinge iniury to his neyghbour. Idelness ydelnes must
be banyshed. It can not be chosen, but men wylle steale,
thoughe they be hanged, excepte they may lyue without
stelyng."[68]

How, then, shall men live without stealing? Both Starkey
and Morison saw the answer to the problem of unemployment in the development of England's natural resources,
and both compared England favorably with continental
countries. Englishmen complain of their poverty, wrote
Starkey: "You schal fynd few that wyl confesse themselfe
ryche, few that wyl say they haue enough. How be hyt, yf
we wyl justely examyn the mater, and compare our pepul
of Englond wyth the pepul of other cuntreys, I thynke we
schal fynd them most rych and welthy of any commyns
aboute vs; for in Fraunce, Italy, and Spayn, the commynys
wythout fayle are more myserabul and pore then they be
here wyth vs."[69] Morison was even more explicit on the

[66] *Remedy*, sig. A iii-A iii[v].
[67] PRO, SP 6/13, fol. 16.
[68] *Remedy*, sig. E iii[v]. Cf. Starkey's *Dialogue*, p. 74.
[69] *Dialogue*, p. 90. See also Herrtage, p. lvii.

same theme: "In Englande the grounde almoste nourisheth vs alone. It is an incredible thinge, to see howe soore men of other nations labour, howe moch we play, howe lytle they consume on their belies, howe moche we deuoure, howe poore they be, and how welthy we are, welthy I saye in comparison of them." In Germany he had observed the people planting trees for fuel, sowing mountainsides, plowing with mattocks, and harrowing with spades; in France they were drawing carts of fagots about the city; in Italy even the rich and wellborn carried on a trade, and as for the commons,

this I am sure, we that haue beene there, haue sayde ones a weke, God saue the welthy comynaltie of England. I wyl not cōpare our kepyng of houses with theirs, where frogges be a dayntie dysshe, snayles, a morsell for a lady, where musshrumpes stande for the seconde course. Ye wolde thynke it a madde syght to see a quarter of a goose runne rounde for burnynge, the rest powdered and kepte in stoore for holydayes. I am assured, the fare in Venys is as good, as is in the moste partes of Italie. Venys is as bygge, or very lyttell lesse, than London with the suburbes: yet is there more fleshe spent in two or thre monethes in London, than is there in a yere . . . We banyshed the best thynge, that euer was with manne, when frugalitie was dryuen away.[70]

England, in Morison's opinion, was even too wealthy, too fertile; for its very wealth had discouraged ingenuity and honest occupations.

But Morison had the more immediate problem of revolt to face. If England was opportunity, what could be done with "Aste and hys soldirs" who seemed to have a very different opinion? At first, Morison, like Henry, could see

[70] *Remedy*, sig. E iv-F ii[v].

no further than their destruction. "Lothe I am, and so is my prince, that they shold thus dy, but if ther be no remedy better they be slayn, thã twyse so many honeste mẽ un- don." [71] His acrimony reflected the genuine alarm of the government in the Yorkshire crisis: "Desperate knaves, that haue nothỹg to lose, but ther lyfe, whych now, after so many mischyfes cõmitted, can not be, but more paỹful unto thẽ, thã dethe, what care they, what be cũ of thẽ? Nay, what greater bẽfitte, cã ye do thẽ now, thã kill thẽ, whych ever more must remẽber how an abbominable acte it is, to go ayenst ther cõtrey." [72]

By the time *A Remedy* reached Berthelet for printing, however, these passages had been deleted, and instead, Morison set forth a remedy for unemployment, and hence a remedy for sedition, which admitted for society as a whole that equality of opportunity by which he himself had been able to rise. Starkey had recently urged a good education for the nobility and the clergy as a correction for the ills of the common wealth; [73] Morison now proposed applying the remedy of education to the commons. Retracting his sen- tence of death, he now held that the need for honest occu- pations could be satisfied only by education in the crafts. [74] "Surely, if it were any thing lyke to be brought to passe, it shulde be moche better to fynde a waye, that none might have wylle to rebell, then to trusse up rebellious people . . . Education, euyll education, is a greatte cause of these and all other myschefes, that growe in a comene welthe." [75] Here was the suggestion, this time not Henry's but Mori- son's own, of a social program. Popular resentment against poverty and a rising cost of living was not likely to be dis- pelled by bombast on obedience; nor were the rumors of a

[71] PRO, SP 6/13, fol. 20ᵛ.
[72] PRO, SP 6/13, fol. 22.
[73] *Dialogue*, pp. 129, 132, 205.
[74] *Remedy*, sig. C iv-C ivᵛ.
[75] *Remedy*, sig. D ii-D iiᵛ.

special tax on white bread, pig, goose, and capon likely to disappear with descriptions of continental peoples as more frugal or more temperate than the English.[76] But a program of education for the eminently practical purpose of providing a living for commoners who had been deprived of their normal means of existence because of widespread changes in the national economy, changes which the Pilgrims would hardly be expected to understand and for which the government could hardly be held responsible—such a program constituted an honest remedy for the social ills Morison alone among the propagandists was able to perceive.

Furthermore, he proposed that the same remedy be applied to religious differences. "Religion agreeth not, where many beareth the swing," he wrote in one of the drafts of A Remedy;[77] in the printed text, he argued that education in a common religious faith would go far to cure the narrow sectionalism which divided North from South.[78]

In general, a notable advance in thought is observable in the final draft of A Remedy. Indeed, it is difficult to believe that he could have given the tract a title until the final draft had been completed. This is clear: that in its printed form A Remedy is the most socially-minded document of the government's campaign, and that Morison, by proposing a system of education on the basis of a frank admission of equality of opportunity, discovered a means of banishing poverty and at the same time indulging the ambitions of the lower classes to rise.

It has been asserted in a recent history of European liberalism that "the emancipation of the individual is a by-product of the Reformation" and that English Reformers did not have "an atom of progressiveness or secularity in

[76] *Remedy*, sig. E iv-F ii. So Starkey's *Dialogue*, p. 95.
[77] PRO, SP 6/13, fol. 38.
[78] *Remedy*, sig. D iii–E.

their outlook." [79] Against any such generalization, Morison's proposal offers sufficient proof. Instructive by contrast was Luther's reaction to the peasant revolt of 1525. The peasants' demand for freedom from serfdom seemed to him sheer robbery, an attempt to interpret Christian freedom in an entirely material sense with the ultimate object of robbing the lord of his property. Social equality was equally abhorrent to him: "This article [the peasants' demand for freedom] would make all men equal and so change the spiritual Kingdom of Christ into an external worldly one. Impossible! An earthly kingdom can not exist without inequality of persons. Some must be free, others serfs; some rulers, others subjects." [80] Luther's complete acceptance of the medieval conception of fixed social degree tended to perpetuate man's servitude rather than enhance his dignity. This can be said in spite of Tawney's observation that Luther recognized a kind of religious equalitarianism in rejecting the mediation of the church and placing all men on an equal footing in their relation toward God. Tawney considered this "an advance, which contained the germ of all subsequent revolutions," and which was "so enormous that all else seems insignificant." [81] But such a view could have little influence on liberal thought unless it could be made to imply that all men were on an equal footing in their relation to each other; and this, of course, was furthest from Luther's intention. In fact, the ideal of Christian equality, placed in the context of Luther' authoritarianism, could only be regarded as humbling and leveling in connotation. As for the other Reformers, Melanchthon, though far more

[79] Harold J. Laski, *The Rise of European Liberalism* (London, 1936), pp. 30-34.

[80] *Werke* (Weimar), xviii, 311-319. Quoted in Jacob S. Schapiro, *Social Reform and the Reformation* (New York, 1909), p. 82.

[81] *Religion and the Rise of Capitalism* (London, 1926), pp. 97-98.

liberal in other respects, was in this bound by much the same social prejudices; and Calvinism, with a similar emphasis on predestination and the irremediability of inequalities, was hardly the perfect ideological approach to the emancipation of the common man.

In the characteristically expanding, acquisitive society of the sixteenth century, there was intellectual sterility in concepts of equality—whether based on the comfortless leveling in the eyes of God which was the extent of Luther's liberalism, or on the ascetic and visionary community of possessions in the Utopian or apostolic sense, in which the individual is subordinate to the group. Short of revolution, a vital concept of equality must rest on a becoming rather than a being. It is not enough that man should exercise himself "in some facyon of lyue conuenyent to the dygnyte and nature of man." "God hath ordeynyd thys, that man schal haue nothyng that ys gud, nothyng perfayt, wythout hys owne labur, dylygence, and cure." [82] In this milieu, the increasing independence of the laborer and the new valuation which he himself set upon his place and work in society made it inevitable that equality should be conceived in terms of opportunity, and that social equalitarianism should achieve its first clear expression in sixteenth-century England.

V

The rapidity of development of social thinking during the reign of Henry VIII may best be measured by comparing the position taken by the government vis à vis the rebels of Devonshire and Norfolk in 1549. In 1536, government spokesmen were accusing the commoners of advocating social equality so that all commoners could be gentlemen;

[82] Starkey's *Dialogue,* pp. 78, 207-208.

in 1549, the commoners were charged with advocating social equality so that gentlemen would be destroyed altogether. A new note of leveling had become articulate.[83] To the demand of the Devonshire rebels "that no Gentleman shal have any mo servants then one, to wait upon him, except he may dispend one hundred mark land, and for every hundred mark we think it reasonable he should have a man," Archbishop Cranmer responded in terms that show his awareness of the new danger: "It was not for good mind, that you bare to the Gentlemen, that you devised this Article; but it appeareth plainly, that you devised it to diminish their strength, and to take away their friends, that you might command Gentlemen at your pleasures." [84] Social equalitarianism seemed now to have become proletarian:

For was it ever seen in any country since the world began, that Commons did appoint the Nobles, and Gentlemen, the number of their Servants? Standeth it with any reason to turn upside down the good order of the whole world, that is every where, and ever hath been? That is to say, the Commoners to be governed by the Nobles, and the Servants by their Masters. Wil you now have the subjects to govern their King, the Vilains to rule the Gentlemen, and the Servants their Masters? If men would suffer this, God wil not; but wil take vengance on al them, that wil break his order.[85]

Writing against the Norfolk rebels in the same year Morison's friend, John Cheke, like Cranmer, was conscious of the leveling motive now implicit in social equalitarianism. Cheke paraphrased Starkey and Morison in warning the

[83] Potentially recurrent, as Professor White points out, in every social rebellion (*Social Criticism*, pp. 118-120).

[84] Strype, *Cranmer*, II, 835-836.

[85] *Ibid.*, II, 837.

rebels that if everyone were rich, the commonwealth would
be destroyed by idleness. But equality had come to mean
quite the reverse of what it meant when Morison wrote
A Remedy. In 1536 Morison, observing the attack on the
rigid system of degree, thought of equality as the opportunity to rise; in 1549 Cheke, observing the threat of leveling
of all ranks, thought of equality as the stultification of it:
"If there should be such equalitie, then ye take awaie all
hope from yours to come to anie better estate than you now
leaue them. And as manie meane mens children doo come
honestlie vp, and are great succour to all their stocke: so
should none be hereafter holpen by you, but bicause ye
seeke equalitie, whereby all can not be rich." [86] Morison
invoked a theory of equality to break down the social barricades to the lower classes; Cheke foresaw the barricades
leveled and the lower classes a victim of their own theory.
You pretend a commonwealth, he mocked, but "if riches
offend you, because yee wish the like, then thinke that to
be no common-wealth, but envie to the common-wealth.
Enuie it is to appaire an other mans estate, without the
amendment of your owne. And to haue no gentlemen,
bicause ye be none your selues, is to bring downe an estate,
and to mend none." Then Cheke addressed himself directly
to the issue of social equality, in the most elaborate analysis
of the motives behind the idea in the Tudor period:

But what meane yee by this equalitie in the commonwealth? If one be wiser than an other, will ye banish him,
because yee intend an equalitie of all things? If one be
stronger than an other, will yee alaie him, bicause ye seeke
an equalitie of all things? If one be well fauorder than an
other, will yee punish him, because yee looke for an equali-

[86] *The Hurt of Sedition*, reprinted in Holinshed's *Chronicles* (London, 1808), III, 990.

tie of all things? If one haue better vtterance than an other,
will ye pull out his toong to saue your equalitie? And if one
be richer than an other, will ye spoile him to mainteine an
equalitie? If one be elder than an other, will ye kill him
for this equalities sake? How iniurious are ye to God him-
selfe, who intendeth to bestow his gifts as he himselfe
listeth: and ye seeke by wicked insurrections to make him
giue them commonlie alike to all men as your vaine fansie
liketh? Whie would ye haue an equalitie in riches & in
other gifts of God? There is no meane sought. Either by
ambition ye seeke lordlinesse much vnfit for you; or by
couetousnesse ye be vnsatiable, a thing likelie inough in ye;
or else by follie ye be not content with your estate, a fansie
to be plucked out of you.[87]

The royal apologists couldn't have it both ways, and subsequent history was to prove that the break in the elaborate
medieval social structure would not be repaired by a mere
reiteration of the principle of degree. But granted that the
points of view were incompatible, the remarkable fact is
that under a Tudor monarch a theory of social equality was
voiced at all. Evaluated as propaganda, it reflects a new
and increasing independence in the commons. It takes on
meaning to the degree that propaganda accurately measures
the minds of its intended audience. Regardless of the motive for its promulgation, it constituted by implication an
unmistakably democratic challenge in the sixteenth century
to the authoritarian tradition.[88] It was inevitable that the

[87] *Ibid.,* pp. 989-990.

[88] Thomas Elyot approached the idea in *The Governour,* edited by
H. H. Croft (London, 1907), I, 6: "They which excel other in this
influence of understanding, and do employ it to the detaining of other
within the bounds of reason, and show hoe to provide for their necessary living; such ought to be set in a more high place than the residue." But Elyot does not face the crucial question of nobility *vs.* men
of noble birth.

same challenge should have been raised wherever in sixteenth-century Europe inquiring minds perceived the incompatibility of the "callings" and Christ's injunction that the first shall be last and the last first. Implicit in the Protestant ethic, was a socially disruptive force. Henry's propagandists were astute enough to put the simple question: If the principle of equalitarianism were divested of its ecclesiastical connotation, what then? [89] In such questionings, the Puritan Revolution germinated.

[89] A. S. P. Woodhouse, *Puritanism and Liberty* (London, 1938), pp. 68-69, 81.

IX

EXILE

The day that Pole sent his opinion on the divorce to Henry, fateful as it was for himself, also marked the breaking of a second career and the making of a third. For Thomas Starkey, the blow was fatal. Despite the fact that his personal defense was accepted, he was relegated to a minor role henceforth in the affairs of state, and the brilliant future that lay ahead of the author of *An Exhortation* was presently blighted by sickness and death. In January 1537 he was presented with a living in London,[1] and served on a witchcraft commission; and in March he received a royal summons to meet with the bishops.[2] The occasion was apparently to issue his directive for preaching, the holograph of which is still extant.[3] In the interest of conformity, he therein ordered that in obscure passages of scripture, preachers should "swarue not at theyr owne lyberty frõ the most cõmỹ & of long tyme receyuyd Interpretatyon therof, made by the anncyent doctorys of our relygyon," and that where their meaning was not plain, preachers should follow "the cõsent & laudabul custome of the church of englond," infringement of the order to be considered as seditious and so prosecuted. Also extant are notes and the

[1] Herrtage, pp. lxiii-lxiv.
[2] *L&P*, XII (1), no. 708.
[3] PRO, SP 1/100, fols. 130-130ᵛ (*L&P*, IX, no. 1160).

sketch of an answer to Pighius's *Hierarchiae ecclesiasticae assertio.*[4]

But Starkey's career was over, and "infirmity and sickness" hastened his end. He may have preached before the King on March 24, 1538,[5] but he died later in the same year. His will, dated August 25, remembered his father for the expense of his education, Lord Montague, brother of Reginald, and "Dr Wotton," presumably Edward, to whom he bequeathed his books, part of which were to help further the education of Wotton's children, part to furnish the library of Magdalen College, part—a characteristic gesture—to be given to poor scholars.[6] It is the testament of a humanist.

Morison, by contrast, had been able to turn Pole's defection to his personal advantage, and the ill wind of the Pilgrimage of Grace had further secured his position as propagandist for Henry. If Fortune had played into Morison's hands on his arrival in England, hard work had brought success. In three months he had risen from suitor to advocate of suitors, an indication of his deep engagement in the affairs of Cromwell, first as his secretary, then after some delay, during which, as Morison complained to Cromwell, "every man took it for a season to be so,"[7] as a member of the Privy Chamber.[8] While the Marchioness of Exeter, stung by her husband's removal from the council, grumbled that "men of noble blood were put out and the King taketh in other at his pleasure,"[9] Morison steadily accumu-

[4] *L&P*, XIII (1), no. 1268 (1538).

[5] *L&P*, XIII (1), no. 1280 (f. 4 b).

[6] Herrtage, p. viii, n. 4.

[7] *L&P*, XIII (1), no. 1296.

[8] He was not in the list of the Privy Chamber entered in *L&P* at the beginning of the years 1538 and 1539. *L&P*, XIII (1), no. 1; XIV (1), no. 2.

[9] *L&P*, XIII (2), no. 802.

lated church preferments and financial rewards.[10] The record of these years of growing affluence is instructive as an illustration of the shift of political power from the old nobility during the Cromwellian regime.

For the nonce, there was little use for Morison's special writing talent: Berthelet finally published *Apomaxis* anonymously in 1537, but a translation of the Pope's *Epistle of Sturmius* [11] and a treatise setting forth Henry's opposition to a general church council at Vicenza,[12] both published by Berthelet in 1538, were the only additions to the anti-papal literature that he found time to do in these rising years.

But while Starkey's dying hand wrote out a bequest of four pounds to "the veray honnerable and my singulier good lorde, my lorde Montague . . . to bie hym a hagg," events were once more casting Morison in the role of protagonist for the government against Reginald Pole.

In June 1538 Cromwell decided to move against the last remaining group of malcontents, the Poles, Courtenays, and Nevilles, whose activities in conjunction with sympathizers on the continent, notably Reginald Pole, had for some time excited his suspicion. So long as potential claimants to the throne remained alive, so long the serpent Sedition lay in wait. Now in the person of the newly-appointed Cardinal Pole, Cromwell recognized the absentee leader of the Pilgrimage of Grace two years since and a fomenter on the continent of England's present grief. The trial and conviction of the conspirators in November and December ended any serious danger from rebellion; but the King was irritated by criticism abroad. On January 19, he requested Wyatt at the court of the Emperor to make representations against "those barking preachers there, slanderously defaming us in so celebre a place, which rather ought to be called false

[10] *L&P*, XIV (1), nos. 733, 771.   [12] *L&P*, XIII (1), no. 709.
[11] *L&P*, XIII (1), no. 622.

SIR THOMAS CROMWELL, BY HANS HOLBEIN
Frick Collection, New York

THOMAS CRANMER, BY GERLACH FLICCIUS
National Portrait Gallery, London

prophets and sheepcloked wolves." [13] From the Netherlands, Wriothesley reported that despite his explanations "folks were very angry with the death of the Marquis [of Exeter]." [14] So unfavorable was the reaction from abroad that Cromwell commissioned Morison to write an official apologia. It was issued from Berthelet's press early in 1539 under the title, *An invectiue ayenste the great and detestable vice, treason*.[15] For the first time, Morison had the satisfaction of viewing his own name on a title page. Henry was highly pleased. On February 13 he sent instructions to Wyatt to point out how odious traitors ought to be to princes and what commonly comes of conferences with them, "whereupon of late there is a pretty book printed in this our realm which ye shall receive herewith." [16]

In *An Invective* Morison intended to show how traitors work their own confusion, and he illustrated by examples from the scriptures and the classic historians before descending to the late unfortunates, each of whom he blamed with ungratefulness. The weight of his censure, however, fell on Reginald Pole, that "arch traitor," who accepted the

[13] *L&P*, XIV (1), no. 82.

[14] *L&P*, XIV (1), no. 208.

[15] *L&P*, XIV (1), no. 401. On February 5, in answer to a request by the favorably disposed Floris D'Egmont, Count of Buren, that "these things about the Marquis, Mountacute, Nevel and Carrowe" be put in print, Cromwell gave assurance that "this was partly done and no doubt would be translated and sent abroad" (*L&P*, XIV (1), no. 233). The reference would seem to indicate that Morison's book was completed in February, though Castillon, the French ambassador, wrote to Montmorency on January 16 that he was sending him "a little book in English by the king about the death of the marquis of Exeter and lord Montague," containing also "something about the king of Scots," with the comment "J'entends que c'est leur proces fait apres leur mort." Castillon may have been referring, of course, to manuscript.

[16] *L&P*, XIV, (1), no. 280. See *L&P*, XV, no. 478 (2) for the circulation of Morison's tracts on the continent in 1540.

King's kindness only to turn against him. Against "old custom," which Pole had defended, Morison praised the change in Henry from Defender of the Faith to Supreme Head of Church and State as the greatest miracle of the time, and concluded that all papists are traitors, at least in intent.

The reward for *An Invective* was not long delayed. On March 17 Morison was appointed to parliament under circumstances which confirm unmistakably the nature of his usefulness as well as his willing subservience to Cromwell and the crown. Said Cromwell to his prince:

> *Amonges other for your graces parliament I have appoincted your Maiesties seruaunt Mr Morisson to be oone of then no doubte he shalbe redy to answer and take vp suche as wold crake or face with literature of lernyng or by Indirecte wayes If any suche shalbe as I thinke there shalbe fewe or noon Forasmoche as I and other your dedicate conseillers be aboutes to bring all thinges so to passe that your Maiestie had never more tractable parlement I have thought the said Morisson very mete to serve your grace therein Wherefore I beseche thesame to have him in your good favour as ye have had hitherto I knowe his hert so good that he is worthy favour in dede.*[17]

Morison's importance in this supine parliament may be judged by the fact that he was the author of the resolution "to support the King with liberality," and that Cromwell corrected the copy.[18]

Soon after his advancement, and apparently under direct surveillance of the King, while England lived in daily ex-

[17] R. B. Merriman, *The Life and Letters of Thomas Cromwell* (Oxford, 1902), II, 199 (March 17, 1539). Calendared in *L&P*, XIV (1), no. 538.

[18] *L&P*, XIV (1), no. 869.

pectation of the appearance of a French armada off the coast, he wrote *An Exhortation to styrre all Englyshemen to the defence of theyr countreye.*[19] As in *An Invective,* Pole was again the point of attack. Morison pictured him as the leader of the threatened French invasion, the Pope as its instigator; but now Morison aimed primarily at demonstrating England's preparedness. If the Pope was by this means trying to break the bond between the prince and his subjects, this traitorous Cardinal Pole could have brought no nation against England that Englishmen had not already beaten many times before. *An Exhortation* was a paean of praise to English valor, from Crécy and Poitiers to Agincourt and the Field of Spurs. "We that haue thus ben used to victories, ofte beaten our enemies of what nation soo euer they be, can we now loke for lesse than great and hygh honour at their handes?"[20] Morison felt sure that the recent rebellion in the North performed an incidental service by preparing England for war; even the coming of Cardinal Pole could hardly cause mistrust hereafter, "except we become chaũgelynges, and for a tryfle leaue that we haue hitherto godly folowed."[21] Henry had

---

[19] Morison addressed Lord Cobham "out of the King's chamber," warning him of sails at North Foreland on April 10 (*L&P*, XIV (1), no. 733). The tract was probably written in March when the fear of French invasion was at its height. The departure of Marillac, the French ambassador, with only vague assurances of a successor looked ominous. Cromwell was pushing general musters, strengthening the defenses on the coast and the Scottish border. He was somewhat sceptical about the rumors of invasion, but none the less cautious (Merriman, *Cromwell,* II, 198-199). The preparations against invasion (see Merriman, *Cromwell,* I, 251-252) were precisely the conditions mirrored in *An Exhortation,* and it seems reasonable to assume, therefore, that Morison had completed writing it before March 28, when Castillon, the new French ambassador, arrived and thereby relieved the tension.

[20] *Exhortation,* sig. C iii-C iv[v].

[21] *Exhortation,* sig. D ii.

already provided spiritual defense by causing the Bible to be translated and printed; [22] now he daily strengthened the military defense by extensive fortifications.[23]

Both *An Invective* and *An Exhortation* exhibit Morison's literary flair; but although he was obviously parading his literary knowledge, he referred to few works not already used in *A Lamentation* or *A Remedy*. Not cited previously were: Pliny (*Invective*, sig. B vi), Cicero's letter to Atticus (*Invective*, sig. B ii), St. Augustine and his unorthodox opinion on the Manichees (*Invective*, sig. D ii), St. Cyprian (*Exhortation*, sig. D ii), and Machiavelli's *Florentine History* (*Invective*, sig. a iiii[v]).[24] The height of Morison's rhetorical power was reached in the closing exordium based on a prophecy, "not lately commen out of Wales," but out of the fourth chapter of Esdras, in which the Lion overcomes the Eagle:

Why may not we thinke, that noble HENRY the VIII is the Lyon, the wynde ordeyned & sente by god, to tosse this wycked tyraunte of Rome, to blowe him out of al Christen regions? Se ye not, to what honour god calleth our nation? may not we reioyce, that god hath chosen our kyng, to worke so noble a feate? God sayth, a Lion shall teare this tirātes auctorite in peces. God sayth, a wynde shal shake hym out of his cheyer: shall we not thynke, this Lyon, this wynde, to be our soueraygne, our kynge, whiche firste of all princes, durst take hym by the bosome? Let this yelling Egle approche towarde us, let her come with all her

---

[22] *Exhortation*, sig. A vii-A vii[v]. An injunction of August 1536, repeated in 1538, required a Latin and an English Bible in every church in the kingdom. The Tyndale-Coverdale (Matthew's) version appeared in August 1537, the Great Bible (Richard Taverner) in April 1539.

[23] Merriman, *Cromwell*, I, 252.

[24] Bk. VIII (ed. Detmold, I, 375).

*byrdes about her, let a traytour cary her standard: doth not
god say, her wynges shall be cut, her kyngedome waxe
feble, the Lyon waxe stronge, and saue the residue of
goddes people, filling them full of ioye and comfort, euen
while the worlde endureth. Let us, let us therfore worke
lustely nowe, we shall play for euer hereafter. Let us fight
this one fielde with englysshe hands, and englysshe hartes,
perpetuall quietness, rest, peace, victorie, honour, welthe,
all is owers.*[25]

Thus spoke a king's hireling fifty years before the sailing of
the Armada, and over a century before Milton, another
secretary to another Cromwell, spoke in a hauntingly similar way on a similar subject.

After the publication of *An Exhortation* and *An Invective,*
Morison apparently gave over writing except on routine
affairs of state. Only one tract, *A discourse touching the
reformation of the laws of England,*[26] is extant to indicate
that after 1539 he made any further use of the literary abilities that first brought him to Cromwell's attention and
eventually gained him a seat in the highest councils of the
realm. Closely associated as he was with Cromwell's career
and policies, his success after the fall of his master was not
built on desertion to his master's enemies. It is to Morison's
credit—and an incidental comment on his conduct toward
Pole—that, to the last, he remained faithful to his patron.
An Exhortation had publicly identified him with the foreign
policy that precipitated Cromwell's fall; [27] yet as late as
May 1540 he expressed his personal loyalty: "My lord Privy
Seal hath so bought me by his noble courtesy that I am all

[25] *Exhortation,* sig. D vii^v-D viii.
[26] Calendared in *L&P,* XVII, appendix no. 2, as a manuscript of 35
pages in a clerk's hand with corrections by Morison, and addressed
to Henry VIII.
[27] Merriman, *Cromwell,* I, 285.

his, and I were a thousand mo, the King's highness and my lord Prince reserved." [28]

II

The problem of Morison's future after Cromwell's death was only a part of the larger problem of what was going to happen to scholarship. As might be expected, the enthusiasms for learning which animated the group under Pole at Padua in the thirties were not communicable in the forties to younger scholars abroad either in the same manner or in the same degree. Even had Pole's household remained intact, Cromwell's fall closed the direct avenue of approach from study to court, and the conditions were not again to be duplicated. It is probably not wholly a matter of chance that Morison's pamphlet-writing career falls largely within the dates of Cromwell's ascendancy. Patronage, of course, did not cease. Henry continued the practice of subsidizing scholars, and it is noticeable that their careers followed the same pattern. Thomas Smith's abilities as a Greek scholar brought Henry's support for study in France and Italy. He took his doctorate in law at Padua, and was then appointed first Regius Professor of civil law at Cambridge. John Cheke, his friend, likewise became King's scholar and first professor of Greek there. But it is true, nevertheless, that during Henry's lifetime neither Smith nor Cheke enjoyed the close association with affairs of state that characterized the careers of Starkey and Morison. They remained for the time being essentially within the academic close.

Even before Cromwell's death, young scholars who hoped to pluck the political and diplomatic plums of their predecessors, found small pickings at court. The case of Antony Barker, student at Paris, will illustrate. Among the English

[28] *L&P*, XV, no. 726. Loyalty, as a matter of fact, was a quality upon which he always prided himself.

Paduans of the previous generation of scholars, John Mason
corresponded with him and Richard Morison probably
knew him. In 1537 his public career seemed to have begun.
On the strength of his literary abilities Cromwell recommended him to Bishop Hugh Latimer for a preferment at
Stratford-on-Avon. Latimer insisted on two things: that "that
poor college" be not bound for the pension, and that Barker
tarry on it and preach "to the reformation of that blind
end of the diocese. For else what are we the better
for his great literature and good conversation?" [29] There
could be no doubt of the young scholar's abilities if scholarship were to be judged by his equipage. He sent over so
many things in canvas that, according to John Bekinsau,
they were taken for "merchandise and not scholar's stuff"; [30]
but less than a year later, he was complaining to Mason of
the infrequency of his visits to court, and wishing he were
in France again, where Mason was then secretary to Wyatt,
the English ambassador. [31] Of the two generations of scholars, Mason, by 1550, had succeeded to the ambassadorship
to France, and Morison had become ambassador to the
Emperor; Barker, for all his great literature and conversation, was destined to remain out of public life. [32]

On the other hand, if the *cul de sac* in which Barker
found himself indicates that for the younger generation of
scholars, at least, the rewards of scholarship had become
less political in the decade after Cromwell's fall, humanistic activity did not cease to be of public importance. Teaching was important when the student was a William Cecil
or a John Ponet. [33] Tutoring was important when royalty

[29] *L&P*, XII (2), no. 909.
[30] *L&P*, XIII (1), no. 1186.
[31] *L&P*, XIII (2), no. 191.
[32] Leland paid a delicate tribute to his learning in *Encomia*, p. 119.
[33] John Strype, *The Life of the Learned Sir Thomas Smith* (Oxford, 1820), pp. 14, 20.

was being taught.[34] Under these circumstances, scholarship was not likely to become atrophied or endemic, and above all, it remained liberal.

The greatest single factor in the continuation of a liberal humanistic tradition was the patronage of Archbishop Cranmer. Strype could say, and with justice, that Cranmer was "a great patron of all solid learning," [35] a comment best illustrated by the fact that Cranmer retained among his chaplains Richard Harman and Richard Cox, erstwhile scholars in Cardinal's College. Harman's association with Cranmer was even earlier than the migration to Oxford.[36] How soon he returned to Cranmer's household after his ousting and flight to France is not known. But that he did return is evidence of the liberal character of the Archbishop's patronage. Cox's early indiscretions at Cardinal's College were all but buried by an academic career that carried him from the mastership of Eton, his own school, back to Oxford as chancellor in 1547. Yet his appointment as chaplain to Cranmer brought him into strategic position for his major role in the revision of the Anglican liturgy during the reign of Edward and afterward in exile. Cranmer's special service to learning was in providing the means of contact between these former Oxford dissidents and the young Cambridge humanists now reading Greek with such avidity under the inspiration of the King's scholars, Cheke and Smith.

The Archbishop's training and associations had all been

[34] Morison's *Apomaxis* was among the books in the library of John Dudley, Duke of Northumberland, tutor to Edward. It is listed as "Item, aponapis of Mr. Monsons" in T. W. Baldwin's *William Shakspere's Small Latine and Lesse Greeke* (Urbana, Illinois, 1944), I, 255. This, so far as I know, is the earliest attribution of *Apomaxis* to Morison. His name did not appear on the title page in 1537.

[35] *Cranmer*, I, 230.

[36] Venn, *Alumni Cantabrigienses*, pt. I, vol. II, p. 308.

connected with Cambridge. It will be recalled that as a student Cranmer was one of those who had received an invitation to migrate to Wolsey's new college but had rejected it "by persuasion of their friends." [37] This loyalty to his university had remained unbroken through his years as Archbishop. Indeed, so close were these ties that, as Strype remarked, "if learning were discountenanced, it was esteemed to cast some disparagement upon him; if it flourished, it was a sign that Cranmer prevailed at court." [38] On the other hand, he had never lost the inquiring spirit that was probably the reason for his being invited to Oxford. What more natural in carrying out his purpose to gather learned men about him than to include among his chaplains liberals of both universities? Besides his contemporaries who had accepted Wolsey's invitation in 1525, he maintained two of the most vigorous malcontents at Cambridge in the forties: Thomas Becon, who had sat under "old father Latimer" at Cambridge twenty years before, and John Ponet, friend of Morison and Ascham, and pupil of Thomas Smith.

Cranmer may have been responsible in some measure also for establishing relations between his scholars at Cambridge and Wolsey's Morison and Starkey. Morison's acquaintance with and respect for Cranmer dated, it will be recalled, from his visit to Cambridge in 1528, and from time to time since then had been renewed.[39] Starkey had come to Cranmer's aid in the divorce proceedings in 1533; [40] he had conferred with him again while in the King's disfavor

[37] John Skip, Walter Haddon, and Matthew Parker were the others who decided to decline, a notable loss to Wolsey. Strype's *Parker*, I, 11.

[38] *Cranmer*, I, 231.

[39] *L&P*, VI, no. 1582; X, no. 224.

[40] See above, pp. 87-90.

in 1536.[41] King's chaplain and Archbishop doubtless enjoyed a continuous friendship until Starkey's death in 1538. The personal and literary influence of Starkey and Morison on the younger Cambridge humanists like Ascham, Cheke, and Ponet, presently to be dealt with, is of no small importance in the continuity of humanism under Edward and Mary.

Whether by Cranmer's auspices or otherwise, this liaison between intellectuals of two generations and two universities perpetuated the liberal tradition after Cromwell's regime when, as a result of Pole's withdrawal, it was in greatest danger. It is useless to speculate on the potentialities of the promising group in Pole's household in Padua if that crisis had not occurred. But the results are plain enough in personal frustrations ending in frank rejection of the active life or in franker Erastianism and negativism. George Lily, after a period of struggle,[42] elected to throw in his lot with Pole, to whom he acted as chaplain, abroad during Edward's reign and at home during Mary's. No one at Padua had been more stimulated by the rediscoveries of his fellow Grecians. Yet when in later life he composed a series of biographical sketches of those who "in our age" were worthy of memory for their erudition and excellence of learning, he recognized none of his former fellow students after Thomas Lupset. Henry Cole, who was with Pole in Padua when his decision was made, evaded the issue as a reformer under Edward and as a Catholic under Mary. He preached the sermon at Cranmer's execution, and lived to act as overseer of Pole's will. Less conspicuously, John Mason followed the same trimmer's course, becoming ambassador to France under Edward and chancellor of Oxford under Mary until he resigned his office to Cardinal Pole in 1556; in that same year he was under suspicion of com-

[41] *L&P*, XI, no. 157; Herrtage, p. xl.   [42] See above, pp. 97-98.

plicity in the arrest of Sir Peter Carew and his relative Sir John Cheke.[43] Each of these men came under the influence of new ideas at Padua, yet not one deserves more than casual mention among Edwardian and Marian humanists, and not one was representative of the continuance of the spirit of policy-making which animated the humanistic activity of Cromwell's protégés in the thirties.

Even among many of the younger Cambridge humanists, with whom Pole's decision could hardly have borne any weight, one senses the same tendency to shrink from public life. It was so with Roger Ascham, who served as secretary to Morison during the period of his ambassadorship under Edward. Enthusiasm for learning created a bond between the two which disparity of age and rank did not affect. Despite the pressure of public affairs, Morison turned for a part of each day to books. Ascham's description of their daily study of the classics together has been one of the most familiar episodes in Morison's life.[44] It might well be expected that contact with Morison would instil political ambitions in the younger man. Yet there was a difference between them to which their reading of Ochino and Machiavelli rather than of the Greek orators and historians is the best index. Ascham's humanism was conventional, acquiescent. In no other way could he have survived as tutor successively to Lady Jane Grey, Mary, and Elizabeth. One can reasonably conjecture the pedantic misgivings of the meticulously proper tutor at the restless and bustling unconventionality of the proselytizing envoy who wrote and thought in his boots.

Here, as earlier, a knowledge of and attitude toward Machiavelli distinguishes Morison as a man of independent judgment. Machiavelli was by no means unknown to the

[43] A. F. Pollard's "John Mason" in *DNB*.
[44] *Works*, I (2), 236, 285.

Cambridge humanists. One, possibly both, of the King's scholars, Thomas Smith and John Cheke, was familiar with Machiavelli's works. Smith, though he expressed no opinion, had the political works in his library, and—we may presume —read them.[45] Cheke's denunciation as "atheists" of hypocritical men who outwardly show religion, even study divinity, but within are empty of good works,[46] is much too vague to identify as a revelation of his attitude toward Machiavelli,[47] but it is identical with the opinion expressed some years later by Ascham, who knew Machiavelli from reading him with Morison.[48] Ascham observed that there are two varieties of scoffers at religion in England, "they that do read, with indifferent judgement, Pygius and Machiavel, two indifferent Patriarches. Of thies two, Religious do know full well what I say trewe."[49] As might be expected from the circumspect secretary, the opposite of a Catholic was a Machiavellian: both dangerous. By the time of Elizabeth, this was to be the normal view. But these attitudes are in marked contrast to Morison's waggish report to William Cecil, from Villach in 1552, of the Emperor's irritation at his purported "preaching" in the imperial household. In characteristic mock surprise, he testified: "I did but read them Bernardine's [Ochino] Prediches for the tongue, and sometimes Machiavel," a tongue-incheek statement which would hardly allay the Emperor's suspicions. Morison's joke was addressed to one already

[45] Strype, *Sir T. Smith*, p. 277.

[46] Dedication of his translation of Plutarch's *Of Superstition* to Henry VIII. John Strype, *The Life of the Learned Sir J. Cheke* (London, 1821), p. 199.

[47] Buckley, *Atheism in the English Renaissance*, p. 36.

[48] *Calendar of State Papers, Foreign, 1547–1553* (London, 1861), no. 550.

[49] *The Scholemaster* (Arber Reprint), p. 83. The punctuation after "Patriarches" and "two" is my own.

familiar with Machiavelli's political discourses,[50] possibly through Morison himself. Cecil approached Machiavelli in the same frame of mind as Morison did. Politically minded as he was, he recognized the novelty of Machiavelli's gift for isolating man as a political animal; and whether Morison can be held responsible for his acquaintance with Machiavelli or not, there can be no doubt that in contrast to Cheke and Ascham, Morison and Cecil stood on common ground.

III

Perhaps it is just as well that humanism in England was not wholly dominated by either its Aschams or its Morisons. For while through Ascham, its more academic qualities would be transmitted to later generations of scholars, through Morison, the active and more characteristic ingredient, applicability to current problems, in the spirit of free inquiry, would again save it from academic sterility. The new generation of humanists might easily have expended their efforts in disputations over the pronunciation of Greek. Cranmer himself achieved a contemporary reputation for scholarship in the sacramentarian controversy. Such questions were matters of learned debate but at best tangential to national policy, and that policy now had to be reëxamined. The accession of Mary automatically placed the whole settlement achieved under Henry for the first time on the defensive. Suddenly it had become necessary to accommodate a theory designed to support a party in power to the *modus vivendi* and the permanent policy of that same party in exile. Cranmer, as titular head of the evicted party, appealed to his scholarly chaplains for an answer, and especially to John Ponet, erstwhile Bishop of Winchester, and his closest intellectual adviser. At the time

[50] *State Papers, Foreign* (1547–1553), no. 550, p. 216.

of Edward's death, no man had greater influence with the Archbishop. A scholar at Cambridge under Thomas Smith, Ponet had begun a prosperous career as one of the Archbishop's learned chaplains, and by 1551 he was signing himself "Winton," a title which he continued to use in exile, thus tenaciously gathering his robes about him. Cranmer had relied upon him to draw up ecclesiastical formularies in conformity with the reformed practice.[51] Now as the highest ranking English churchman in Germany, a bigger job confronted him.

Significant for the continuity and vitality of humanism during the reign of Mary is the fact that while Ponet was formulating the theory to accommodate the exigency of banishment, he was living in daily contact in Strasbourg with the most gifted humanists of the day: Richard Cox, John Cheke, and Richard Morison.[52] All were experienced propagandists, and now found their talents in demand again. As religious exiles, they plunged into a revision of the Prayer Book, and instituted a pamphlet war against the return of Catholicism with a vigor reminiscent of the campaign for its eviction. Politically, this involved a *volte-face*, in which a theoretic justification of disobedience was substituted for the Tudor maxim of obedience. Nevertheless, although they faced a situation tactically novel, their strategy was the same. Once more, the stress of a national crisis forced a liberalizing of current theory. Once more, the theories so created, while drawing their immediate strength

[51] Garrett, *The Marian Exiles,* p. 253.

[52] Winthrop S. Hudson, *John Ponet* (University of Chicago, 1942), p. 71: "Of that group of young humanist scholars which had centered around Cheke and Smith at Cambridge, practically all who fled from the Marian regime came to this city. In addition, we find at Strasbourg at this time almost all the members of the court circle who had affiliated themselves with that Cambridge group during the first years of Edward's reign."

from expediency, were rooted in tradition. And once more, in building for the present, they determined the shape of things to come. Formal expression of these objectives was Ponet's *A Shorte Treatise of Politike Power*.

Mere propinquity makes it understandable that Ponet should have been influenced by Morison, and it is probably through Morison that he became acquainted with the writing of Starkey, none of whose works, except *An Exhortation*, was in print. But whatever the circumstances, there can be little doubt that Ponet found his bearings in the theory which Starkey had erected, and at the same time expanded it to fit the current situation. How the ideas of these men migrated to the upper Rhine requires further consideration.

The trek of Morison and his associates to Strasbourg was leisurely. Men in exile are not in a hurry, and there was plenty of time to indulge the humanist's desire to cross the Alps into Italy first. Many of them made the journey before taking up a more permanent residence along the Rhine, and for those who visited Padua, there was an English welcome. Pole's household had been long dispersed, but one of its most enthusiastic and liberal supporters, Edmund Harvel, had remained close by in Venice as a kind of ex-officio ambassador there after Pace's death,[53] and continued to offer hospitality to his native countrymen who traveled into Italy.[54] How many of them were students and how long they stayed is conjectural; but that his house was a resort for the exiles during Mary's reign is certain.[55] In fact, if all the reformers who came to Padua during that period frequented Harvel's house, it would have been a busier place

[53] *Ven. Cal.*, 1534–1554, no. 354.
[54] *Camden Miscellany*, X. 8. Cited in Garrett, *Marian Exiles*, p. 181.
[55] Church, *The Italian Reformers*, p. 150. Cited in Garrett, *Marian Exiles*, p. 181.

than Pole's two decades before. What emerges from Miss Garrett's census of exiles is a fact which she herself does not stress: between 40 and 50 of a total of the 472 exiled Englishmen included in the census visited Padua or Venice, many of them as students.

As students, however, they appear to have been far less serious than the earlier group supported by Pole, who were primarily poor, youthful scholars hoping for a political career through their studies. Most of the present visitors had education and rank, and gave the appearance of making the grand tour as a pastime before settling in Strasbourg or Frankfort. Nevertheless, the company, including Morison, believed by Miss Garrett to be the controlling body of the migration, in terms of intellectual history was without doubt the most important group of Englishmen on the continent at the time. In the spring of 1554, Sir John Cheke started for Italy, having obtained permission to travel abroad. He was apparently accompanied by Sir Thomas Wrothe, Sir Anthony Cooke, and Sir Richard Morison at the beginning of the journey, though Cooke left the party in Strasbourg, and Morison before they arrived in Padua in July. Their purpose is suggested by Wrothe's comment that he was coming to Italy to learn the Italian tongue and "philosophically to course over the civil law." [56] One might conjecture that the stimulus to these studies was suggested by his recent traveling companion, Morison, long familiar with both. Cheke, meanwhile, is reported to have lectured on Demosthenes to the English student colony then in Padua.[57] In August, the Hobys, Sir Philip and Sir Thomas, arrived on the scene, followed shortly after by Cooke, who had stayed in Strasbourg where Peter Martyr was lecturing

[56] *SP, Foreign*, 1553–1558, p. 112. Cited in Garrett, *Marian Exiles*, p. 115.

[57] Strype's *Cheke*, p. 96. Cited in Garrett, *Marian Exiles*, p. 115.

and where *The Confession of the Banished Ministers* was then being composed.[58] The whole group including Cheke and Wrothe joined in a pleasure trip to Mantua in October, after which they settled in Padua for the winter. In the summer of 1555 they left Padua at various times and journeyed northward again, Cooke, Cheke, and Wrothe going to Strasbourg, where in September Morison and Cooke with Edwin Sandys,[59] until Mary's accession vice-chancellor of Cambridge University, had applied for residence.[60]

The trip to Padua was not a meeting of strangers. Cooke and Wrothe had both been present at the disputations on the sacraments held in the houses of Morison and Cecil in 1551.[61] During the summer of 1553 the Hobys had been with Morison in Brussels, and Sir Thomas returned with Morison at the time of his recall by Mary.[62] Cheke and Cooke, because of their suspected complicity in the affair of Lady Jane Grey, were imprisoned together in the Tower. All were knit by the common bond of exile.

Morison was the only one of the group who did not get to Italy, possibly only because Italy could hardly have held the attraction for him that it did for the others, who were making the trip for the first time, but possibly also because his services as a propagandist would have been especially valuable in the pamphlet campaign soon to be launched against Mary from Strasbourg. As the author of *The Hurt of Sedition,* Cheke also had proved his value; and it is not strange, therefore, that it was he who made the first move to return to Germany in the spring of 1555.[63]

[58] Garrett, *Marian Exiles,* p. 125.
[59] *Ibid.,* p. 345.
[60] *Ibid.,* p. 125.
[61] Strype's *Cranmer,* p. 386. Cited in Garrett, *Marian Exiles.*
[62] Garrett, *Marian Exiles,* pp. 229-230.
[63] *Ibid.,* p. 115.

IV

In the meantime, Morison had established friendly contacts in Strasbourg with John Ponet.[64] Like Morison, Ponet had spoken for authority, and he must therefore have welcomed the elder scholar into the exiled community as an experienced propagandist. When Cheke arrived in Strasbourg in the fall, the three men set up a close liaison.[65] According to Miss Garrett, Cheke directed the campaign of propaganda against Mary;[66] but though it may be doubted that he was "the brain of the whole campaign," the important fact is the association of the three men in a project eminently suited to their abilities.

Obviously, their task was representative. They were not speaking for themselves alone, nor for the group of exiles alone, but for a great and indeterminate part of the English people, perhaps a majority. In view of the current situation, it would not be enough to attempt a settlement of the ecclesiastical issues; the relation between monarch and subject must be reviewed and a principle evolved—must be, that is, if the radical courses that then seemed necessary were to be successfully implemented by theory. Moreover, they were living in the meantime among strangers, and their point of view was bound to be affected by the social acci-

[64] The first explicit evidence is the baptism of Ponet's son in December 1554 (*ibid.*, p. 255). On p. 230, Miss Garrett seems to date this event erroneously a year later.

[65] *Ven. Cal.*, 1555–1556, pp. 258, 282. Cited in Garrett, *Marian Exiles*, p. 106.

[66] Garrett, *Marian Exiles*, pp. 116-117. Miss Garrett is not always consistent as to Cheke's whereabouts during the period of greatest activity. On p. 106, she places him unequivocally, and probably correctly, in Strasbourg during November, but on p. 116, she builds a case on circumstantial evidence for his presence for three months before February 18, 1556 in Emden.

dent of isolation.[67] In spite of the distinctions in rank among the exiles, the necessity of daily intercourse had imposed a new kind of practical equalitarianism. Miss Garrett has noted the results of this situation in the increasingly democratic conceptions of church government which sprang up in the community at Frankfort, and there is no reason for believing that conditions at Strasbourg were any different. There were also important political implications. Indeed, political equalitarianism was inevitably concomitant to their opposition to Mary. To take such an attitude meant a reversal of the principle of obedience to constituted authority unless sovereignty could be understood to reside in the people, not as a "rude and ignorant" commons but as a politically responsible coalition of all classes. The acceptance of this provision opened the way to Ponet's conception of uncontractual agreement between "people" and king, the most important contribution of the exiles to the history of English thought.

Such practical expediential considerations found a way to pour new wine into old bottles. Yet in this process, Ponet's thought was tempered as much by the liberal views of his humanist associates and predecessors as by the exigencies of exile. It is a strange kind of retributive justice tinged with irony that Pole's *Pro ecclesiasticae unitatis defensione* had just been published in Strasbourg, and that Pole, as "Carnal Phoole," should have served Ponet's argument for limitation of the powers of the monarch,[68] proof incidentally of Pole's early liberalism.

Ponet's intellectual contact with Starkey was more congenial than with any of the other humanists, his dependence on him more pervasive. This influence, however, has been

[67] *Ibid.*, pp. 21-22.
[68] *A Shorte Treatise of Politike Power*, edited by Winthrop S. Hudson (University of Chicago, 1942), sig. G iii.

generally denied. Winthrop Hudson, in pointing out the availability of sources for Ponet's theory of contractual government, failed to stress what he was certainly aware of— the immediate inspiration for the idea in Starkey's *Dialogue*.[69] Hudson, as a matter of fact, was merely following the conventional view that Starkey was an "isolated voice," possibly following the lead of J. W. Allen who had already come to the categorical conclusion that "it was not on the basis of the assumptions of Starkey's *Dialogue* that opposition to Tudor orthodoxy in politics developed in sixteenth-century England."[70] However, it should be kept in mind that both of these judgments were based on an examination of the *Dialogue* alone, and therefore suffer the common fault of all evaluations of Starkey's importance in English thought. Yet even disregarding Starkey's other work, there is sufficient evidence to show that, far from being an isolated voice, Starkey was once more to offer the readiest means of liberalizing current political theory, and so far as Ponet was concerned, opened the way to his popular limitation of the powers of a monarch oblivious to the interests of the commonwealth.

In the *Dialogue*, Starkey assigned the argument for limitation to Pole. Pole reminds Lupset that for many years English princes "have judged all things pertaining to the state of our realm to hang only upon their will and fantasy," a custom which "without doubt . . . hath ever been the greatest destruction to this realm, yea and to all other" (pp. 100-101). Such use of power is "the open gate to all tyr-

[69] *Ponet*, p. 124, n. 35. Cf. *Dialogue*, pp. 168-169. The more remarkable inasmuch as Hudson repeatedly calls attention to the similarity of Ponet's and Starkey's views. See particularly, *Ponet*, pp. 138, 152, 158, 175-176.

[70] *History of Political Thought*, p. 151. Though elsewhere (p. 143), he calls the *Dialogue* the most remarkable piece of political writing in England under Henry VIII with the exception of More's *Utopia*.

anny" (p. 103). Starkey denies the commonly accepted opinion that the tyranny of kings is a righteous punishment for the sins of the people, on the ground that the power of the prince does not derive from God nor from hereditary right, but from the people, a grant within man's power to continue or revoke (p. 167). The office of the king should therefore be elective and his administration of it restrained by "the common counseyl of the realm and parliament, assembled here in our country" (p. 102). A tyrant may even be deposed (p. 167), though active steps to that end need not be taken so long as England is ruled by its present beneficent sovereign (p. 105); in the long run, however, the best protection for the people against the rule of a prince "aftur hys owne lyberty and wyl" is the laws, which, insofar as they follow reason are not bondage but "veray true lyberty" (p. 103). To this end, "consyderyng the nature of pryncys, ye, and the nature of man as hyt ys indede," Aristotle's "mixed state" is the best safeguard against tyranny (p. 181).

With all of this, Ponet was in substantial agreement. Rulers, who "wolde be taken for Goddes," claim and exercise power "to doo what they lust" (sig. B iii); but to accept this conduct would make God the author of evil (sig. C vi). The making and breaking of princes, as in Starkey, lies within the power of the people (sig. G vi). And, like Starkey, he believed that "by long continuaunce" men have judged the mixed state to be the best sort of all (p. 9).

The most significant point of comparison between the two writers is their approach to the question of sovereignty through analysis of the origins and history of legal prerogative. Starkey's views on this subject have been discussed at length in connection with his development of a *via media.* It will be necessary in examining Ponet's use of them to review them here.

Fundamental in this regard was Ponet's theory of the origin of society. There is nothing in *Politike Power* to give credence to Miss Garrett's suggestion that through familiarity with Richard Eden's translation of Peter Martyr of Angleria's *Decades of the New World* (1555), Ponet may have become the first to base a political philosophy on the noble savage.[71] But it is important to note in considering the genesis of Ponet's thought that he was nevertheless a primitivist, though in a juridical rather than a naturalistic sense. Ponet followed the conventional Christian view that there was never a time in man's history when he was without law. Even before man-made law existed, there was a law of nature instituted by God to which the Decalogue in later time would conform.[72] "Before Magistrates were, Goddes lawes were." [73] He was equally conventional in expressly denying the belief of "the ethnics" that it was merely a law of reason which brought men together for the first time into social communities. If this were true, how should it be explained that their civilizations were so easily overthrown? "Wher is the wisdome of the Grecianes? wher is the fortitude of the Assirianes? wher is bothe the wisdome and force of the Romaynes become? All is uanished awaye, nothing almost lefte to testifie that they were, but

[71] Garrett, *Marian Exiles*, pp. 256-257. Eden's sentiments, to the contrary, are clear from his praise of "the manhodde and pollicie of the Spanyardes," who in their conquest of the Indies "consumed these naked people . . . this deuelysshe generation . . . partely by the slaughter of suche as coulde by no meanes be brought to ciuilitie, and partly by reseruynge such as were ouercome in the warres, and conuertynge them to a better mynde." Sig. A ii[v].

[72] Cf. Eden's belief (*Decades of the New World*, sig. C vii[v]) that the aborigines in the New World "may also cheflyer bee allured to the Christian fayth, for that it is more agreable to the lawe of nature then eyther the cerimonious lawe of Moises, or portentous fables of Mahometes Alcharon."

[73] *Politike Power*, sig. B iv.

that which well declareth, that their reason was not hable
to gouerne them." [74] God took upon himself the order and
government of man, and prescribed him a rule. This rule is
the law of nature, "furst planted and graffed only in the
mynde of mã," and after his sin set forth in the Ten Com-
mandments.[75] Ponet has little to say about the state of society in this earliest period, but he does state that there was
no corporal punishment, even for Cain and Lamech, until
the destruction of the world by flood, and that up to that
time, God ruled with gentleness and patience. Then God
was constrained to change his lenity to severity and to
institute politic power, thereby giving authority to men to
make law.[76]

Ponet's insistence on the God-given origin of law looks
very much like a refutation, generally of the "ethnics," but
particularly of Starkey's view of the beginnings of society.
Nowhere in English thought of the sixteenth century is the
primitivistic note franker or more unmistakable than in the
Dialogue, the more remarkable in that it seems to be wholly
dependent on classic rather than Christian thought. At the
beginning, according to Starkey, man lived for many years
in the wild forest without civil policy. Of man's life during
this earliest time, the *Dialogue* gives two distinct and anti-
thetic pictures, identifiable in the current terminology as
"soft" and "hard" primitivism.[77] The inconsistency is apparently the result of Starkey's wide but uncritical use of the
classics. Sometimes, in the idyllic tradition of Hesiod and
Ovid, Starkey thought of man's existence in this earliest
time as "lyuyd more vertusely, and more accordyng to the

[74] *Ibid.,* sig. A ii-ii^v.
[75] *Ibid.,* sig. A ii^v.
[76] *Ibid.,* sig. A iiii. Hardly a description of a "state of nature," as
Hudson apparently interpreted this passage (*Ponet,* p. 135).
[77] A. O. Lovejoy and George Boas, *Primitivism and Related Ideas
in Antiquity* (Baltimore, 1935), pp. 9-11.

dygnyte of hys nature, then he doth now . . . as hyt ys sayd men dyd in the golden age";[78] at other times, closely paraphrasing Cicero's *Pro Sestio*,[79] he thought of it as a rude existence, without city or town, law or religion, in which man "wan[d]eryd abrode in the wyld feldys and wodys, non other wyse then you see now brute bestys to dow . . . lad and drawen wythout reson and rule by frayle fantasy and inordynate affectys."[80] After many years of this sort of life, "certayn men of gret wytt and pollycy, wyth perfayte eloquence and hye phylo[so]phy" induced them by slow degrees to some order and civility, first by building towns and later by devising laws,

at the fy[r]st begynnyng also . . . vnperfayt and somewhat rude, accordyng to the tyme and nature of the pepul; for hyt was not possybul sodeynly, by exacte law and pollycy, to bryng such a rude multytude to perfayt cyuylyte, but euer as the pepul, by processe of tyme, in vertue incresyd, so partycular lawys by polytyke men were deuysyd. And thus in long tyme, by perfayt eloquence and hye phylosophy men were brought, by lytyl and lytyl, from the rude lyfe in feldys and wodys, to thys cyuylyte, wych you now se stablyschyd and set in al wel rulyd cytes and townys.[81]

How could such an account square with the Biblical story of the Garden of Eden? Plainly, man's life as a political animal, in Starkey's view, began as a purely secular process,

[78] *Dialogue,* p. 9.

[79] *Pro Sestio,* xlii, 91-92, quoted in Lovejoy and Boas, *Primitivism and Related Ideas in Antiquity,* pp. 243-244. There is a striking parallel in Alcuin (*Dialogus de rhetorica et virtutibus*), quoted in Carlyle, *Mediaeval Political Theory in the West,* I, 211-212, though Alcuin was admittedly borrowing it.

[80] *Dialogue,* pp. 10, 52.

[81] *Dialogue,* pp. 52-53. The men of "great wit and policy" Starkey earlier (p. 2) identifies as Plato, Lycurgus, and Solon.

a conception sufficiently heterodox to call forth Ponet's denunciation at the very beginning of *Politike Power* of "those worldlings" who took their own reason rather than God to be "the only cause, that men furst assembled together in companies, that common welthes were made, that policies were well gouerned and long continued." [82] Both men conceived of a radical and primitive law of nature. But to Starkey, this rule is "rotyd" in men's hearts by the power of nature, "inclynyng hym euer to the cyuyle lyfe, accordyng to the excellent dygnyte of hys nature" (pp. 14-15). To Ponet, this rule "which we haue not learned, receaued or reade, but haue taken, sucked, and drawne it out of nature: wherunto we are not taught, but made: not instructed, but seasoned: and (as S. Paule saieth) mannes conscience bearing witnesse of it" (pp. 107-108), was "furst planted and graffed only in the myndes of mã" by God (pp. 4, 22).

But if Ponet's insistence that civil order originated in the mind of God rather than in the mind of man was a correction of Starkey's view, it was only by way of accepting Starkey's fundamental distinction between natural law as the universal foundation of civil order and positive law as derivative from it. "Bi this all mẽnes lawes be discerned, whether they be iuste or uniuste, godly or wicked.[83] That distinction was as essential to Ponet's argument in 1555 as it was to Starkey's twenty years before, but with the immense difference that the theory was now being propounded by an "out" rather than an "in." Law to the King's chaplain, writing in defense of royal authority, was essentially restrictive; to a bishop unfrocked by that same authority, it was essentially permissive. Hence, for Starkey, the law of nature, when identified with the law of God, became an instrument for inducing obedience to the higher powers, and positive law a matter of indifference; for Ponet, positive

[82] Sig. A ii. [83] *Politike Power*, sig. A iii.

law remained a matter of indifference, but the law of nature became, as an inevitable consequence of exile, a justification for disobedience to the same powers.

For this new point of view, Ponet had much to gain from the *Dialogue,* where Starkey had strictly limited the powers of the king. So long as England was ruled by a prince as "nobul and wyse" as Henry VIII (pp. 104, 214), Starkey characterized Pole as arguing, no reason existed for invoking the restrictive powers inhering in the people; but that this was merely an interim arrangement and that authority should presently be restored to the lower estates, he left no doubt. It would be necessary, "aftur the decesse of the prynce, by electyon of the commyn voyce of the parlyament assemblyd to chose one, most apte to that hye offyce and dygnyte, wych schold not rule and gouerne al at hys owne plesure and lyberty, but euer be subiecte to the ordur of hys lawys." [84] That anticipated situation had now arrived, and Ponet's task was clear: he must make law independent of the monarch. Starkey had placed "in mannys powar" both the election and the deposition of kings.[85] Ponet's problem in 1555, before Mary's death solved it for him, was to translate these desiderata into theory. On a purely theoretic level, Starkey had already shown the way by erecting the law of nature to a place of preëminence over other forms of law. But the law of nature was an ideal rather than a practical reality. It would be little to his purpose in overthrowing the royal prerogative unless a further limitation over the powers of the monarch were discovered in positive law. As might be expected, he turned again to the writings of Starkey for support. In Starkey's conception of the nature and scope of positive or human law, and specifically in his theory of indifferent things as set forth in *An Exhortation,*

[84] *Dialogue,* p. 168.   [85] *Dialogue,* p. 167.

Ponet's dependence on the earlier theorist becomes clear. Here again, in an opposite context, Starkey's theories were to bear strange fruit.

Incidental to the immediate purpose of justifying intransigence to the legitimate monarch, Ponet adopted whole cloth Starkey's conception of juristic *adiaphora:* things neither good nor bad as defined in God's word, and things indifferent, that is, neither prohibited nor commanded but left to worldly policy. On this basis, all those laws which evolve from local or national custom and hence vary according to the circumstance were delegated to the administration of the king as the duly constituted authority, and if they were not contrary to God's law, they should be obeyed. But whereas Starkey in *An Exhortation* had willingly also committed immutable law, that is, the law of nature or God, to the administration only of a benevolent king, Ponet, under the duress of present circumstance, found it necessary and convenient to revert to the theory of limited obedience, as set forth in the *Dialogue,* whereby a monarch remained in office contingent upon the tolerance of the people, who could elect or depose him. He had thus ultimately effected a basic shift of authority from the monarch to the subject.

True it is, that in maters indifferent, that is, that of them selues be neither good nor euil, hurtfull or profitable, but for a decent ordre: Kinges and Princes (to whom the people haue geuen their autoritie) maie make suche lawes, and dispense with them. But in maters not indifferent, but godly and profitably ordayned for the common wealthe, ther can they not (for all their autoritie) breake thẽ or dispense with them. For Princes are ordained to doo good, not to doo euil: to take awaie euil, not to increace it: to geue example of well doing, not to be procurers of euil: to procure the

wealthe and benefite of their subiectes, and not to worke
their hurt or vndoing.[86]

Obviously, the strength or weakness of such a position
depended upon the clarity with which a line of demarcation
could be drawn between a thing indifferent and a thing essential. Starkey's use of the same distinction had not involved such ambiguities. The Act of Six Articles having been
established, there were the essential things. Starkey's emphasis was on the rest, the indifferent things, that could be
brought under restriction. But what were "maters godly
and profitably ordayned," when a prince's conduct was to
be judged by them? If they were the same things that
Starkey held to be essential in 1535, their legitimacy could
no longer be established on the same grounds, for parliament had rejected them. That is why Ponet, while taking
up Starkey's position, shifted emphasis from a natural to a
theistic origin of civil life. God has taken upon himself
"thordre and gouernement of man his chief creature, and
prescribed him a rule, how he should behaue him self,
what he should doo, and what he maye not doo." It is this
rule which is the law of nature.[87] Thus Ponet, in effect, restricted appreciably the range of acceptance of Starkey's
principle. His was a narrow theology which identified the
law of nature as the law of God; to identify the law of
God as the law of nature as Starkey had done was to speak
in the accents of the Renaissance.

<h2 style="text-align:center">V</h2>

Ponet had, of course, gained his immediate objective. In
indifferent matters, a king could continue to exercise jurisdiction, but he must not interfere with God's laws as al-

[86] *Politike Power*, sig. B v[v].   [87] *Politike Power*, sig. A ii[v].

ready established for the common weal. Practically speaking, Ponet had thus justified the reforms under Henry and Edward and condemned Mary's abrogations. But his practical objective hardly measures his importance in the history of English thought. Nor can it be said, in the light of Starkey's proposals in the *Dialogue,* that his justification of the limitation of royal power constituted an original contribution to English political theory.[88] His importance lies rather in the incidental but explicit increase of power thereby given to the people. Of this he was sure, that rulers who claimed and exercised an absolute power transgressed both natural and positive law,[89] and that it was in accordance with the law of nature to depose such rulers.[90] In the end, as Ponet left the deposition of Mary to God alone, so he knew that deposition would not solve the larger problem of the source of authority. Counter to the conventional notion that the king was superior to his subjects as the belly was to the other members of the body, Ponet not only placed country and commonwealth a degree above the king, and the whole commonwealth above any of its members including kings; he asserted repeatedly that states and kings are ordained merely for "the wealthe and benefite of the people." [91] This, he claimed, was a law of nature.[92] Once, he committed the flat social heresy of labeling kings as unnecessary: "Common wealthes mai stande well ynough and florishe, albeit ther be no kinges, but contrary wise without a common wealthe ther can be no king. Common wealthes and realmes may liue, whan the head is cut of, and may put on a newe head, that is, make them a newe

[88] Hudson, *Ponet,* pp. 165 ff., reviews precursive thought on the subject.

[89] *Politike Power,* sig. B iii.

[90] *Politike Power,* sig. [G iv].

[91] *Politike Power,* sig. A v; E vii^v; G i^v-ii.

[92] *Politike Power,* sig. G vi^v.

gouernour, whan they see their olde head seke to muche his owne will and not the wealthe of the hole body, for the which he was only ordained." [93]

In the same vein, all members of the commonwealth, including kings, enjoy equality in the observance as well as the benefits of the law.[94] Quoting Moses, "Whan ye sitte to iudge, ye shal not haue respecte of persones, whether they be riche or poore, great or smal." [95] Lawmakers should observe "an equalitie in paynes" so that "they punishe not thinnocent or smal offendour for malice, and let the mightie and great thefe escape." [96] There is more than an echo of the equalitarian position of earlier theorists in his explanation of the origin of nobility:

Wherof came the name of Nobilitie, or how were those that be called heroical or noble personages diuided from others, and had in suche honour and reuerence, seing all men came of one man and one woman? was it for their lustie hawking and hunting? for their nimble diceing and cōning carding? . . . No, no, ther was no suche thing. The respecte only of their vertue ād loue to their coūtrey brought them therto. Bicause they reuenged and deliuered the oppressed people out of the handes of their gouernours, who abused their autoritie, ād wickedly, cruelly and tirannously ruled ouer them: the people of a grate and thākefull minde, gaue them that estimacion and honour.[97]

The extent to which these ideas are referable to Ponet's English associates at Strasbourg must be left to conjecture. Ponet made no specific acknowledgment of any of them in

[93] *Politike Power*, sig. [D vii].
[94] *Politike Power*, sig. [C vi^v].
[95] *Politike Power*, sig. H i.
[96] *Politike Power*, sig A iv^v.
[97] *Politike Power*, sig. [G vii-vii^v]. See above, pp. 207 ff.

Politike Power. And as a matter of fact, by 1555 some of them had become widely current on the continent. Adiaphorism was the basis of the Augsburg Interim of 1548, and the social implications of equalitarianism might have derived, as has been suggested, from the living conditions of the English community at Strasbourg as easily as from the consciously held conviction of its members. Nevertheless, considering the close contact of these men, exiles for a cause, with the special bond of language in a strange land, it is not unnatural to assume that here among these expatriates was the most immediate inspiration for Ponet's ideas.

The specific source of Ponet's inspiration, however, is of less importance than the fact that he is to be unmistakably identified with the liberal tradition with which this book is primarily concerned. From the point of view of political theory, he too conceived of the relation between church and state as a *via media,* a norm between complete obedience and complete liberty. Allowing for the fact that in the meantime Catholicism had come to power, there is a striking similarity between Ponet's position under Mary and Starkey's under Henry. Like Starkey, Ponet struck a mean between the Anabaptists, who in the name of Christian liberty "wolde haue all politike power taken awaye: and so in dede no obedience," [98] and the English papists, who "wil nedes haue ciuile power obeied in all thinges." Both were in error, according to Ponet, the Anabaptists so mistaking Christian liberty as to think "that men maye liue without sinne," forgetting that since the fall of man, God found it necessary to ordain civil power to rule him; the papists

[98] Cf. Starkey's *Exhortation,* sig. F iv-F iv^v: "For these men [the Anabaptists] vnder the pretence of libertie, couertly purpose to distroye all christen policie, and soo in conclusion bringe al to manyfest ruine and vtter confusion."

neglecting the fact that there are some matters, affairs of soul and conscience, over which the civil power has no authority, and wrenching the command of Peter for servants to obey their masters, though they be froward and churlish, to refer to "free subiectes vnder a king: as if bounde men and free men were all one, and kinges and bondesmens lordes hade like authoritie." [99]

This is the middle position of Starkey with a new note added, the consciousness of freedom of the individual as distinct from his obligations to the state. And not merely religious freedom. In discussing the limitation of royal power by parliament, Ponet warned present powers in England that Mary was queen only because parliament rejected Edward's bequest of the crown. The king and queen "haue the Crowne to minister iustice, but the Realme being a bodi of free men and not of bondemen, he nor she can not geue or sell them as slaues and bondemen." They cannot give away or sell Calais or Berwick without the consent of the commons, "for it was purchaced with their blood ād moneie." [100]

On these grounds, Ponet's *Shorte Treatise of Politike Power* can be associated on the one hand with the liberal humanism of the reign of Henry VIII, and on the other with the liberal thought of the seventeenth century. It is not chance that Ponet was reading Starkey's *Dialogue* in 1555,[101] and that the *Shorte Treatise* should have been republished during the exciting events of 1642, in the same year as Henry Parker's *Observations*. In a very real sense, Ponet took up the battle which Starkey might well have thought at his death that he had won. He would conserve for England an Anglican polity which circumstance had

[99] *Politike Power*, sig. [C viii]-D i.
[100] *Politike Power*, sig. E iii-iii^v.
[101] Hudson, *Ponet*, p. 176, especially n. 39.

now disenfranchised. The battle for freedom had to be fought once more, and against a familiar opponent. Again, Pole's *Pro ecclesiasticae unitatis defensione* could and did provide, by a curious and ironic inversion, ammunition for the deposition of princes;[102] again, Starkey was Ponet's philosophical antecedent. Freedom from papal domination motivated the thinking of both men, just as tradition, but not a Catholic tradition, was the common background of both their philosophies and the *via media* of the Anglican church a practical expression of it. Yet Ponet realized that freedom and tradition were not necessarily compatible. The papists, he declared in answer to Gardiner, "fixe ther whole hope apō Traditions, Customes, Cannons, Lawes, and inuentions of men," and seek, like the Spaniards, "to destroy the libertie of the English nation, wher by no doubt shortly the noses of the nobilitie shal be holden to the gryndstone and the necks of the commons tyed vnder the priests gyrdels."[103] Against this claim of tradition, Ponet insisted that long custom doesn't make a law, and that evil customs, however old, are not to be endured.[104] "The liberty of the English nation" was, as for Starkey, his primary concern.

Ponet's vigorous sense of personal liberty, however, grew out of the current situation rather than his predecessors in the liberal tradition. When Ponet claimed the title of a free subject under a king, he was suggesting a relation which could have been of no concern to Starkey; but he was laying down a principle which anticipated by almost a hundred years Milton's declaration of the individual's independence from the state. For Milton, the doctrine of in-

[102] It was first published in Strasbourg in 1555, possibly by Ponet himself. Hudson, *Ponet,* p. 176.

[103] *An Apologie fully aunsweringe by Scriptures and aunceāt Doctors a blasphemose book gatherid by D. Steph. Gardiner and D. Smyth of Oxford* (Zurich, 1555), sig. A 3-3ᵛ; [H 7ᵛ].

[104] *Politike Power,* sig. [B viᵛ].

different things which had been a means of liberty to Starkey had now become a fetter:

> But [the Protestant] is wont to say he enjoyns only things indifferent. Let them be so still; who gave him authority to change their nature by injoyning them? If by his own Principles, as is prov'd, he ought to tolerate controverted points of Doctrine not slightly grounded on Scripture, much more ought he not impose things indifferent without Scripture. In Religion nothing is indifferent, but, if it come once to be Impos'd, is either a command or a Prohibition, and so consequently an addition to the word of God, which he professes to disallow. Besides, how unequal, how uncharitable must it needs be, to Impose that which his conscience cannot urge him to impose, upon him whose conscience forbids him to obey? What can it be but love of contention for things not necessary to be done, to molest the conscience of his Brother, who holds them necessary to be not done? [105]

Far from preserving the liberties of Englishmen, England had now forced men to seek freedom elsewhere:

> What numbers of faithfull, and freeborn Englishmen, and good Christians have bin constrain'd to forsake their dearest home, their friends, and kindred, whom nothing but the wide Ocean, and the savage deserts of America could hide and shelter from the fury of the Bishops. O Sir, if we could but see the shape of our deare Mother England, as Poets are wont to give a personal form to what they please, how would she appeare, think ye, but in a mourning weed, with ashes upon her head, and teares abundantly flowing from her eyes, to behold so many of her children expos'd

[105] "Of True Religion" in The Works of John Milton, edited by F. A. Patterson (New York, 1932), VI, 170-171.

at once, and thrust from things of dearest necessity, because their conscience could not assent to things which the Bishops thought indifferent. *What more binding then Conscience?* what more free then indifferency? *cruel then must that* indifferency *needs be, that shall violate the strict necessity of Conscience, merciles, and inhumane that free choyse, and liberty that shall break asunder the bonds of Religion.*[106]

Thus, through the exigency of circumstance, the conception of liberty had shifted its ground. To the Puritan party, indifferent things had become essential, and that same doctrine of indifferency, which had provided a convenient and legal means of escape from papal domination in the sixteenth century, had now become, by reason of its legal establishment, an intolerable personal tyranny.

[106] "Of Reformation in England" in *The Works of John Milton,* III (1), 49-50.

X

QUAM SIT HUMANITER VIVENDUM

From the foregoing account of English humanism during the crucial years of the sixteenth century, certain generalizations will have become clear. In the first place, it would be hard to overestimate the importance of the intellectual crisis precipitated by Pole's decision to break with Henry. Up to that time, the community of scholars was unbroken; after that time, the schism among men of learning was as inevitable as it was irreparable. English humanists were faced at once with the choice either of *rapprochement* with Rome following Pole's example, or of a plunge into the arena of active policy-making for which indeed they had been preparing but which was suddenly no longer a merely academic ideal but a royal command. Cromwell's and Henry's offers were flattering. Never had the student of political theory hope of attaining so high a market value. Never had learning been so genuinely a commodity. The whole prospect was remarkably stimulating.

The task which Henry had set for his scholars was formidable. It was, in fact, no less than a justification of his whole political and social program. Their first and immediate task was to provide a political justification for the break with Rome; their second was to provide a social justification for those who were chiefly responsible for it. In these aims they were successful, but the most striking characteristic of their work is that in so doing, they fell upon principles so broad and far-reaching. Starting from motives of pure expediency, they evolved formulae which anticipated the most important ideals of the seventeenth century and beyond. The *via media,* which began as a means of silencing the opposition to the royal supremacy from the right and left, survived the reign of Mary and the Commonwealth. Social equalitarianism, seized upon during the heat of a rebellion of the commons to legitimize Henry's advancement of men of no rank, found wide enough support in a newly constituted English society not only to outmode the accepted principle of fixed degree, which was its immediate purpose, but to set up a permanent basis for the continuing equalitarian impulse of the next century.

Official awareness of these new political and social currents might, in fact, have meant little were it not for the dynamic character of the principles themselves. Indeed, it is difficult to see how otherwise they would have survived conservative Tudor opinion. Upon what nice interpretations the *via media* rested was apparent as soon as it was put in practice. So long as the political-ecclesiastical position laid down by Henry's agents could be generally accepted as unessential, the fact that Henry was the sole judge of its essentiality did not matter. Intellectual peace under these circumstances rested on the stability of opinion of the monarch and popular sentiment. Hypothetically, this popular sentiment constituted a restriction on royal power which there was no reason to exercise so long as the King remained benevolent. No sooner did Henry attempt to abandon this subtle equilibrium than a hitherto acceptable Act of Six Articles became a "whip of six strings." And when Mary came to the throne and forced the *via media* into migration along with the Anglican clergy, it is notable that Ponet as their spokesman, while continuing to uphold the principle that the ruler has control over indifferent things, based his demand for Mary's deposition on the ground that she had violated essential doctrine, namely the law of God. Thus, although he ignored the Tudor principle of obedience, he stood firm on the doctrine of indifferent things. Under the Commonwealth, this shift of authority from earthly to heavenly rule made it possible for Milton to assert that essentiality theoretically resided in anything regarded hitherto as indifferent, and that any attempt at imposition or command in such matters by that very fact denied its indifferency. What had begun as a plea for tolerance had in the course of a hundred years become a symbol of tyranny.

The doctrine of equality, though showing no such remarkable metamorphosis, demonstrated a similar power of survival. Its appearance in the reign of Henry was clearly a defense measure to offset popular pressure by a superficial concession to the rising middle class. But a concession once made was irretrievable, the consequence inevitable. Continuing popular pressure could end only in the democratic principles of the Levellers.

It is highly improbable that any such iconoclastic implications were anticipated by the authors of Henry's new program. Yet that they were not wholly unaware of its liberal character there is abundant evidence. For this reason, however novel the doctrine, Henry's propagandists invariably appealed to tradition of greater authority than the tradition being displaced. Thus canon law was superseded by civil law and the law of God. The law of nature superseded the law of man or positive law. An aura of legalism made new departures acceptable. It is not necessary, however, to conclude from this approach to policies of state that they were indulging in an elaborate piece of chicanery, as is sometimes inferred. One need look no further than their training in the civil law for a sufficient explanation of their legalistic bias. On merely professional grounds, they were disposed to find a law to hang a policy on.

And this juristic foundation was broadened and colored by their humanistic training. Their easy command over Biblical and classical literatures, over the early church fathers, made also available to them the sum of accepted learning as proof of the authenticity of their position. Yet the surest sign of their humanism is the fact that they were not scholiasts, humanists in the narrowest sense. The professional lawyer's tendency to venerate the past was balanced by a healthy awareness of the currents of doctrine in their own day. If national policy was to be rooted in tradition, the leaven of contemporary thought would quicken it. Their years of study in Italy had not brought them the classics without acquainting them also with Machiavelli. And as for their debt to German thought, the learning of the past and present united in no living person to their greater profit than in that great eclectic, Melanchthon. For them, Germany during Mary's reign was no intellectual exile.

At the same time, neither Renaissance Italy nor Reformation Germany became a land of adoption; nor did Florence any more than Basle migrate to England. Englishmen from abroad returned eclectics but Englishmen still. Their travels on the continent made them acutely conscious of the comparison between economic and social conditions at home and abroad, and the comparison led them invariably to the same conclusion: the superiority of living conditions in England. While much was written in the early Tudor period of the decay of the commonwealth, More's and Starkey's accounts being the most familiar, the important fact is that the traveled Englishman recognized that, socially, Englishmen fared much better than foreigners.

This national consciousness was even more apparent when they turned to the political scene. The crisis of 1536 inspired glowing appeals for civil obedience. "Then shall we be inexpugnable," one chauvinist predicted. "Then all nacons shall quake and tremble at the name of Englande."[1] In 1539, when the danger of French invasion was at its height, a foreign ambassador on returning from abroad is reputed to have publicly remarked of the English, "They haue bene of good hartes, couragyouse, bolde, valyaunt in martiall feates: But those Englyshe men are deade." To which Morison retorted, "As longe as Englyshe bodies remayn in Englande, they shall also fynde Englysshe stomackes, Englysshe handes, Englysshe hartes." Recollecting English victories over the French from Crécy to the Field of Spurs, as admitted by French historians, and listing in detail the fortifications being thrown up with the revenue from taxes and ecclesiastical confiscations, his words were exuberant, heroic: "What a realme woll Englande be whan his grace hath set walles accordyng to the dyches, that runne rounde about vs? England wol than be moch liker a castel, than a realme."[2] The legend of "the tight little isle" was obviously already in being, the intellectual climate already favorable for the writing of *The Faerie Queene*.

The deaths of More and Fisher were without doubt a serious blow to learning. But in the light of the evidence, it would seem to misrepresent fact to conclude that the

[1] PRO, SP 6/4, fols. 197-198.

[2] *Exhortation*, sig. C iii-iv; D iii. For similar patriotic expressions, see Morison's *Lamentation*, sig. A ii^v; *Remedy*, sig. C ii; *Exhortation*, sig. A ii, D vii^v-viii; Tunstal's *Palm Sunday Sermon*, sig. E ii^v; Becon's *The Policy of War* (Parker Society, 1843), p. 245.

history of humanism in England was gravely affected or seriously interrupted thereby. As one looks at the course of humanism through the rest of the century, it becomes apparent that the determining point for English humanists was not the death of More in 1535 but the Act of Royal Supremacy in 1534. Henry's declaration of independence might well have been impossible were it not for the fact that humanism had also become newly independent.

Historic accident determined some of the outward and most conspicuous characteristics of English humanism. It was Protestant, but its protest was against religious restriction of whatever sort, and humanists set their sights on a new unity of Christendom which Rome had been unable to achieve. It is true that the first effects of the new program were to accent England's insularity. But Morison's observation that Henry's England was becoming "moch liker a castel than a realme" was the direct result of real and imminent danger from without the realm, not of a policy of isolation. A union of Protestant states remained a dream of English policy-makers long after those words were spoken.

But these were superficial characteristics. The animating and persistent force of the humanists who formulated English policy in the sixteenth century was their fundamental liberalism. In spite of its immediate and local objective, the very necessity of recognizing dissent in the body politic insured that the new program would be grounded on principles of tolerance. The best proof of that liberal spirit in the Tudor founders of English polity is the striking identity in opinion of those who two and a half centuries later revolted against that same polity as intolerable, and found it necessary to establish in "the savage deserts of America" a new polity on basic principles. It is very possible that in casting off the form of that polity they were ironically unaware of their inheritance. In *A Defence of the Constitu-*

tions of Government, John Adams found the period of the Reformation to be the first of three periods in English history in which the principles of government have been most anxiously studied. Two writers, Machiavelli and Ponet, he singled out for special mention, Machiavelli as "the great restorer of the true politics," Ponet as the theorist whose *Politike Power* contained every essential principle of liberty which was afterwards dilated on by Algernon Sidney and John Locke.[3] And all the more significant because its likeness to Starkey's discourse was almost certainly unconscious, is Adams' observation to Thomas Jefferson: "When People talk of the Freedom of Writing Speaking or Thinking, I cannot choose but laugh. No such thing ever existed. No such thing now exists: but I hope it will exist. But it must be hundreds of years after you and I shall write and speak no more."[4] With this statement of principle, the founders of English and American polity, thus far separated in time and circumstance, faced a similar task, spoke a common language.

[3] *Works,* edited by Charles F. Adams (Boston, 1851), VI, 3-4.
[4] July 15, 1817. Jefferson Collection, The Library of Congress, Washington, D. C.

CHECK LIST OF WORKS CITED

Adams, John. MS. letter to Jefferson, July 15, 1817. Jefferson Collection, The Library of Congress, Washington, D. C.

Adams, John. *Works,* edited by Charles F. Adams, Boston, 1851.

Agapetus. *The preceptes teachyng a prynce or a noble estate his duetie,* translated by Thomas Paynell, London, n. d.

Allen, J. W. *A History of Political Thought in the Sixteenth Century,* London, 1928.

Andrich, Io. Aloys. *De natione Anglica et Scota iuristarum Universitatis Pativinae,* Padua, 1892.

Anon. *Articles to stablish Christian quietness,* London, 1536.

Anon. *Howe to Reforme the Realme in settyng them to werke,* c. 1535–6. Reprinted in *Tudor Economic Documents,* III, 115-129.

Anon. *A Letter sent to the comons that rebell, wherin louyngely is shewed to them, how they every way ryse to they owne extreme ruine and distruction.* Entitled also *Admonicōn to the Rebells in the North to desiste* and *A book of Rebellyon agaynste it.* PRO, SP 1/113, fols. 250-255ᵛ. Calendared in *L&P,* XI, app. no. 12.

Anon. *Praier and complaynt of the Ploweman vnto Christ,* 1531.

Anon. "The prynce of Oratores Marius Tullius Cicero whose facundious eloquence was dailie exercised in makyng orations . . ." Closing legend: "This boke entreateth of obedience to Princes." PRO, SP 6/9, fols. 173-210. Calendared in *L&P,* XI, no. 1420.

Archaeologia, or Miscellaneous Tracts Relating to Antiquity, Society of Antiquarians of London, London, 1773–1819.

Ascham, Roger. *The Whole Works of Roger Ascham . . .,* edited by Rev. Dr. Giles, 1864–65.

Ascham, Roger. *The Scholemaster* (Arber Reprint), London, 1870.

Ashley, W. J. *English Economic History and Theory,* London, 1925.

Augustine, Saint. In *A Select Library of the Nicene and Post-Nicene Fathers,* edited by Phillip Schaff, New York, 1888.

Bainton, Roland H. *Castellio Concerning Heretics,* New York, 1935.

Bainton, Roland H. "The Struggle for Religious Liberty," *Church History,* X (1941), 95-124.

Bainton, Roland H. Review of Baumer's *Early Tudor Theory of Kingship,* in *Review of Religion,* V (1941), 239-240.

Bale, John. *Illustrium Maioris Britanniae scriptorum,* [Wesel, D. van den Straten], Gippiswici, per J. Overton, 1548.

Bale, John. *Index Britanniae Scriptorum,* edited by R. L. Poole, Oxford, 1902.

Bale, John. *Scriptorum Illustriũ maioris Brytanniẽ,* Basle, 1559.

Baron, Hans. "The Historical Background of the Florentine Renaissance," *History,* n. s., XXII (1938), 315-327.

Baskervill, C. R. "Sir Richard Morison as the author of two anonymous tracts on sedition," *Library,* fourth series (1936), 83-87.

Baskerville, Geoffrey. *English Monks and the Suppression of the Monasteries,* London, 1937.

Bateson, Mary. "Robert Aske's Narrative of the Pilgrimage of Grace," *English Historical Review,* V (1890), 330-345, 550-573.

Baumer, Franklin Le Van. *The Early Tudor Theory of Kingship,* New Haven, 1940.

Baumer, Franklin Le Van. "Thomas Starkey and Marsilius of Padua," *Politica,* II (1936), 188-205.

Beccatelli, Ludovico. *The Life of Cardinal Reginald Pole,* London, 1766.

Becon, Thomas. *Works,* edited by John Ayre, Parker Society, 1843-44.

Biographia Britannica, edited by White Kennett, London, 1760.

Bloxam, J. R. *Register of Magdalen College,* Oxford, 1863.

Bourilly, V. L. *Guillaume du Bellay,* Paris, 1904.

Brewer, J. S. *The Reign of Henry VIII,* London, 1884.

Buckley, George T. *Atheism in the English Renaissance,* Chicago, 1937.

Burnet, Gilbert. *History of the Reformation of the Church of England,* edited by Nicholas Pocock, Oxford, 1865.

Bush, Douglas. "Tudor Humanism and Henry VIII," *University of Toronto Quarterly,* VII (1938), 162-177.

Calendar of State Papers, Foreign, 1547–1553, London, 1861.

Calendar of State Papers, Spanish, London, 1862–.

Calendar of State Papers, Venetian, London, 1864–1898.

Camden Miscellany, vol. X., no. 2. See Hoby, Sir Thomas.

Carlyle, R. W. and A. J. *A History of Mediaeval Political Theory in the West,* Edinburgh, 1928–1936.

Chambers, R. W. *The Place of St. Thomas More in English Literature and History,* London, 1937.

Chambers, R. W. *Thomas More,* New York, 1935.

Cheke, Sir John. *The hurt of sedition howe greuous it is to a communewelth,* London, 1549. Reprinted in *Holinshed's Chronicles of England, Scotland, and Ireland* (London, 1807–08), III, 987-1011.

Cheyney, Edward P. *Social Changes in England in the Sixteenth Century*, University of Pennsylvania, 1895.

Church, Frederic C. *The Italian Reformers*, New York, 1932.

Constant, Gustave. *The Reformation in England: the English Schism*, New York, 1935.

Cooper, C. H. and T. *Athenae Cantabrigienses*, Cambridge, 1858–1861.

Corpus Iuris Civilis, edited by Rudolf Schoell, Berlin, 1928.

Correspondence of Edward, Third Earl of Derby, edited by T. Northcote Toller, Chetham Society, 1890.

Cranmer, Thomas. *Miscellaneous Writings and Letters*, edited by J. E. Cox, Parker Society Publications, vols. XV-XVI, Cambridge, 1844–1846.

Dictionary of National Biography, London, 1885–1900.

Dodds, M. H. and R. *The Pilgrimage of Grace and the Exeter Conspiracy*, Cambridge, 1915.

Dudley, Edmund. *The Tree of Commonwealth*, Manchester, 1859.

EHR. English Historical Review.

Eliot, T. S. *Essays Ancient and Modern*, New York, 1932.

Elliot-Binns, L. E. *The Reformation in England*, London, 1937.

Elyot, Thomas. *The Governour*, edited by H. H. Croft, London, 1883.

Erasmus, Desiderius. *Prouerbes or adagies with newe addicions, gathered out of the Chiliades of Erasmus by R. Taverner*, London, 1539.

Erasmus, Desiderius. *Opus epistolarum*, edited by P. S. Allen, Oxford, 1906–.

Fiddes, Richard. *The Life of Cardinal Wolsey*, London, 1724.

Foster, Joseph. *Alumni Oxonienses: the members of the university of Oxford, 1500–1714*, Oxford, 1891–92.

Fowler, Thomas. *The History of Corpus Christi College*, Oxford, 1893.

[Fox, Edward]. *Opus eximium de vera differentia regiae potestatis et ecclesiasticae*, London, 1534.

Foxe, John. *Actes and monuments*, edited by Stephen Cattley and George Townsend, London, 1837–1841.

Froude, J. A. *The History of England from the Fall of Wolsey to the Defeat of the Spanish Armada*, London, 1856–1870; revised edition, 1862–1870.

Gairdner, James. *Lollardy and the Reformation in England*, London, 1908.

Galen. *Opera omnia*, Venice, 1525.

Garrett, Christina H. *The Marian Exiles*, Cambridge, 1938.

Gasquet, F. A. *Cardinal Pole and his Early Friends*, London, 1927.

Gee, John A. *Life and Works of Thomas Lupset*, New Haven, 1928.

Gooch, G. P. *English Democratic Ideas in the Seventeenth Century*, 2nd edition with notes and appendices by H. J. Laski, Cambridge, 1927.

Haile, Martin. *Life of Reginald Pole*, London, 1910.

Hall, Edward. *The Union of the two noble and illustre famelies of Lancastre & Yorke*, London, 1548, 1550.

Hanford, J. H. "A Platonic Passage in 'Troilus and Cressida,'" *Studies in Philology*, XIII (1916), 105.

Harwood, Thomas. *Alumni Etonienses*, London, 1797.

Henry VIII. *An Epistle of . . . Henry the . . . viii . . . to the Emperours Maiestie . . . why the Kynges hyghenes owght neyther to sende nor go to the Councill indicted at Vincence*, London, 1538.

Henry VIII. *Answere made by the kynges hyghnes to the petitions of the rebelles in Yorkeshire*, London, 1536.

Henry VIII. *Answere to the petitions of the traytours and rebelles in Lyncolneshyre*, London, 1536.

[Henry VIII]. *A Protestation made for the . . . kynge of Englande and his hole counsel˜ ınd clergie, wherin is declared, that neyther his hyghenes, nor his prelates, neyther any other prynce, or prelate, is bounde to come or sende, to the pretended councell, that Paule byshoppe of Rome, first by a bul indicted at Mantua . . . & nowe a late by an other bull, hath proroged to a place, no man can telle where*, London, 1537.

Herbert, Lord Edward (of Cherbury). *The life and raigne of king Henry the eighth*, London, 1649.

Herrtage. See Thomas Starkey, *England in the Reign of Henry VIII: Starkey's Life and Letters*.

Hoby, Sir Thomas. *The Travels and Life of Sir Thomas Hoby, Kt of Bisham abbey, written by himself, 1547–1564*, edited by Edgar Powell, *Camden Miscellany*, vol. X, no. 2 (1902).

Holdsworth, W. S. *A History of English Law*, London, 1937.

Holinshed, Raphael. *Holinshed's Chronicles of England, Scotland, and Ireland*, London, 1807–08.

Hook, Walter F. *Lives of the Archbishops of Canterbury*, London, 1868.

"Household Book of Henry VIII," *Trevelyan Papers Prior to 1558*, edited by J. Payne Collier, Camden Society, no. 67 (1857).

Hudson, Winthrop S. *John Ponet (1516?–1556), Advocate of Limited Monarchy*, Chicago, 1942.

Janelle, Pierre. *L'Angleterre catholique à la veille du schisme*, Paris, 1935.

Janelle, Pierre. *Obedience in Church and State*, Cambridge, 1930.

Jewel, John. *Works*, edited by John Ayre, Parker Society, 1845–1850.

Jones, P. V. *The Household of a Tudor Nobleman*, Cedar Rapids, Iowa, 1918.

Jordan, W. K. *The Development of Religious Toleration in England from the Beginning of the English Reformation to the Death of Queen Elizabeth,* London, [1932].

Kohn, Hans. *The History of Nationalism* (1940).

L&P. See *Letters and Papers, Foreign and Domestic, of the Reign of Henry VIII.*

Leach, A. F. *Memorials of Beverley Minster: the Chapter Act Book,* Surtees Society, vol. CVIII (1903).

Leadam, I. S. *Select Cases in the Court of Requests,* Selden Society, vol. XII (1898).

Leland, John. *Principum ac illustrium aliquot et eruditorum in Anglia virorum Encomia.* In *De rebus britannicis collectanea,* London, 1774.

Letters and Papers, Foreign and Domestic, of the Reign of Henry VIII, 1509-47, London, 1862-1932.

Liljegren, S. J. *The Fall of the Monasteries and the Social Changes in England Leading up to the Great Revolution,* Lund, 1924.

Lloyd, David, *State Worthies,* London, 1766.

Lovejoy, A. O., and George Boas. *Primitivism and Related Ideas in Antiquity,* Baltimore, 1935.

Machiavelli, Niccolò. *The Prince* and *The Discourses of Livy,* edited by Max Lerner, New York, 1940.

Machiavelli, Niccolò. *The Historical, Political, and Diplomatic Writings of Niccolò Machiavelli,* edited by C. E. Detmold, Boston, 1882.

McIlwain, Charles H. *The Growth of Political Thought in the West,* New York, 1932.

Macray, William D. *Register of the Members of St. Mary Magdalen College, Oxford, from the Foundation of the College,* London, 1894-.

Maitland, F. W. *English Law and the Renaissance,* Cambridge, 1901.

Mallet, Charles E. *A History of the University of Oxford,* London, 1924.

Martyr of Angleria, Peter. *The decades of the newe worlde or west India, conteynyng the navigations and conquestes of the Spanyardes,* translated by Richard Eden, London, 1555.

Melanchthon, Philipp. *Philippi Melanthonis opera quae supersunt omnia,* edited by Bretschneider, 1834-1860. [*Corpus Reformatorum,* vols. 1-28.]

Melanchthon, Philipp. *The confessyon of fayth . . . to Charles the .V.,* translated by Robert Syngylton, n. d.

Melanchthon, Philipp. *The confessyon of the faythe of the Garmaynes to . . . Charles the .v . . . To which is added the Apologie of Melancthon,* translated by Richard Taverner, London, 1536.

Melanchthon, Philipp. *A waying and considering of the Interim,* translated by John Rogers, London, 1548.

Merriman, Roger B. *The Life and Letters of Thomas Cromwell,* Oxford, 1902.

Meylan, Edward F. "The Stoic Doctrine of Indifferent Things and the Conception of Christian Liberty in Calvin's *Institutio religionis Christianae,*" *Romanic Review,* XXVIII (1937), 135–145.

Milton, John. *The Works of John Milton,* edited by F. A. Patterson, New York, 1932.

More, Thomas. *Utopia,* edited by J. C. Collins, Oxford, 1904.

[Morison, Richard.] Commonplace book, PRO, SP 6/4.

Morison, Richard. *De rebus gestis ab Henrico octauo.* Folger MS. 1283-1. Single sheet headed: "Ex oratione Cardinalis Campagii ad Henricum octavum Anno regni decimo habetur in Libro morisoni de rebus gestis Hy: 8."

[Morison, Richard.] MS drafts of *A Remedy for Sedition:*
PRO, SP 6/8, fols. 303-304. *L&P,* XII (2), no. 405.
PRO, SP 6/13, fols. 31-47, 49-61, 63-67. *L&P,* XI, no. 1409.
PRO, SP 240, fol. 192. *L&P,* XI, Addendum 1143.

[Morison, Richard.] Notes and sketch of an answer to Pighius's *Hierarchiae ecclesiasticae assertio. L&P,* XIII (1), no. 1268.

[Morison, Richard.] *Apomaxis calumniarum, convitiorumque,* London, 1537.

Morison, Richard. *An Exhortation to styrre all Englyshemen to the Defence of theyr countreye,* London, 1539.

Morison, Richard. *An inuectiue ayenste the great and detestable vice, treason,* London, 1539.

[Morison, Richard.] *A lamentation in whiche is shewed what Ruyne and destruction cometh of seditious rebellyon,* London, 1536.

[Morison, Richard.] *A Remedy for sedition, wherein are conteyned many thynges, concernynge the true and loyall obeysance, that commēs owe unto their prince and soveraygne lorde the kynge,* London, 1536; reprinted with a foreword by E. M. Cox, London, 1933.

Muller, James A. *Stephen Gardiner and the Tudor Reaction,* New York, 1926.

Narratives of the Days of the Reformation, edited by John G. Nichols, Camden Society, no. 77 (1859).

Nelson, William. *John Skelton, Laureate,* New York, 1939.

Newman, George. *Interpreters of Nature,* London, 1927.

Nine Historical Letters of the Reign of Henry VIII, edited by J. P. Collier, London, 1871.

Original Letters Illustrative of English History, edited by Henry Ellis, London, 1824–1846.

Parker, Henry. *Dives and Pauper,* London, 1534 [1536].

Passerin d'Entreves, A. *The Medieval Contribution to Political Thought,* Oxford, 1939.

Phillimore, J. S. "Blessed Thomas More and the Arrest of Humanism in England," *Dublin Review*, CLIII (1913), 1-26.

Phillips, James E., Jr. *The State in Shakespeare's Greek and Roman Plays*, New York, 1940.

[Phillips, Thomas.] *The History of the Life of Reginald Pole*, London, 1767.

Pickthorn, Kenneth. *Early Tudor Government: Henry VIII*, Cambridge, 1934.

PMLA. Publications of the Modern Language Association.

Pocock, Nicholas. *Records of the Reformation*, Oxford, 1870.

Pole, Reginald. *Pro ecclesiasticae unitatis defensione* [Rome, 1536].

Pollard, A. F. "Council, Star Chamber and Privy Council under the Tudors," *EHR*, XXXVIII (1923), 42-60.

Pollard, A. F. Review of Baumer's *Early Tudor Theory of Kingship*, in *EHR*, LVI (1941), 311.

Pollard, A. F. *Wolsey*, London, 1929.

Ponet, John. *A Shorte Treatise of Politike Power* [Strasbourg?], 1556.

Ponet, John. *An Apologie fully aunsweringe by Scriptures and aunceāt Doctors a blasphemose book gatherid by D. Steph. Gardiner and D. Smyth of Oxford*, Zurich, 1555.

Praz, Mario. "Machiavelli and the Elizabethans," *Proceedings of the British Academy*, XIV (1928).

Previté-Orton, C. W. "Marsilius of Padua," *Proceedings of the British Academy*, XXI (1935), 137-183.

Privy Purse Expenses of King Henry the Eighth, from November MDXXIX, to December MDXXXII, edited by N. H. Nicolas, London, 1827.

PRO. Public Record Office.

Reid, Rachel R. *The King's Council in the North*, London, 1921.

Sadoleto on Education, edited by E. T. Campagnac and K. Forbes, Oxford, 1916.

St. German, Christopher. *A treatise concernynge the diuision betwene the spiritualtie and temporaltie*, London [1532?].

Sampson, Richard. *Oratio quae docet horatur admonet omnes potissimum Anglos*, London, 1534.

Schirmer, W. K. *Der englische Frühhumanismus*, Leipzig, 1931.

Smyth, C. H. *Cranmer and the Reformation under Edward VI*, Cambridge, 1926.

SP. State Papers.

[Starkey, Thomas.] Conclusion of some discourse on the liberty of speaking and writing. PRO, SP 1/75, fol. 240. *L&P*, VI, no. 414 (ii).

[Starkey, Thomas.] "Primi fructus distribuendi pauperibus . . ." PRO, SP 1/75, fol. 240. *L&P*, VI, no. 414 (ii).

[Starkey, Thomas.] Letter to Cromwell on the two polities, civil and heavenly. PRO, SP 1/89, fols. 135-138. Margin in another contemporary hand: "of worldly & spuall lyvinge a discourse."

[Starkey, Thomas.] "What ys pollycy aftur the setēce of Arystotyl." PRO, SP 1/89, fols. 220-230. *L&P*, VIII, no. 216 (iii).

[Starkey, Thomas.] Instructions for preaching. PRO, SP 1/100, fols. 130-130ᵛ. *L&P*, IX, no. 1160.

[Starkey, Thomas.] *An Inductyon to Concord to the pepul of Englond.* Called also *A côfyrmacyon of concord.* PRO, SP 6/9, fols. 219-221. *L&P*, XI, no. 936.

Starkey, Thomas. *A Dialogue between Cardinal Pole and Thomas Lupset, Lecturer in Rhetoric at Oxford,* edited by J. W. Cowper, Early English Text Society, extra series, no. XII (1871).

[Starkey, Thomas.] *An exhortation to the people instructynge theym to unitie and obedience* [London, 1535-6].

Starkey, Thomas. *England in the Reign of Henry VIII: Starkey's Life and Letters,* edited by S. J. Herrtage, Early English Text Society, extra series, no. XXXII (1878).

State Papers published under the authority of His Majesty's Commission, King Henry VIII, London, 1830-1852.

Strype, John. *Annals of the Reformation and Establishment of Religion, Oxford,* 1820-1840.

Strype, John. *Ecclesiastical Memorials,* London, 1822.

Strype, John. *The Life and Acts of Matthew Parker,* Oxford, 1821.

Strype, John. *The Life of the Learned Sir J. Cheke,* London, 1821.

Strype, John. *The Life of the Learned Sir T. Smith,* London, 1820.

Strype, John. *Memorials of the Most Reverend Father in God Thomas Cranmer,* Oxford, 1812.

Sturge, Charles. *Cuthbert Tunstal,* London, 1938.

Sturmius, Johan. *The Epistle that Iohan Sturmius . . . sent to the Cardynalles and prelates, that were chosen . . . by the Bysshop of Rome, to serche out the abuses of the churche,* translated by *Richard Morison,* London, 1538.

Symonds, John A. *The Renaissance in Italy,* London, 1900.

Tawney, R. H. *The Agrarian Problem in the Sixteenth Century,* London, 1912.

Tawney, R. H. *Religion and the Rise of Capitalism,* London, 1926.

Thompson, Henry L. *Christ Church,* London, 1900.

Thompson, Maclaren. "A Glimpse of Padua," *The Diplomate,* XVI (1944), 302-308.

Three Chapters of Letters relating to the Suppression of Monasteries, edited by Thomas Wright, Camden Society, XXVI (1843).

Troeltsch, Ernest. *The Social Teaching of the Christian Churches,* London, 1931.

Tudor Economic Documents, edited by R. H. Tawney and Eileen Power, London, 1924.

Tunstal, Cuthbert. *A sermon of Cuthbert Bysshop of Duresme vpon Palme Sondaye before Kynge Henry the viii*, London, 1539.

Van Dyke, Paul. *Renascence Portraits*, New York, 1905.

Ven. Cal. Calendar of State Papers, Venetian.

Venn, J. and J. A. *Alumni Cantabrigienses*, Cambridge, 1927.

Vetter, Theodor. *Relations between England and Zurich during the Reformation*, London, 1904.

Vives, Juan Luis. *Introducción á la Sabiduría*, Madrid, 1918.

von Martin, Alfred. *Sociology of the Renaissance*, New York, 1944.

Wegg, Jervis. *Richard Pace*, London, 1932.

Weiss, Roberto. *Humanism in England during the Fifteenth Century*, Oxford, 1941.

Weissberger, L. Arnold. "Machiavelli and Tudor England," *Political Science Quarterly*, XLII (1927), 589-607.

White, Helen C. *Social Criticism in Popular Religious Literature of the Sixteenth Century*, New York, 1944.

White, Olive B. "Richard Taverner's Interpretation of Erasmus in *Proverbes or Adagies*," *PMLA*, LIX (1944), 928-943.

Whitgift, John. *Works*, edited by John Ayre, Parker Society, 1851–1853.

Whitney, E. A. "Erastianism and Divine Right," *Huntington Library Quarterly*, II (1939), 373-398.

Wood, Anthony à. *Athenae Oxonienses*, edited by Philip Bliss, Oxford, 1813–1820.

Wood, Anthony à. *Fasti Oxonienses*, edited by Philip Bliss, London, 1815.

Wood, Anthony à. *The History and Antiquities of the Colleges and Halls in the University of Oxford*, Oxford, 1786.

Woodhouse, A. S. P. *Puritanism and Liberty*, London, 1938.

Zeeveld, W. Gordon. "Richard Morison, Public Apologist for Henry VIII," *PMLA*, LV (1940), 406-425.

Zimmerman, Athanasius. *Kardinal Pole, sein Leben und seine Schriften*, Regensburg, 1893.

INDEX